ISBN 0-8373-0574-8

C-574   CAREER EXAMINATION SERIES

This is your
PASSBOOK® for...

WITHDRAWN

Parole Officer

Test Preparation Study Guide

Questions & Answers

NATIONAL LEARNING CORPORATION

Copyright © 2006 by

National Learning Corporation

212 Michael Drive, Syosset, New York 11791

(516) 921-8888
(800) 645-6337
FAX: (516) 921-8743
www.passbooks.com
email: sales @ passbooks.com
info @ passbooks.com

PRINTED IN THE UNITED STATES OF AMERICA

PASSBOOK®
NOTICE

PASSBOOK SERIES®

THE *PASSBOOK SERIES®* has been created to prepare applicants and candidates for the ultimate academic battlefield—the examination room.

At some time in our lives, each and every one of us may be required to take an examination—for validation, matriculation, admission, qualification, registration, certification, or licensure.

Based on the assumption that every applicant or candidate has met the basic formal educational standards, has taken the required number of courses, and read the necessary texts, the *PASSBOOK SERIES®* furnishes the one special preparation which may assure passing with confidence, instead of failing with insecurity. Examination questions— together with answers—are furnished as the basic vehicle for study so that the mysteries of the examination and its compounding difficulties may be eliminated or diminished by a sure method.

This book is meant to help you pass your examination provided that you qualify and are serious in your objective.

The entire field is reviewed through the huge store of content information which is succinctly presented through a provocative and challenging approach—the question- and-answer method.

A climate of success is established by furnishing the correct answers at the end of each test.

You soon learn to recognize types of questions, forms of questions, and patterns of questioning. You may even begin to anticipate expected outcomes.

You perceive that many questions are repeated or adapted so that you gain acute insights, which may enable you to score many sure points.

You learn how to confront new questions, or types of questions, and to attack them confidently and work out the correct answers.

You note objectives and emphases, and recognize pitfalls and dangers, so that you may make positive educational adjustments.

Moreover, you are kept fully informed in relation to new concepts, methods, practices, and directions in the field.

You discover that you are actually taking the examination all the time: you are preparing for the examination by "taking" an examination, not by reading extraneous and/or supererogatory textbooks.

In short, this PASSBOOK®, used directedly, should be an important factor in helping you to pass your test.

PAROLE OFFICER

DUTIES

Under general supervision, a Parole Officer makes investigations of inmates eligible for release on parole and does social casework and community protection in the supervision and guidance of parolees. He counsels inmates and investigates their prospective homes employment, and general environment. He secures, for the Parole Board, information regarding inmates' criminal records, conduct, and other pertinent information. He supervises persons released on parole and assists parolees in their rehabilitation. He investigates employment opportunities and arranges for placement of parolees. He maintains case records and makes reports, interprets the work of the Division of Parole in the community, and may act as liaison between the institution and parolee in preparing inmates for release.

SUBJECT OF EXAMINATION

There will be a written test designed to test for knowledge, skills, and/or abilities in such areas as:
1. Preparing written material;
2. Interviewing;
3. Human behavior; and
4. Principles and practices of casework and counseling in a correctional/parole rehabilitation setting.

HOW TO TAKE A TEST

I. YOU MUST PASS AN EXAMINATION
   A. *WHAT EVERY CANDIDATE SHOULD KNOW*

Examination applicants often ask us for help in preparing for the written test. What can I study in advance? What kinds of questions will be asked? How will the test be given? How will the papers be graded?

As an applicant for a civil service examination, you may be wondering about some of these things. Our purpose here is to suggest effective methods of advance study and to describe civil service examinations.

Your chances for success on this examination can be increased if you know how to prepare. Those "pre-examination jitters" can be reduced if you know what to expect. You can even experience an adventure in good citizenship if you know why civil service examinations are given.

   B. *WHY ARE CIVIL SERVICE EXAMINATIONS GIVEN?*

Civil service examinations are important to you in two ways. As a citizen, you want public jobs filled by employees who know how to do their work. As a job-seeker, you want a fair chance to compete for that job on an equal footing with other candidates. The best known means of accomplishing this two-fold goal is the competitive examination.

Examinations are widely publicized throughout the nation. They may be administered for jobs in federal, state, city, municipal, town, or village governments or agencies.

Any citizen may apply, with some limitations, such as the age or residence of applicants. Your experience and education may be reviewed to see whether you meet the requirements for the particular examination. When these requirements exist, they are reasonable and are applied consistently to all applicants. Thus, a competitive examination may cause you some uneasiness now, but it is your privilege and safeguard.

   C. *HOW ARE CIVIL SERVICE EXAMINATIONS DEVELOPED?*

Examinations are carefully written by trained technicians who are specialists in the field known as "psychological measurement," in consultation with recognized authorities in the field of work that the test will cover. These experts recommend the subject matter areas or skills to be tested; only those knowledges or skills important to your success on the job are included. The most reliable books and source materials available are used as references. Together, the experts and technicians judge the difficulty level of the questions.

Test technicians know how to phrase questions so that the problem is clearly stated. Their ethics do not permit "trick" or "catch" questions. Questions may have been tried out on sample groups, or subjected to statistical analysis, to determine their usefulness.

Written tests are often used in combination with performance tests, ratings of training and experience, and oral interviews. All of these measures combine to form the best known means of finding the right man for the right job.

II. HOW TO PASS THE WRITTEN TEST

A. *NATURE OF THE EXAMINATION*

To prepare intelligently for civil service examinations, you should know how they differ from school examinations you have taken. In school you were assigned certain definite pages to read or subjects to cover. The examination questions were quite detailed and usually emphasized memory. Civil service examinations, on the other hand, try to discover your present ability to perform the duties of a position, plus your potentiality to learn these duties. In other words, a civil service examination attempts to predict how successful you will be. Questions cover such a broad area that they cannot be as minute and detailed as school examination questions.

In the public service similar kinds of work, or positions, are grouped together in one "class." This process is known as "position-classification." All the positions in a class are paid according to the salary range for that class. One class title covers all these positions, and they are all tested by the same examination.

B. *FOUR BASIC STEPS*

1. Study the Announcement.--How, then, can you know what subjects to study? Our best answer is: "Learn as much as possible about the class of positions for which you have applied." The examination will test the knowledge, skills, and abilities needed to do the work.

Your most valuable source of information about the position you want is the official announcement of the examination. This announcement lists the training and experience qualifications. Check these standards and apply only if you come reasonably close to meeting them.

The brief description of the position in the examination announcement offers some clues to the subjects which will be tested. Think about the job itself. Review the duties in your mind. Can you perform them, or are there some in which you are rusty? Fill in the blank spots in your preparation.

Many jurisdictions preview the written test in the examination announcement by including a section called "Knowledge and Abilities Required," "Scope of Examination," or some similar heading. Here you will find out specifically what fields will be tested.

2. Review Your Own Background.-- Once you learn in general what the position is all about, and what you need to know to do the work, ask yourself which subjects you already know fairly well and which need improvement. You may wonder whether to concentrate on improving your strong areas or on building some background in your fields of weakness. When the announcement has specified "some knowledge" or "considerable knowledge," or has used adjectives such as "beginning principles of ...." or "advanced .....methods," you can get a clue as to the number and difficulty of questions to be asked in any given field. More questions, and hence broader coverage, would be included for those subjects which are more important in the work. Now weigh your strengths and weaknesses against the job requirements and prepare accordingly.

3. Determine the Level of the Position.-- Another way to tell how intensively you should prepare is to understand the level of the job for which you are applying. Is it the entering level? In other words, is this the position in which beginners in a field of work are hired? Or is it an intermediate or advanced level? Sometimes this is indicated by such words as "Junior" or "Senior" in the class title.Other jurisdictions use Roman numerals to designate the level: Clerk I,

Clerk II, for example. The word "Supervisor" sometimes appears in the title. If the level is not indicated by the title, check the description of duties. Will you be working under very close supervision, or will you have responsibility for independent decisions in this work?

4. Choose Appropriate Study Materials.-- Now that you know the subjects to be examined and the relative amount of each subject to be covered, you can choose suitable study materials. For beginning level jobs, or even advanced ones, if you have a pronounced weakness in some aspect of your training, read a modern, standard textbook in that field. Be sure it is up-to-date and has general coverage. Such books are normally available at your library, and the librarian will be glad to help you locate one. For entry level positions, questions of appropriate difficulty are chosen -- neither highly advanced questions, nor those too simple. Such questions require careful thought but not advanced training.

If the position for which you are applying is technical or advanced, you will read more advanced, specialized material. If you are already familiar with the basic principles of your field, elementary textbooks would waste your time. Concentrate on advanced textbooks and technical periodicals. Think through the concepts and review difficult problems in your field.

These are all general sources. You can get more ideas on your own initiative, following these leads. For example, training manuals and publications of the government agency which employs workers in your field can be useful, particularly for technical and professional positions. A letter or visit to the government department involved may result in more specific study suggestions, and certainly will provide you with a more definite idea of the exact nature of the position you are seeking.

II. KINDS OF TESTS

Tests are used for purposes other than measuring knowledge and ability to perform specified duties. For some positions, it is equally important to test ability to make adjustments to new situations or to profit from training. In others, basic mental abilities not dependent upon information are essential. Questions which test these things may not appear as pertinent to the duties of the position as those which test for knowledge and information. Yet they are often highly important parts of a fair examination. For very general questions, it is almost impossible to help you direct your study efforts. What we can do is to point out some of the more common of these general abilities needed in public service positions and describe some typical questions.

1. General Information

Broad, general information has been found useful for predicting job success in some kinds of work. This is tested in a variety of ways, from vocabulary lists to questions about current events. Basic background in some field of work, such as sociology or economics, may be sampled in a group of questions. Often these are principles which have become familiar to most persons through "exposure" rather than through formal training. It is difficult to advise you how to study for these questions; being alert to the world around you is our best suggestion.

2. Verbal Ability

An example of an ability needed in many positions is verbal or language ability. Verbal ability is, in brief, the ability to use and understand words. Vocabulary and grammar tests are typical measures of this ability. "Reading comprehension" or "paragraph interpretation" questions are common in many kinds of civil service tests. You are given a paragraph of written material and asked to find its central meaning.

3. Numerical Ability

Number skills can be tested by the familiar arithmetic problem, by checking paired lists of numbers to see which are alike and which are different, or by interpreting charts and graphs. In the latter test, a graph may be printed in the test booklet which you are asked to use as the basis for answering questions.

4. Observation

A popular test for law-enforcement positions is the observation test. A picture is shown to you for several minutes, then taken away. Questions about the picture test your ability to observe both details and larger elements.

5. Following Directions

In many positions in the public service, the employee must be able to carry out written instructions dependably and accurately. You may be given a chart with several columns, each column listing a variety of information. The questions require you to carry out directions involving the information given in the chart.

6. Skills and Aptitudes

Performance tests effectively measure some manual skills and aptitudes. When the skill is one in which you are trained, such as typing or shorthand, you can practice. These tests are often very much like those given in business school or high school courses. For many of the other skills and aptitudes, however, no short-time preparation can be made. Skills and abilities natural to you or that you have developed throughout your lifetime are being tested.

Many of the general questions just described provide all the data needed to answer the questions and ask you to use your reasoning ability to find the answers. Your best preparation for these tests, as well as for tests of facts and ideas, is to be at your physical and mental best. You, no doubt, have your own methods of getting into an exam-taking mood and keeping "in shape." The next section lists some ideas on this subject.

IV. KINDS OF QUESTIONS

Only rarely is the "essay" question, which you answer in narrative form, used in civil service tests. Civil service tests are usually of the short-answer type. Full instructions for answering these questions will be given to you at the examination. But in case this is your first experience with short-answer questions and separate answer sheets, here is what you need to know.

1. Multiple-Choice Questions

Most popular of the short-answer questions is the "multiple-choice" or "best-answer" question. It can be used, for example, to test for factual knowledge, ability to solve problems, or judgment in meeting situations found at work.

A multiple-choice question is normally one of three types:

(1) It can begin with an incomplete statement followed by several possible endings. You are to find the one ending which *best* completes the statement, although some of the others may not be entirely wrong.

(2) It can also be a complete statement in the form of a question which is answered by choosing one of the statements listed.

(3) It can be in the form of a problem -- again you select the best answer.

Here is an example of a multiple-choice question with a discussion which should give you some clues as to the method for choosing the right answer.

SAMPLE QUESTION:

When an employee has a complaint about his assignment, the action which will *best* help him overcome his difficulty is

(A) to discuss his difficulty with his co-workers
(B) to take the problem to the head of the organization
(C) to take the problem to the person who gave him the assignment
(D) to say nothing to anyone about his complaint

In answering this question you should study each of the choices to find which is best. Consider choice (A). Certainly an employee may discuss his complaint with fellow employees, but no change or improvement can result, and the complaint remains unsolved. Choice (B) is a poor choice since the head of the organization probably does not know what assignment you have been given, and taking your problem to him is known as "going over the head" of the supervisor. The supervisor, or person who made the assignment, is the person who can clarify it or correct any injustice. Choice (C) is, therefore, correct. To say nothing, as in choice (D), is unwise. Supervisors have an interest in knowing the problems employees are facing, and the employee is seeking a solution to his problem.

2. True-False Questions

The "true-false" or "right-wrong" form of question is sometimes used. Here a complete statement is given. Your problem is to decide whether the statement is right or wrong.

SAMPLE QUESTION:

A person-to-person long distance telephone call costs less than a station-to-station call to the same city.

This question is wrong, or "false," since person-to-person calls are more expensive.

This is not a complete list of all possible question forms, although most of the others are variations of these common types. You will always get complete directions for answering questions. Be sure you understand *how* to mark your answers -- ask questions until you do.

V. RECORDING YOUR ANSWERS

For an examination with very few applicants, you may be told to record your answers in the test booklet itself. Separate answer sheets are much more common. If this separate answer sheet is to be scored by machine -- and this is often the case -- it is highly important that you mark your answers correctly in order to get credit.

An electric test-scoring machine is often used in civil service offices because of the speed with which papers can be scored. Machine-scored answer sheets must be marked with a special pencil, which will be given to you. This pencil has a high graphite content which responds to the electrical scoring machine. As a matter of fact, stray dots may register as answers, so do not let your pencil rest on the answer sheet while you are pondering the correct answer. Also, if your pencil lead breaks or is otherwise defective, ask for another.

Since the answer sheet will be dropped in a slot in the scoring machine, be careful not to bend the corners or get the paper crumpled.

The answer sheet normally has five vertical columns of numbers, with 30 numbers to a column. These numbers correspond to the question numbers in your test booklet. After each number, going across the page, are four or five pairs of dotted lines. These short dotted lines have small letters or numbers above them. The first two pairs may also have a "T" and "F" above the letters. This indicates that the first two pairs only are to be used if the questions are of the true-false type. If the questions are multiple-choice, disregard this "T" and "F" completely, and pay attention only to the small number or letters.

Answer your questions in the manner of the sample that follows. Proceed in the sequential steps outlined below.

Assume that you are answering question 32, which is:

    32. The largest city in the United States is:

        A. Washington, D.C.   B. New York City   C. Chicago
        D. Detroit   E. San Francisco

1. Choose the answer you think is best.
   New York City is the largest, so choice B is correct.
2. Find the row of dotted lines numbered the same as the question you are answering.
   This is question number 32, so find row number 32.
3. Find the pair of dotted lines corresponding to the answer you have chosen.
   You have chosen answer B, so find the pair of dotted lines marked "B".
4. Make a solid black mark between the dotted lines.
   Go up and down two or three times with your pencil so plenty of graphite rubs off, but do not let the mark get outside or above the dots.

VI. BEFORE THE TEST

Common sense will help you find procedures to follow to get ready for an examination. Too many of us, however, overlook these sensible measures. Indeed, nervousness and fatigue have been found to be the most serious reasons why applicants fail to do their best on civil service tests. Here is a list of reminders.

1. Begin Your Preparation Early

Don't wait until the last minute to go scurrying around for books and materials or to find out what the position is all about.

2. Prepare Continuously

An hour a night for a week is better than an all-night cram session. This has been definitely established. What is more, a night a week for a month will return better dividends than crowding your study into a shorter period of time.

3. Locate the Place of the Examination

You have been sent a notice telling you when and where to report for the examination. If the location is in a different town or otherwise unfamiliar to you, it would be well to inquire the best route and learn something about the building.

4. Relax the Night Before the Test

Allow your mind to rest. Do not study at all that night. Plan some mild recreation or diversion; then go to bed early and get a good night's sleep.

5. Get Up Early Enough to Make a Leisurely Trip to the Place for the Test

Then unforeseen events, traffic snarls, unfamiliar buildings, will not upset you.

6. Dress Comfortably

A written test is not a fashion show. You will be known by number and not by name, so wear something comfortable.

7. Leave Excess Paraphernalia at Home

Shopping bags and odd bundles will get in your way. You need bring only the items mentioned in the official notice sent to you; usually everything you need is provided. Do not bring reference books to the examination. They will only confuse those last minutes and be taken away from you when in the test room.

8. Arrive Somewhat Ahead of Time

If because of transportation schedules you must get there very early, bring a newspaper or magazine to take your mind off yourself while waiting.

9. Locate the Examination Room

When you have found the proper room, you will be directed to the seat or part of the room where you will sit. Sometimes you are given a sheet of instructions to read while you are waiting. Do not fill out any forms until you are told to do so; just read them and be ready.

10. Relax and Prepare to Listen to the Instructions

11. If you have any physical problem that may keep you from doing your best, be sure to tell the test administrator. If you are sick, or in poor health, you really cannot do your best on the test. You can come back and take the test some other time.

AT THE TEST

The day of the test is here and you have the test booklet in your hand. The temptation to get going is very strong. Caution! There is more to success than knowing the right answers. You must know how to identify your papers and understand variations in the type of short-answer question used in this particular examination. Follow these suggestions for maximum results from your efforts:

1. Cooperate with the Monitor

   The test administrator has a duty to create a situation in which you can be as much at ease as possible. He will give instructions, tell you when to begin, check to see that you are marking your answer sheet correctly. He is not there to guard you, although he will see that your competitors do not take unfair advantage. He wants to help you do your best.

2. Listen to All Instructions

   Don't jump the gun! Wait until you understand all directions. In most civil service tests you get more time than you need to answer the questions. So don't get in a hurry. Read each word of instructions until you clearly understand the meaning. Study the examples. Listen to all announcements. Follow directions. Ask questions if you do not understand what to do.

3. Identify Your Papers

   Civil service examinations are usually identified by number only. You will be assigned a number; you must not put your name on your test papers. Be sure to copy your number correctly. Since more than one examination may be given, copy your exact examination title.

4. Plan Your Time

   Unless you are told that a test is a "speed" or "rate-of-work" test, speed itself is not usually important. Time enough to answer all the questions will be provided. But this does not mean that you have all day. An overall time limit has been set. Divide the total time (in minutes) by the number of questions to get the approximate time you have for each question.

5. Do Not Linger Over Difficult Questions

   If you come across a difficult question, mark it with a paper clip (useful to have along) and come back to it when you have been through the booklet. One caution if you do this -- be sure to skip a number on your answer sheet too. Check often to be sure that you have not lost your place and that you are marking in the row numbered the same as the question you are answering.

6. Read the Questions

   Be sure you know what the question asks! Many capable people are unsuccessful because they failed to *read* the questions correctly.

7. Answer All Questions

   Unless you have been instructed that a penalty will be deducted for incorrect answers, it is better to guess than to omit a question.

8. Speed Tests

   It is often better *not* to guess on speed tests. It has been found that on timed tests people are tempted to spend the last few seconds before time is called in marking answers at random -- without even reading them -- in the hope of picking up a few extra points. To discourage this practice, the instructions may warn you that your score will be "corrected" for guessing. That is, a penalty will be applied. The incorrect answers will be deducted from the correct ones, or some other penalty formula will be used.

9. Review Your Answers

   If you finish before time is called, go back to the questions you guessed or omitted to give further thought to them. Review other answers if you have time.

10. Return Your Test Materials

If you are ready to leave before others have finished or time is called, take *all* your materials to the monitor and leave quietly. Never take any test material with you. The monitor can discover whose papers are not complete, and taking a test booklet may be grounds for disqualification.

VIII. EXAMINATION TECHNIQUES

1. Read the *general* instructions carefully. These are usually printed on the first page of the examination booklet. As a rule, these instructions refer to the timing of the examination; the fact that you should not start work until the signal and must stop work at a signal, etc. If there are any *special* instructions, such as a choice of questions to be answered, make sure that you note this instruction carefully.

2. When you are ready to start work on the examination, that is as soon as the signal has been given, read the instructions to each question booklet, underline any key words or phrases, such as *least, best, outline, describe,* and the like. In this way you will tend to answer as requested rather than discover on reviewing your paper that you *listed without describing,* that you selected the *worst* choice rather than the *best* choice, etc.

3. If the examination is of the objective or so-called multiple-choice type, that is, each question will also give a series of possible answers: A, B, C, or D, and you are called upon to select the best answer and write the letter next to that answer on your answer paper, it is advisable to start answering each question in turn. There may be anywhere from 50 to 100 such questions in the three or four hours allotted and you can see how much time would be taken if you read through all the questions before beginning to answer any. Furthermore, if you come across a question or a group of questions which you know would be difficult to answer, it would undoubtedly affect your handling of all the other questions.

4. If the examination is of the esssay-type and contains but a few questions, it is a moot point as to whether you should read all the questions before starting to answer any one. Of course if you are given a choice, say five out of seven and the like, then it is essential to read all the questions so you can eliminate the two which are most difficult. If, however, you are asked to answer all the questions, there may be danger in trying to answer the easiest one first because you may find that you will spend too much time on it. The best technique is to answer the first question, then proceed to the second, etc.

5. Time your answers. Before the examination begins, write down the time it started, then add the time allowed for the examination and write down the time it must be completed, then divide the time available somewhat as follows:

(a) If $3\frac{1}{2}$ hours are allowed, that would be 210 minutes. If you have 80 objective-type questions, that would be an average of $2\frac{1}{2}$ minutes per question. Allow yourself no more than 2 minutes per question, or a total of 160 minutes, which will permit about 50 minutes to review.

(b) If for the time allotment of 210 minutes, there are 7 essay questions to answer, that would average about 30 minutes a question. Give yourself only 25 minutes per question so that you have about 35 minutes to review.

6. The most important instruction is *to read each question* and make sure you know what is wanted. The second most important instruction is to *time yourself properly* so that you answer every question. The third most important instruction is to *answer every question*. Guess if you have to but include something for each question. Remember that you will receive no credit for a blank and will probably receive some credit if you write something in answer to an essay question. If you guess a letter, say "B" for a multiple-choice question, you may have guessed right. If you leave a blank as the answer to a multiple-choice question, the examiners may respect your feelings but it will not add a point to your score.

7. Suggestions

a. <u>Objective-Type Questions</u>

(1) Examine the question booklet for proper sequence of pages and questions.

(2) Read all instructions carefully.

(3) Skip any question which seems too difficult; return to it after all other questions have been answered.

(4) Apportion your time properly; do not spend too much time on any single question or group of questions.

(5) Note and underline key words -- *all, most, fewest, least, best, worst, same, opposite.*

(6) Pay particular attention to negatives.

(7) Note unusual option, e.g., unduly long, short, complex, different or similar in content to the body of the question.

(8) Observe the use of "hedging" words -- *probably, may, most likely, etc.*

(9) Make sure that your answer is put next to the same number as the question.

(10) Do not second-guess unless you have good reason to believe the second answer is definitely more correct.

(11) Cross out original answer if you decide another answer is more accurate; do not erase.

(12) Answer all questions; guess unless instructed otherwise.

(13) Leave time for review.

b. <u>Essay-Type Questions</u>

(1) Read each question carefully.

(2) Determine exactly what is wanted. Underline key words or phrases.

(3) Decide on outline or paragraph answer.

(4) Include many different points and elements unless asked to develop any one or two points or elements.

(5) Show impartiality by giving pros and cons unless directed to select one side only.

(6) Make and write down any assumptions you find necessary to answer the question.

(7) Watch your English, grammar, punctuation, choice of words.

(8) Time your answers; don't crowd material.

8. Answering the Essay Question

Most essay questions can be answered by framing the specific response around several key words or ideas. Here are a few such key words or ideas:

M's: manpower, materials, methods, money, management;
P's: purpose, program, policy, plan, procedure, practice, problems, pitfalls, personnel, public relations.

a. Six Basic Steps in Handling Problems:
   (1) Preliminary plan and background development
   (2) Collect information, data and facts
   (3) Analyze and interpret information, data and facts
   (4) Analyze and develop solutions as well as make recommendations
   (5) Prepare report and sell recommendations
   (6) Install recommendations and follow up effectiveness

b. Pitfalls to Avoid
   (1) *Taking things for granted*
       A statement of the situation does not necessarily imply that each of the elements is necessarily true; for example, a complaint may be invalid and biased so that all that can be taken for granted is that a complaint has been registered.
   (2) *Considering only one side of a situation*
       Wherever possible, indicate several alternatives and then point out the reasons you selected the best one.
   (3) *Failing to indicate follow-up*
       Whenever your answer indicates action on your part, make certain that you will take proper follow-up action to see how successful your recommendations, procedures, or actions turn out to be.
   (4) *Taking too long in answering any single question*
       Remember to time your answers properly.

IX. AFTER THE TEST

Scoring procedures differ in detail among civil service jurisdictions although the general principles are the same. Whether the papers are hand-scored or graded by the electric scoring machine we have described, they are nearly always graded by number. That is, the person who marks the paper knows only the number -- never the name -- of the applicant. Not until all the papers have been graded will they be matched with names. If other tests, such as training and experience or oral interview ratings have been given, scores will be combined. Different parts of the examination usually have different weights. For example, the written test might count 60 percent of the final grade, and a rating of training and experience 40 percent. In many jurisdictions, veterans will have a certain number of points added to their grades.

After the final grade has been determined, the names are placed in grade order and an eligible list is established. There are various methods for resolving ties between those who get the same final grade: probably the most common is to place first the name of the person whose application was received first. Job offers are made from the eligible list in the order the names appear on it.

You will be notified of your grade and your rank order as soon as all these computations have been made. This will be done as rapidly as possible.

People who are found to meet the requirements in the announcement are called "eligibles." Their names are put on a list of eligibles. An eligible's chances of getting a job depend on how high he stands on this list and how fast agencies are filling jobs from the list.

When a job is to be filled from a list of eligibles, the agency asks for the names of people on the list of eligibles for that job.

When the civil service commission receives this request, it sends to the agency the names of the three people highest on the list. Or, if the job to be filled has specialized requirements, the office sends the agency, from the general list, the names of the top three persons who meet those requirements.

The appointing officer makes a choice from among the three people whose names were sent to him. If the selected person accepts the appointment, the names of the others are put back on the list to be considered for future openings.

That is the rule in hiring from all kinds of eligible lists, whether they are for typist, carpenter, chemist, or something else. For every vacancy, the appointing officer has his choice of any one of the top three eligibles on the list. This explains why the person whose name is on top of the list sometimes does not get an appointment when some of the persons lower on the list do. If the appointing officer chooses the No.2 or No.3 eligible, the No.1 eligible does not get a job at once, but stays on the list until he is appointed or the list is terminated.

X. HOW TO PASS THE INTERVIEW TEST

The examination for which you applied requires an oral interview test. You have already taken the written test and you are now being called for the interview test -- the final part of the formal examination.

You may think that it is not possible to prepare for an interview test and that there are no procedures to follow during an interview.

Our purpose is to point out some things you can do in advance that will help you and some good rules to follow and pitfalls to avoid while you are being interviewed.

A. WHAT IS AN INTERVIEW SUPPOSED TO TEST?

The written examination is designed to test the technical knowledge and competence of the candidate; the oral is designed to evaluate intangible qualities, not readily measured otherwise, and to establish a list showing the relative fitness of each candidate, *as measured against his competitors*, for the position sought. Scoring is not on the basis of "right" or "wrong," but on a sliding scale of values ranging from "not passable" to "outstanding." As a matter of fact, it is possible to achieve a relatively low score without a single "incorrect" answer because of evident weakness in the qualities being measured,

Occasionally, an examination may consist entirely of an oral test -- either an individual or a group oral. In such cases, information is sought concerning the technical knowledges and abilities of the candidate, since there has been no written examination for this purpose. More commonly, however, an oral test is used to supplement a written examination.

B. WHO CONDUCTS INTERVIEWS?

The composition of oral boards varies among different jurisdictions. In nearly all, a representative of the personnel department serves as chairman. One of the members of the board may be a representative of the department in which the candidate would work. In some cases, "outside experts" are used, and, frequently, a business man or some other representative of the general public is asked to serve. Labor and management or other special groups may be represented. The aim is to secure the services of experts in the appropriate field.

However the board is composed, it is a good idea (and not at all improper or unethical) to ascertain in advance of the interview who the members are and what groups they represent. When you are introduced to them, you will have some idea of their backgrounds and interests, and at least you will not stutter and stammer over their names.

C. WHAT TO DO BEFORE THE INTERVIEW

While knowledge about the board members is useful and takes some of the surprise element out of the interview, there is other preparation which is more substantive. It *is* possible to prepare for an oral -- in several ways:

1. <u>Keep a Copy of Your Application and Review it Carefully Before the Interview</u>

   This may be the only document before the oral board, and the starting point of the interview. Know what experience and education you have listed there, and the sequence and dates of it. Sometimes the board will ask *you* to review the highlights of your experience for them; you should not have to hem and haw doing it.

2. <u>Study the Class Specification and the Examination Announcement</u>

   Usually, the oral board has one or both of these to guide them. The qualities, characteristics, or knowledges required by the position sought are stated in these documents. They offer valuable clues as to the nature of the oral interview. For example, if the job involves supervisory responsibilities, the announcement will usually indicate that knowledge of modern supervisory methods and the qualifications of the candidate as a supervisor will be tested. If so, you can expect such questions, frequently in the form of a hypothetical situation which you are expected to solve. *Never* go into an oral without knowledge of the duties and responsibilities of the job you seek.

3. <u>Think Through Each Qualification Required</u>

   Try to visualize the kind of questions *you* would ask if you were a board member. How well could you answer them? Try especially to appraise your own knowledge and background in each area, *measured against the job sought,* and identify any areas in which you are weak. Be critical and realistic -- do not flatter yourself.

4. <u>Do Some General Reading in Areas in Which You Feel You May be Weak</u>

   For example, if the job involves supervision and your past experience has *not,* some general reading in supervisory methods and practices, particularly in the field of human relations, might be useful. *Do not* study agency procedures or detailed manuals. The oral board will be testing your understanding and capacity, *not* your memory.

5. <u>Get a Good Night's Sleep and Watch Your General Health and Mental Attitude</u>

   You will want a clear head at the interview. Take care of a cold or other minor ailment, and, of course, *no hangovers.*

D. WHAT TO DO THE DAY OF THE INTERVIEW

Now comes the day of the interview itself. Give yourself plenty of time to get there. Plan to arrive somewhat ahead of the scheduled time, particularly if your appointment is in the fore part of the day. If a previous candidate fails to appear, the board might be ready for you a bit early. By early afternoon an oral board is almost invariably behind schedule if there are many candidates, and you may have to wait. Take along a book or magazine to read, or your application to review. But leave any extraneous material in the waiting room when you go in for your interview. In any event, relax and compose yourself.

The matter of dress is important. The board is forming impressions about you -- from your experience, your manners, your attitudes, and from your appearance. Give your personal appearance careful attention. Dress your *best*, but not your flashiest. Choose conservative, appropriate clothing, and be sure it and you are immaculate. This is a business interview, and your appearance should indicate that you regard it as such. Besides, being well-groomed and properly dressed will help boost your confidence.

Sooner or later, someone will call your name and escort you into the interview room. *This is it.* From here on you are on your own. It is too late for any more preparation. But, remember, you asked for this opportunity to prove your fitness, and you are here because your request was granted.

E. WHAT HAPPENS WHEN YOU GO IN?

The usual sequence of events will be as follows: The clerk (who is often the board stenographer) will introduce you to the chairman of the oral board, who will introduce you to each other member of the board. Acknowledge the introductions before you sit down. Do not be surprised if you find a microphone facing you or a stenotypist sitting by. Oral interviews are usually recorded, in the event of an appeal or other review.

Usually the chairman of the board will open the interview by reviewing the highlights of your education and work experience from your application -- primarily for the benefit of the other members of the board, as well as to get the material into the record. Do not interrupt or comment unless there is an error or significant misinterpretation; if so, do not hesitate. But do not quibble about insignificant matters. Usually, also, he will ask you some question about your education, your experience, or your present job -- partly to get you started talking, to establish the interviewing "rapport." He may start the actual questioning, or turn it over to one of the other members. Frequently each member undertakes the questioning on a particular area, one in which he is perhaps most competent. So you can expect each member to participate in the examination. And because the time is limited, you may expect some rather abrupt switches in the direction the questioning takes. Do not be upset by it. Normally, a board member will not pursue a single line of questioning unless he discovers a particular strength or weakness.

After each member has participated, the chairman will usually ask whether any member has any further questions, then will ask you if you have anything you wish to add. Unless you are expecting this question, it may floor you. Or worse, it may start you off on an extended, extemporaneous speech. The board is not usually seeking more information. The question is principally to offer you a last opportunity to present further qualifications or to indicate that you have nothing to add. So, if you feel that a significant qualification or characteristic has been overlooked, it is proper to point it out in a sentence or so. Do not compliment the board on the thoroughness of their examination -- they have been sketchy, and you know it. If you wish, merely say, "No thank you, I have nothing further to add." This is a point where you can "talk yourself out" of a good impression or fail to present an important bit of information. *Remember, you close the interview yourself.*

The chairman will then say, "That is all, Mr. Smith, thank you." Do not be startled; the interview is over, and quicker than you think. Say, "Thank you and good morning," gather up your belongings and take your leave. Save your sigh of relief for the other side of the door.

F. *HOW TO PUT YOUR BEST FOOT FORWARD*

Throughout all this process, you may feel that the board individually and collectively is trying to pierce your defenses, to seek out your hidden weaknesses, and to embarrass and confuse you. Actually, this is not true. They are obliged to make an appraisal of your qualifications for the job you are seeking, and they *want to see you in your best light.* Remember, they must interview all candidates and a noncooperative candidate may become a failure in spite of their best efforts to bring out his qualifications. Here are fifteen(15) suggestions that will help you:

1. Be Natural. Keep Your Attitude Confident, But Not Cocky

If *you* are not confident that you can do the job, do not expect the *board* to be. Do not apologize for your weaknesses, try to bring out your strong points. The board is interested in a positive, not a negative presentation. Cockiness will antagonize any board member, and make him wonder if you are covering up a weakness by a false show of strength.

2. Get Comfortable, But Don't Lounge or Sprawl

Sit erectly but not stiffly. A careless posture may lead the board to conclude you are careless in other things, or at least that you are not impressed by the importance of the occasion to you. Either conclusion is natural, even if incorrect. Do not fuss with your clothing, or with a pencil or an ashtray. Your hands may occasionally be useful to emphasize a point; do not let them become a point of distraction.

3. Do Not Wisecrack or Make Small Talk

This is a serious situation, and your attitude should show that you consider it as such. Further, the time of the board is limited; they do not want to waste it, and neither should you.

4. Do Not Exaggerate Your Experience or Abilities

In the first place, from information in the application, from other interviews and other sources, the board may know more about you than you think; in the second place, you probably will not get away with it in the first place. An experienced board is rather adept at spotting such a situation. Do not take the chance.

5. If You Know a Member of the Board, Do Not Make a Point of It, Yet Do Not Hide It.

Certainly you are not fooling him, and probably not the other members of the board. Do not try to take advantage of your acquaintanceship -- it will probably do you little good.

6. Do Not Dominate the Interview

Let the board do that. They will give you the clues -- do not assume that you have to do all the talking. Realize that the board has a number of questions to ask you, and do not try to take up all the interview time by showing off your extensive knowledge of the answer to the first one.

15

7. Be Attentive

You only have twenty minutes or so, and you should keep your attention at its sharpest throughout. When a member is addressing a problem or a question to you, give him your undivided attention. Address your reply principally to him, but do not exclude the other members of the board.

8. Do Not Interrupt

A board member may be stating a problem for you to analyze. He will ask you a question when the time comes. Let him state the problem, and wait for the question.

9. Make Sure You Understand the Question

Do not try to answer until you are sure what the question is. If it is not clear, restate it in your own words or ask the board member to clarify it for you. But do not haggle about minor elements.

10. Reply Promptly But Not Hastily

A common entry on oral board rating sheets is "candidate responded readily," or "candidate hesitated in replies." Respond as promptly and quickly as you can, but do not jump to a hasty, ill-considered answer.

11. Do Not Be Peremptory in Your Answers

A brief answer is proper -- but do not fire your answer back. That is a losing game from your point of view. The board member can probably ask questions much faster than you can answer them.

12. Do Not Try To Create the Answer You Think the Board Member Wants

He is interested in what kind of · mind you have and how it works -- not in playing games. Furthermore, he can usually spot this practice and will usually grade you down on it.

13. Do Not Switch Sides in Your Reply Merely to Agree With a Board Member

Frequently, a member will take a contrary position merely to draw you out and to see if you are willing and able to defend your point of view. Do not start a debate, yet do not surrender a good position. If a position is worth taking, it is worth defending.

] Do Not Be Afraid to Admit an Error in Judgment if You Are Shown to Be Wrong

The board knows that you are forced to reply without any opportunity for careful consideration. Your answer may be demonstrably wrong. If so, admit it and get on with the interview.

15. Do Not Dwell at Length on Your Present Job

The opening question may relate to your present assignment. Answer the question but do not go into an extended discussion. You are being examined for a *new* job, not your present one. As a matter of fact, try to phrase *all* your answers in terms of the job for which you are being examined.

G. BASIS OF RATING

Probably you will forget most of these "do's" and "don'ts" when you walk into the oral interview room. Even remembering them all will not insure you a passing grade. Perhaps you did not have the qualifications in the first place. But remembering them *will* help you to put your best foot forward, without treading on the toes of the board members.

Rumor and popular opinion to the contrary notwithstanding, an oral board wants you to make the best appearance possible. They know you are under pressure -- but they also want to see how you respond to it as a guide to what your reaction would be under the pressures of the job you seek. They will be influenced by the degree of poise you display, the personal traits you show, and the manner in which you respond.

EXAMINATION SECTION

EXAMINATION SECTION
TEST 1

DIRECTIONS: Each question or incomplete statement is followed by
several suggested answers or completions. Select the
one that BEST answers the question or completes the
statement. *PRINT THE LETTER OF THE CORRECT ANSWER IN
THE SPACE AT THE RIGHT.*

1. The primary aim of the traditional treatment-oriented   1.___
    model of reintegrating offenders is
      A. the cultivation of remorse and conscience
      B. the establishment of a routine that will limit an
         offender's behavioral options
      C. long-term change in offender behavior
      D. the creation of an undesignated *buffer* between the
         offender and potential victims

2. What is the term for a judicial or quasi-judicial proceed-   2.___
    ing held to determine whether it is appropriate to continue
    to hold a juvenile in a shelter facility?
      A. Demand waiver   B. Detention hearing
      C. Delinquency petition   D. Detainer warrant

3. Which of the following is considered to be an advantage   3.___
    of indeterminate sentencing in relation to parole?
    It
      A. forces society to confront the underlying causes of
         crime
      B. involves concrete, easily followed guidelines for the
         designation of some offenders as mentally ill
      C. offers maximum protection to society from hard-core
         recidivists
      D. supplies much positive motivation to prisoners for
         their own rehabilitation

4. Status offenses that are removed from the jurisdiction of   4.___
    juvenile court or secure-custody facilities are described
    as
      A. deinstitutionalized   B. commutated
      C. desanctioned   D. readjudicated

5. The most common organizational model for adult paroling   5.___
    authorities is the _____ model.
      A. institutional   B. consolidation
      C. intensive   D. autonomous

6. The substations or satellite offices of regular probation   6.___
    and parole agencies are commonly referred to as
      A. annexes   B. PORTs
      C. outreach centers   D. halfway houses

7. When parole was first practiced in some form in Europe   7.___
   in the 1700s, it was largely instituted in response to
      A. excessive sentencing by judges
      B. a growing reform movement that emphasized rehabili-
         tation
      C. political corruption involved in early release
      D. prison overcrowding

8. *Avertable recidivist* is a term that refers to   8.___
      A. a new concept based on the correctional goal of
         offender reintegration into the community
      B. the phenomenon of gradually progressing to more
         serious forms of offending
      C. an offender who would still have been in prison
         serving a sentence at a time when a new offense was
         committed
      D. one who commits a misdemeanor

9. The first true use of parole in the United States occurred   9.___
   in
      A. 1790, in Pennsylvania   B. 1817, in New York
      C. 1846, in Tennessee   D. 1884, in Massachusetts

10. Collectively, probation, diversion, and community-based   10.___
    correctional programs are described as _____ solutions
    to jail and prison overcrowding.
      A. front-end   B. contractive
      C. halfway   D. nominal

11. Juvenile intensive supervision probation (JISP) programs   11.___
    are typically characterized by each of the following
    EXCEPT
      A. high levels of offender control
      B. low levels of offender responsibility
      C. frequent checks for arrests, substance abuse, and
         employment/school attendance
      D. low officer/client caseloads

12. The collective term used for the constraints imposed on   12.___
    some probationers or parolees to increase the restrictive-
    ness or painfulness of probation or parole is
      A. treatment conditions   B. strictures
      C. civil disabilities   D. punitive conditions

13. The MOST reliable indicator of recidivism, as well as the   13.___
    most valid definition of the term, is
      A. revocation or unsatisfactory termination
      B. reconviction
      C. technical rule violations
      D. rearrest

14. Correction officers sometimes attempt to predict the   14.___
    future behavior of inmates based on a class of offenders
    considered for parole. This process is known as
      A. matching   B. actuarial prediction
      C. anamnestic prediction   D. clinical prediction

15. Currently, the most important factor in parole board   15.___
    decision-making appears to be
      A. the increasing emphasis on public safety
      B. the growth of the community corrections movement
      C. prison overcrowding
      D. the spread of presumptive sentencing

16. Currently, the federal corrections system grants federal   16.___
    prisoners up to _____ days per year as good-time credit
    against their original sentence lengths.
      A. 36   B. 54   C. 88   D. 120

17. The functions of most work release programs include   17.___
      I. participation in vocational or educational training
     II. provision of food and shelter
    III. promotion of self-respect
     IV. community reintegration

    The CORRECT answer is:
      A. I, II   B. I, III, IV
      C. II, IV   D. I, III

18. The Federal Tort Claims Act of 1946 permits   18.___
      A. correctional officers and parole or probation super-
         visors to sue inmates or clients for punitive damages
         arising from harm associated with the officer/inmate
         or PO-client relation
      B. victims of crimes to sue the offender for punitive
         damages arising from the harm associated with the
         commission of the crime, regardless of criminal
         conviction
      C. federal prisoners and those under federal parole or
         probation supervision the right to sue their super-
         visors and/or administrators for punitive damages
         arising from harm associated with officer/inmate or
         PO-client relation
      D. defendants to sue for punitive damages arising from
         the harm associated with wrongful prosecution

19. Which of the following comparative statements about   19.___
    probation and parole is generally TRUE?
      A. Probation usually has a higher success rate.
      B. Probation is not granted to violent criminals.
      C. Parole has traditionally been more punishment-oriented.
      D. Parole involves a more intensive one-on-one monitor-
         ing effort.

20. Which of the following is a basic measure of the occurrence 20.___
    of a crime?
      A. Technical infraction   B. Expense
      C. Victimization   D. Increased risk or threat

21. Among corrections professionals, the term *furlough* is often used interchangeably with
    A. conditional prerelease   B. standard parole
    C. unconditional prerelease D. work release

21.___

22. What is the term for a parole board decision-making system that emphasizes the functions of parole supervision and management?
    _____ system.
    A. Congregate   B. Jurist value
    C. Controller value   D. Specialized caseloads

22.___

23. Which of the following is a policy implication involved in the rehabilitation model of probation practice?
    A. Reduced judicial discretion
    B. Mandated sentencing ranges
    C. Decriminalization
    D. Proportional sentencing

23.___

24. The portion of a presentence investigation report prepared by a parole officer or agency, in which a description of the offense and the offender is provided, and which culminates in and justifies a recommendation for a specific sentence to be imposed on the offender by the judges, is called the
    A. portrait parle   B. narrative
    C. needs assessment   D. presentment

24.___

25. Nationwide, approximately what percentage of parole terms currently end in successful completion?
    A. 15   B. 35   C. 50   D. 75

25.___

KEY (CORRECT ANSWERS)

1. C		11. B	
2. B		12. D	
3. C		13. B	
4. A		14. B	
5. D		15. C	
6. C		16. B	
7. D		17. B	
8. C		18. C	
9. D		19. C	
10. A		20. C	

21. D
22. C
23. C
24. B
25. B

TEST 2

DIRECTIONS: Each question or incomplete statement is followed by several suggested answers or completions. Select the one that BEST answers the question or completes the statement. *PRINT THE LETTER OF THE CORRECT ANSWER IN THE SPACE AT THE RIGHT.*

1. In the _____ model of supervision, the probation/parole officer serves primarily as a counselor, dispensing *treatment* to *clients* in a one-on-one therapeutic relationship.
   A. justice   B. casework   C. brokerage D. medical

   1.___

2. At the departmental level, the most important goal of officers is typically identified as
   A. successful completion of the parole term
   B. the reintegration of the client
   C. rehabilitation
   D. the safety of the community

   2.___

3. Evidence or material that demonstrates or supports a defendant's innocence is described as
   A. exculpatory   B. mitigating
   C. injunctive   D. recusive

   3.___

4. Which of the following is NOT generally perceived to be a difference between modern jails and modern prisons?
   A. Jails have a greater diversity of inmates.
   B. The physical plants of prisons are in poorer condition.
   C. Jails are not usually partitioned into areas of differing security.
   D. Prison inmate culture is more pronounced and persistent.

   4.___

5. The United States Supreme Court ruling in the 1983 <u>Bearden v. Georgia</u> case established that
   A. probationers and parolees are entitled to legal representation at any revocation hearing
   B. a probationer who is indigent may not have probation revoked because of a failure to pay fines or make restitution
   C. the legal procedural requirements for probation revocation are the same as that for parole
   D. judges are not generally obligated to consider alternatives to incarceration before revoking an offender's probation

   5.___

6. A petty crime, punishable by a fine only, is described as a
   A. summary offense   B. nugatory offense
   C. status offense   D. misdemeanor

   6.___

7. Which of the following statements about probationer/parolee   7.___
   rights relative to program conditions is FALSE?
       A. A probationer/parolee who is in custody is not
          entitled to a Miranda warning.
       B. Search and seizure grounds are less stringent for POs
          who itend to search a client's home for contraband.
       C. Statements made to a PO during questioning are
          admissible under almost any circumstances as evidence
          in court for supporting new criminal cases.
       D. Restitution is a legitimate condition of probation/
          parole, but not always an efforceable condition.

8. What is the term for any authorized, unescorted leave   8.___
   from confinement granted for a specific purpose and for
   a designated time period?
       A. Pass   B. Release-on-recognizance
       C. Furlough   D. Parole

9. Which of the following offers the best explanation for why   9.___
   some probation/parole officers choose to overlook certain
   technical violations by offenders?
       A. The officer has developed a sympathetic attitude
          toward the offender.
       B. It is not considered evidence of criminal activity.
       C. Reincarceration of the offender may only serve to
          aggravate the overcrowding problem.
       D. The violation may have been committed intentionally.

10. Circumstances of a crime that enhance an offender's   10.___
    sentence are described as
       A. aggravating   B. mitigating
       C. amplifying   D. augmenting

11. Though community-based corrections programs vary in size   11.___
    and scope, they tend to share common characteristics.
    Which of the following is NOT one of these?
       A. On-call support services (medical, social, psycholo-
          gical)
       B. Heightened staff accountability to the court concern-
          ing offender progress
       C. Centralized control of program resources
       D. 24-hour availability of administrators on premises

12. Which of the following is not considered to be an *inter-*   12.___
    mediate sanction?
       A. Probation   B. House arrest
       C. Community service   D. Restitution

13. Which of the following is NOT typically a goal of home   13.___
    confinement?
    To
       A. reduce the costs of offender supervision
       B. demonstrate faith in the offender's word
       C. maintain a controlled community presence
       D. enable offenders to assume familial responsibility

14. For most of the current period, beginning in the 1970s,   14.____
    the prevailing philosophy operating in United States
    corrections has shifted to that of
    A. isolation   B. rehabilitation
    C. retribution   D. deterrence

15. The official document that is filed in juvenile courts   15.____
    on the juvenile's behalf, specifying the reasons for the
    court appearance, is the
    A. conferral B. bid   C. petition   D. linkage

16. In evaluating a parole program's effectiveness in assess-   16.____
    ing an offender's suitability for placement, which of the
    following would be the most appropriate performance
    indicator?
    A. Number of drug-free and/or alcohol-free days during
       supervision
    B. Number and type of technical violations during super-
       vision
    C. Accuracy and completeness of presentence investiga-
       tions
    D. Extent of victim satisfaction with service and
       department

17. In 1931, a report was released on the status of United   17.____
    States parole practices by the Wickersham Commission,
    a National Commission on Law Observance and Enforcement.
    Which of the following were findings of the report?
      I. Victims were dissatisfied with the amount of prison
         time served by offenders.
     II. Parole caused the release of many dangerous, unre-
         habilitated criminals into society.
    III. A suitable system for determining parole eligibility
         did not exist.

    The CORRECT answer is:
    A. I, II   B. I, III
    C. II, III   D. I, II, III

18. The *logical consequences* model, an emerging model in   18.____
    juvenile probation, is based on a number of assumptions.
    Which of the following is NOT one of these?
    A. It is not usually necessary to include serious punish-
       ments in a juvenile probation program; the emphasis
       should be on needs assessment and rehabilitation.
    B. Juvenile offenders have free will and should be held
       responsible for what they do.
    C. It is possible to develop effective relationships
       with juvenile probationers once they decide to take
       probation seriously.
    D. Youthful offenders will only modify their behavior
       when the cost of their behavior becomes too high.

19. Under the conventional model of caseload assignment, probation or parole officers are assigned to clients
    A. randomly
    B. according to the nature of the offense
    C. geographically
    D. according to the training of the officer

19.____

20. Approximately what percentage of inmates who enter parole supervision each year in the United States have committed violent offenses?
    A. 10   B. 25   C. 35   D. 45

20.____

21. The correctional model based on the concept of *just desserts* is the _____ model.
    A. penal   B. justice
    C. presumptive   D. medical

21.____

22. A parole officer may issue a warrant for a parolee's return to prison only after the warrant has been issued by the
    A. local law enforcement agency
    B. parole board
    C. local court
    D. corrections department

22.____

23. Which of the following is NOT an example of an intermittent sentence?
    An
    A. offender's location is electronically monitored
    B. offender must serve weekends in jail
    C. offender must spend specific weeknights in home confinement
    D. offender must adhere to a curfew

23.____

24. Which of the following is most commonly a criticism of halfway houses?
    They
    A. do not provide for the basic needs of clients
    B. tend to cost more than incarceration
    C. don't tend to support the long-term maintenance of client employment
    D. are not effective in preventing criminal behavior

24.____

25. Based on parole officers' experiences, which of the following factors is least likely to function as a predictor of a parolee's successful reintegration?
    A. Marital status
    B. Participation in academic or vocational programs
    C. Good prison behavior
    D. Prior problems with drug/alcohol abuse

25.____

KEY (CORRECT ANSWERS)

1.	B		11.	C
2.	D		12.	A
3.	A		13.	B
4.	B		14.	C
5.	B		15.	C
6.	A		16.	C
7.	A		17.	C
8.	C		18.	A
9.	B		19.	A
10.	A		20.	B

21. B
22. B
23. A
24. C
25. C

TEST 3

DIRECTIONS: Each question or incomplete statement is followed by several suggested answers or completions. Select the one that BEST answers the question or completes the statement. *PRINT THE LETTER OF THE CORRECT ANSWER IN THE SPACE AT THE RIGHT.*

1. What is the term for a document given to a prisoner as a result of accumulating good-time marks, which obligates the prisoner to remain under limited jurisdiction and supervision of local police?
   A. ROR
   B. Ticket-of-leave
   C. Conditional release
   D. Provisional certificate

   1.__

2. In contrast to other post-release correctional programs, work release programs emphasize
   A. responsibility for dependents
   B. community service
   C. the provision of shelter
   D. victim restitution

   2.__

3. The probation/parole officer work-role in which the offender seeks to instruct and assist offenders in dealing with problems as they arise is the _____ role.
   A. promoter   B. enabler   C. enforcer   D. broker

   3.__

4. In recent years, criticisms of probation and parole programs in the United States have included
   I. insufficient licensing mechanisms for officer certification
   II. PO training based on same military model used for police training
   III. lack of coordination with other criminal justice agencies
   IV. selection procedures for officers based on physical attributes and security considerations

   The CORRECT answer is:
   A. I, III, IV
   B. II, III
   C. III, IV
   D. I, II, III, IV

   4.__

5. Which of the following was NOT a reason for the decline in the significance and influence of the rehabilitative model in United States corrections?
   A. Unacceptable levels of recidivism
   B. The rise of victims' rights movement
   C. Rising crime rates
   D. General dissension among corrections professionals

   5.__

6. The average length of time for an offender to spend on parole is about _____ months.
   A. 8   B. 19   C. 27   D. 38

   6.__

7. Judges often sentence low-risk offenders to incarceration   7.___
   with a strong warning that they be encouraged to apply for
   intensive probation supervision programs. This process is
   known as
      A. alternative sentencing   B. backdooring
      C. screening   D. stacking

8. Which of the following is a commonly perceived DISADVANTAGE   8.___
   associated with electronic monitoring?
      A. Studies show higher recidivism rates than standard
         probation
      B. More costly than standard monitoring procedures
      C. Those chosen for participation tend to be those who
         do not require monitoring anyway
      D. Does not accommodate special-needs clients

9. The primary distinguishing feature between probation and   9.___
   parole is that
      A. parole involves a clear instance of conviction
      B. parole involves indeterminate sentencing
      C. probation is granted or imposed as a sentence by a
         judge
      D. probation is a fixed-term situation

10. Among paroling agencies, the most desirable outcome measure   10.___
    for the effectiveness of a parole program is
       A. family stability
       B. new arrests
       C. the number of supervision terms completed
       D. the amount of restitution collected

11. What is the term for a parole board decision-making system   11.___
    that regards such decisions as a natural part of the
    criminal justice process, and in which fairness and equity
    predominate?
       A. Specialized caseloads systems
       B. Jurist value system
       C. Controller value system
       D. Regulator value system

12. Which of the following is most commonly used as an item   12.___
    in a paroling authority's release risk instruments?
       A. Drug use
       B. Number of prior convictions
       C. Total years incarcerated
       D. Number of parole revocations

13. Standard conditions of probation and parole typically   13.___
    include
       I. reporting a change of address
      II. remaining employed
     III. performing community service
      IV. not leaving the jurisdiction without permission

    The CORRECT answer is:
       A. I, II   B. I, III, IV
       C. I, II, IV   D. III, IV

14. Most state work release programs require that eligible   14.___
    candidates must have served at LEAST _____% of their
    incarcerative sentence.
      A. 10   B. 30   C. 50   D. 70

15. What is the term for the administratively authorized   15.___
    early release of an offender from custody?
      A. Abrogation   B. Commutation
      C. Rescission   D. Surrogation

16. In the traditional model of parole agency orientation,   16.___
    the emphasis is most often placed on
      A. the specialization of officers in certain kinds of
        problems
      B. offender change
      C. increased accountability for service availability
      D. even distribution of caseloads among officers

17. Each of the following is generally a difference between   17.___
    probationers and parolees in United States corrections
    EXCEPT
      A. the offenses of parolees are more serious
      B. parolees have been convicted
      C. parolees have been incarcerated for a portion of
        their sentences
      D. the conditions of probation are not as stringent

18. Which of the following statements about recidivism is   18.___
    generally TRUE?
      A. The greater the intensity of supervision, the less
        likely the recidivism
      B. The earlier offenders begin their careers, the more
        likely the recidivism
      C. The longer the time served in prison, the less likely
        the recidivism
      D. Violent offenders are more likely to recidivate than
        property offenders

19. The Federal Sentencing Reform Act of 1984   19.___
      A. encouraged the states' adoption of *three strikes*
        sentencing statutes
      B. established a mechanism for investigating charges of
        sentencing disparity
      C. provided federal judges and others with discretionary
        powers to provide alternative sentencing
      D. extended the death penalty to a number of drug crimes

20. Participants in day reporting programs should probably   20.___
    NOT include
      A. those with an established residence
      B. inmates within 6 months of release
      C. sex offenders
      D. those without an identified victim

21. Which of the following is most likely to be considered a latent function of parole?
    A. Integrating offenders into a structured community
    B. Separating offenders from the criminal element
    C. Alleviating prison overcrowding
    D. Preventing recidivism

21.___

22. Compared to routine court procedures related to fine assessment and payment, day-fine structures involve the advantage of
    I. fewer warrants for nonappearance at postsentence hearings
    II. greater victim satisfaction
    III. fewer court appearances
    IV. more extended terms of payment for larger fines

    The CORRECT answer is:
    A. I, II   B. I, III, IV
    C. II, IV   D. III, IV

22.___

23. The most important factor distinguishing between a *halfway in* and a *halfway out* house is
    A. whether the goal of the program is reintegration
    B. whether participants are probationers or parolees
    C. the variety of services available to participants
    D. the amount of time served by participating inmates

23.___

24. Most recidivists tend to
    A. be under correctional supervision when committing new offenses
    B. commit progressively more serious offenses
    C. be under 30 years of age
    D. be unemployed when committing new offenses

24.___

25. Approximately what percentage of adult prisoners being held in jails today are pretrial detainees?
    A. 10   B. 30   C. 50   D. 70

25.___

KEY (CORRECT ANSWERS)

1. B	6. B	11. B	16. D	21. C
2. D	7. B	12. D	17. B	22. B
3. B	8. C	13. C	18. B	23. B
4. D	9. C	14. A	19. C	24. C
5. B	10. D	15. B	20. C	25. C

EXAMINATION SECTION
TEST 1

DIRECTIONS: Each question or incomplete statement is followed by several suggested answers or completions. Select the one that BEST answers the question or completes the statement. *PRINT THE LETTER OF THE CORRECT ANSWER IN THE SPACE AT THE RIGHT.*

1. The institution of parole rests on the concepts of   1.___
   I. retribution   II. contract of consent
   III. custody   IV. grace or privilege

   The CORRECT answer is:
   A. I, III   B. II, IV
   C. II, III, IV   D. I, II, III, IV

2. _____ sentencing occurs when the court is required to   2.___
   impose an incarcerative sentence of a specified length,
   without the option for probation, suspended sentence, or
   immediate parole eligibility.
   A. Guidelines-based   B. Mandatory
   C. Presumptive   D. Determinate

3. Each of the following is generally considered to be an   3.___
   advantage associated with community service as a form
   of corrections EXCEPT
   A. unambiguous punishment
   B. court benefit of sentencing alternatives
   C. community benefit of restitution
   D. reintegration of offenders in responsible, law-
      abiding roles

4. Some electronic monitoring devices function by telephoning 4.___
   an offender at random hours to verify that he is where he
   is supposed to be. These are _____ devices.
   A. programmed contact   B. vicarious monitoring
   C. random access   D. continuous signaling

5. Which of the following is the basic change strategy   5.___
   involved in the deterrence model of probation practice?
   A. Care and control   B. Punishment
   C. Surveillance   D. Threats

6. Which of the following is NOT considered to be a goal   6.___
   common to all community corrections programs?
   A. Maintaining some degree of ostracism
   B. Facilitating offender reintegration
   C. Heightening offender accountability
   D. Fostering rehabilitation

7. Which of the following court cases established the 7.__
minimum due process requirements for offenders undergoing
parole revocation proceedings?
A. *In re Gault* (1967)
B. *Mempa v. Rhay* (1967)
C. *McKeiver v. Pennsylvania* (1970)
D. *Morrissey v. Brewer* (1972)

8. The SFS/81 guidelines for parole release decisions include 8.__
each of the following scoring items EXCEPT
A. heroin/opiate dependence
B. recent commitment-free period
C. age at current offense/prior commitments
D. employment history

9. Which of the following is/are a type of unconditional 9.__
release?
I. Mandatory parole   II. Expiration
III. Commutation   IV. Parole board release

The CORRECT answer is:
A. I, III   B. I, IV   C. II, III   D. II, IV

10. Other than the requirement to obey all federal, state, 10.__
and local laws, the condition of parole most often imposed
by United States paroling authorities is that the offender
A. meet family responsibilities and support dependents
B. remain within the jurisdiction of the court and notify
the officer of any change in residence
C. maintain gainful employment
D. report to the parole officer as directed and answer
all reasonable inquiries

11. Which of the following was a ruling in the 1975 *Breed v.* 11.__
Jones case?
A. Deliberate indifference by prison authorities to
serious medical disorders of prisoners violates the
Eighth Amendment as *cruel and unusual punishment.*
B. A juvenile may not be adjudicated as delinquent in
juvenile courts and then tried as adults in criminal
courts later on the same charges.
C. A probationer is entitled to have court-appointed
counsel at hearings concerning violations of the
terms of probation.
D. Female inmates must receive equal corrections program-
ming.

12. A parole officer and an offender list a high number of 12.__
supervision objectives in their parole plan. This
generally indicates a
A. lack of trust between the officer and the offender
B. high emphasis on control for the officer
C. high degree of centralized bureaucratic control
D. high emphasis on assistance for the officer

13. When an offender is placed in prison for a brief period, primarily to give him a sense of prison life, and then released into the custody of a probation or parole officer, the offender has undergone
   A. role ambiguity   B. mixed sentencing
   C. unconditional diversion   D. shock probation
13.___

14. In juvenile corrections, the equivalent of a presentence investigation is the
   A. delinquency petition   B. predispositional report
   C. detention hearing   D. demand waiver
14.___

15. The significant problems in providing correctional treatment for white-collar offenders include
  I. not requiring job training
  II. their not being receptive to counseling
 III. their correctional term is typically too short to be influential
  IV. they are likely to come from an environment plagued by social problems

The CORRECT answer is:
   A. I, II   B. I, II, III
   C. I, III, IV   D. II, III, IV
15.___

16. In the *numbers game* model of assignment for probation or parole officers,
   A. the total number of offender-clients is divided by the number of officers
   B. the number of cases assigned to an officer is proportional to his/her years of experience
   C. each officer tries to outperform the other by taking on an escalating number of clients
   D. the number of cases worked by an officer is constantly changing
16.___

17. Which of the following is LEAST likely to be a statutory element of a parole board's decision to grant parole release?
   A. Probability of recidivism
   B. Sufficiency of the parole plan
   C. Offense seriousness
   D. The conduct of the offender while in the correctional institution
17.___

18. A corrections department formulates a restitution program that emphasizes the offender's accountability and service to pay for damages inflicted on the victims, as well as to defray a portion of prosecution expenses.
This program could be said to be following the ____ model.
   A. medical-reintegration
   B. financial-community service
   C. victim-offender mediation
   D. victim reparations
18.___

19. It is generally agreed among corrections professionals
    that the period of greatest vulnerability for formerly
    drug-dependent inmates who reenter the community is the
    _____ release.
    A. first six months following
    B. period beginning six months after
    C. first two years following
    D. period beginning one year after

    19.___

20. The _____ value system is used by parole boards in early-
    release decision making in which the amount of time
    served is equated with the seriousness of the conviction
    offense.
    A. sanctioner   B. selective
    C. punitive   D. regulator

    20.___

21. In the juvenile justice system, what is the equivalent
    of a formal charge?
    A. Disposition   B. Adjudication
    C. Intake   D. Petition

    21.___

22. What is the term used to denote taking only the most
    qualified offenders for succeeding in rehabilitative
    programs?
    A. Skimming   B. Backdooring
    C. Creaming   D. Screening

    22.___

23. Which of the following would be an element of a regular
    or differential scheme for juvenile parole supervision?
    A. 2 face-to-face contacts per month with parents
    B. 3 face-to-face contacts per month with placement staff
    C. 6 face-to-face contacts per month with youth alone
    D. 3 contacts with school officials

    23.___

24. A _____ sentence has a different meaning from the others.
    A. mandatory   B. straight
    C. determinate   D. fixed

    24.___

25. In evaluating a parole program's effectiveness in enforcing
    court-ordered sanctions, the most appropriate performance
    indicator would be
    A. number and type of arrests during supervision
    B. number of favorable discharges
    C. payment of restitution
    D. employment during supervision

    25.___

KEY (CORRECT ANSWERS)

1. C	6. A	11. B	16. A	21. D
2. B	7. D	12. D	17. C	22. C
3. A	8. D	13. D	18. B	23. A
4. A	9. C	14. B	19. A	24. A
5. D	10. D	15. A	20. A	25. B

TEST 2

DIRECTIONS: Each question or incomplete statement is followed by several suggested answers or completions. Select the one that BEST answers the question or completes the statement. *PRINT THE LETTER OF THE CORRECT ANSWER IN THE SPACE AT THE RIGHT.*

1. The _____ value system is the term for a parole board   1.___
    decision-making system that is oriented toward the
    inmates' reactions to parole board decisions.
    A. regulator   B. jurist value
    C. controller   D. congregate

2. The reintegrative tasks of a probation department typically 2.___
    include
      I. assessing the willingness of the community to accept
         offender reintegration
     II. encouraging and conducting research designed to
         develop and improve reintegrative techniques for
         offenders
    III. providing information and recommendations to the
         courts that will assist in achieving dispositions
         favorable to reintegration
     IV. assessing the personal and social conditions of
         persons referred for probation services

    The CORRECT answer is:
    A. I, II   B. II, III, IV
    C. III, IV   D. I, III

3. According to the _____ philosophy of probation and parole   3.___
    management, the goal is to maximize the caseload while
    minimizing supervisory costs, time expenditures, and
    client criminality.
    A. conservationist   B. cost/benefit
    C. due process   D. economic

4. Which of the following is LEAST likely to be an effect of   4.___
    the growth of presumptive and determinate sentencing on
    inmate furlough programs?
    A. Impossibility of conforming to statutory prohibitions
    B. Decreased success rate
    C. Reductions in inmate incentives to abide by institu-
       tional rules
    D. Higher administrative costs

5. One approach to criminology is based on the assumption   5.___
    that human behavior is a product of biological, economic,
    psychological, and social factors, and that the scientific
    method can be used to establish the causes of an indivi-
    dual's behavior.

This school of thought is known as the _____ school.
- A. determinist
- B. behaviorist
- C. positivist
- D. empirical

6. Which of the following is NOT typically a formal role expectation for a parole officer?   6.__
- A. Gathering information necessary for the parole board to make a parole decision
- B. To recommend, when necessary, an issue for a warrant returning a parolee to prison
- C. Providing presentence reports
- D. Insuring that parolees receive their due process rights during revocation hearings

7. Approximately what percentage of conditional inmate releases are mandatory in nature?   7.__
- A. 10
- B. 33
- C. 50
- D. 66

8. In general, it is recommended that day reporting programs operate under each of the following conditions EXCEPT   8.__
- A. twice-weekly urinalysis
- B. notification of the police department in the offender's hometown
- C. control of the offender's daily itinerary
- D. performance of spot-checks of the offender's home

9. In the late 19th century, the state of California began to implement its first parole system. Which of the following were purposes of this adoption?   9.__
- I. Effecting rehabilitation among offenders
- II. Minimizing the use of clemency by governors
- III. Alleviating prison overcrowding
- IV. Correcting or modifying excessive prison sentences in relation to certain crimes

The CORRECT answer is:
- A. I, III
- B. I, II, III
- C. II, IV
- D. II, III, IV

10. Corrections officers sometimes attempt to predict the future behavior of inmates based on past circumstances. This process is known as   10.__
- A. analogous foretoken
- B. actuarial prediction
- C. anamnestic prediction
- D. clinical prediction

11. The factor most likely to be associated with community-based corrections programs is   11.__
- A. state government funding
- B. affiliation with work release
- C. application of electronic monitoring
- D. some degree of home confinement

12. The United States Sentencing Commission's guidelines recommend that a defendant shall notify a parole officer within _____ hours of any change of residence or employment.   12.__
- A. 24
- B. 48
- C. 64
- D. 72

13. The ability of a person to obtain compliance by the
    manipulation of symbolic rewards is known as _____ power.
    A. coercive   B. legitimate
    C. normative   D. administrative

13.____

14. Which of the following statements concerning judicial
    actions and probationer/parolee rights is TRUE?
    A. Judges may revoke a program or probation or parole
       and impose a new sentence that the offender must
       serve the remainder of the term in confinement.
    B. Defendants may not refuse probation of the court
       imposes it as a sentence.
    C. Probationers may not be obligated to pay supervision
       fees to defray program expenses, even if they are
       financially able to do so.
    D. Ordinarily, sentences of probation may be served
       simultaneously with sentences of incarceration.

14.____

15. The collective term for attempts to categorize the future
    behaviors of persons charged with or convicted of crimes
    is
    A. screening   B. risk assessment
    C. augury   D. needs assessment

15.____

16. What is the term for an action filed by a juvenile and
    his/her attorney to have a case in juvenile court trans-
    ferred to the jurisdiction of criminal courts?
    A. Demand waiver   B. Bench warrant
    C. Detainer warrant   D. Delinquency petition

16.____

17. Correctional methods such as home incarceration and
    electronic monitoring are often referred to as
    A. community-based corrections
    B. intermediate punishments
    C. intermittent sentences
    D. diversions

17.____

18. Which of the following is considered to be a DISADVANTAGE
    associated with home confinement programs?
    It
    A. is not cost-effective
    B. focuses on offender surveillance
    C. is not responsive to local citizen needs
    D. has no perceivable social benefits

18.____

19. Among most corrections agencies, the most popular type
    of juvenile parole is
    A. determinate parole set by administrative agency
    B. indeterminate parole with a specified maximum and a
       discretionary minimum length of supervision
    C. indeterminate or purely discretionary parole
    D. presumptive minimum with discretionary extension of
       supervision for an indeterminate period

19.____

20. In the _____ model of supervision, the probation/parole officer focuses on helping offenders comply with the conditions of their release.
    A. justice
    B. casework
    C. brokerage
    D. community resource management

21. Each of the following is a commonly-encountered problem in providing treatment for street offenders EXCEPT they
    A. see no need for rehabilitation
    B. are more likely to commit violent crimes than other types of offenses
    C. tend to come from problem environments
    D. often belong to prison gangs or a subculture that disapproves of participation in treatment

22. The numerical score used by parole boards and agencies to forecast an offender's risk to the public and future dangerousness is known as a(n) _____ score.
    A. public risk   B. offense probability
    C. salient factor   D. clearance

23. According to most research, the act of exiting from crime appears to depend on a set of interrelated processes. Which of the following is NOT typically one of these?
    A. Developing an escalating fear of punishment
    B. Having successful community experiences
    C. Maturing out of crime
    D. Developing internal resources

24. *Cleared by arrest* is a term used by the FBI in its UNIFORM CRIME REPORTS to indicate that someone has been
    A. arrested and charged for a reported crime
    B. arrested for a reported crime
    C. charged for a crime and prosecution has been initiated
    D. arrested and confessed to a reported crime

25. The typical period of incarceration for an offender under-going shock probation is _____ days.
    A. 10-30   B. 15-60   C. 30-120   D. 120-240

KEY (CORRECT ANSWERS)

1. A	6. C	11. B	16. A	21. B
2. B	7. B	12. D	17. B	22. C
3. D	8. C	13. C	18. B	23. A
4. B	9. C	14. A	19. C	24. B
5. C	10. C	15. B	20. A	25. C

TEST 3

DIRECTIONS: Each question or incomplete statement is followed by several suggested answers or completions. Select the one that BEST answers the question or completes the statement. *PRINT THE LETTER OF THE CORRECT ANSWER IN THE SPACE AT THE RIGHT.*

1. In the initial stages of parole supervision, a strong attachment tends to exist between the
   A. bureaucracy and the community
   B. parolee and the officer
   C. officer and the bureaucracy
   D. parolee and the bureaucracy

   1.___

2. Which of the following statements about recidivism is generally TRUE?
   A. Females are more likely than males to recidivate.
   B. Parolees who recidivate tend to do so for crimes different from the ones for which they were originally imprisoned.
   C. Recidivism decreases as participation in programs such as furlough, study release, and other prerelease programs increase.
   D. The number of prior arrests does not correlate strongly with recidivism.

   2.___

3. What is the term for a prosecutor-initiated charge against a criminal defendant?
   A. Information   B. Imputation
   C. Indictment   D. Billing

   3.___

4. Each of the following elements is considered to be essential for the success of community-corrections programs EXCEPT
   A. use of a specific formula for fund allocation
   B. financial subsidies provided to local government and community agencies
   C. targeting offenders who are not prison- or jail-bound
   D. local advisory boards in each community

   4.___

5. Which of the following statements about potential parolees who are released into home confinement programs is TRUE? They
   A. have troubled institutional records
   B. are more likely to have drug or alcohol dependencies
   C. have stable home environments
   D. are generally younger than other potential parolees

   5.___

6. Which of the following items of federal legislation   6.__
   authorizes the allocation of a certain amount of work
   releasee wages for restitution and a general victim
   compensation fund?
   A. Victim and Witness Protection Act of 1982
   B. Victims of Crime Act of 1984
   C. Victims of Child Abuse Act of 1990
   D. Crime Control Act of 1994

7. Which of the following was a ruling in the 1984 *Schall v.*   7.__
   Martin case?
   A. Parole revocation hearings must consist of two stages:
      determination of probable cause that a violation has
      occurred, and punishment.
   B. Courts have a right to order the pretrial detention of
      a juvenile deemed to be dangerous.
   C. Juveniles are not entitled to a jury as a matter of
      course.
   D. The state takes precedence over the family in deciding
      the best interests of children.

8. What is the term for rehabilitative treatment that focuses   8.__
   on how a person interacts with others, especially in
   situations that reveal personal problems?
   A. Unit management   B. Transactional analysis
   C. Behavioral reintegration D. Utilitarianism

9. In jurisdictions where the *parole as grace* concept   9.__
   operates, parole officers are generally granted which of
   the following powers?
   The
     I. search of a parolee's living quarters without warning
        or warrant
    II. suspension of parole pending a board hearing
   III. arrest of a parolee for suspected violations without
        the possibility of bail
    IV. use of incriminating statements made by a parolee
        during noncustodial questioning

   The CORRECT answer is:
   A. I *only*   B. I, II, III
   C. II *only*   D. II, III, IV

10. The convicted offender's version of events leading to   10.__
    the conviction offense, often included in records relating
    to a specific offense, is known as the
    A. offense sequential   B. impact statement
    C. incident report   D. sentencing memorandum

11. One philosophy of parole is that the parolee is still   11.__
    under the supervision of the parole authorities or the
    prison, and that his constitutional rights are limited.
    This is the _____ theory.
    A. contract   B. continuing custody
    C. degree of justice   D. medical

12. For most of the period between 1900 and 1960, the   12.___
    principle of _____ was of primary importance in the
    operation of United States corrections.
       A. isolation   B. rehabilitation
       C. retribution   D. deterrence

13. What is the term for a charge issued by a grand jury upon   13.___
    its own authority against a specific criminal defendant?
       A. Charge bill   B. Arraignment
       C. Conferral   D. Presentment

14. What is the term for a notice of criminal charges or   14.___
    unserved sentences pending against a prisoner in the same
    or other jurisdictions?
       A. Presentment   B. Demand waiver
       C. Detainer warrant   D. Detention hearing

15. Though the functions of parole boards often vary from   15.___
    state to state, most share some common functions. These
    include
       I. evaluating juveniles to determine their eligibility
          for release from detention
      II. providing investigative and supervisory services to
          smaller jurisdictions within the state
     III. review pardons and executive clemency decisions made
          by governors
      IV. commuting death penalties or granting reprieves

    The CORRECT answer is:
       A. I, II   B. I, III
       C. II, III, IV   D. I, II, III, IV

16. The tendency for social control mechanisms to encompass   16.___
    a larger (or different) population than originally intended
    is known as
       A. mission creep   B. outlawry
       C. role conflict   D. net widening

17. Nationwide, which of an offender's due process rights is   17.___
    least likely to be provided at a revocation hearing?
       A. Written statement of reasons for the revocation deci-
          sion
       B. Written notice of alleged violation
       C. Representation by counsel
       D. Opportunity to confront and cross-examine witnesses

18. The legal term applicable to juveniles who have not   18.___
    attained the age of majority (in most states, 18) is
       A. slip   B. infant
       C. adolescent   D. minor

19. What is the term for a parole board decision-making system   19.___
    that is concerned with appealing to the public interests
    and seeing that community expectations are met?
    _____ value system.
       A. Citizen   B. Jurist   C. Treater   D. Regulator

20. Which of the following is a form of probation imposed before a plea of guilt that can result in a dismissal of the charges?
   A. Nominal disposition   B. Presentment
   C. Pretrial diversion   D. Deferred adjudication

20._

21. Which of the following statements about presumptive sentencing is FALSE?
It
   A. usually results in a universal sentence for particular crimes
   B. is designed to reduce sentencing disparities associated with race, gender, ethnicity, or socio-economic status
   C. specifies ranges of time for different degrees of offense seriousness
   D. takes an offender's prior record into account

21._

22. The fear aroused by the construction of halfway houses for parolees is often referred to as the fear of
   A. community degeneration   B. criminal contamination
   C. crimogenesis   D. assured recidivism

22._

23. The primary manifest goal of community-based corrections is
   A. crime control   B. restitution
   C. deterrence   D. societal reintegration

23._

24. The purpose of a preliminary hearing in criminal proceedings is to
   A. determine if a person charged with a crime should be held for trial
   B. examine a defendant's prior criminal history
   C. present evidence relating to the defendant's character
   D. discuss the possibility of intermediate punishment for a crime

24._

25. On average, parole accounts for about _____% of all correctional time served for United States offenders in all categories.
   A. 20   B. 40   C. 60   D. 80

25._

KEY (CORRECT ANSWERS)

1. C	6. B	11. B	16. D	21. A
2. C	7. B	12. B	17. C	22. B
3. A	8. B	13. D	18. B	23. D
4. C	9. B	14. C	19. A	24. A
5. C	10. D	15. D	20. C	25. B

EXAMINATION SECTION
TEST 1

DIRECTIONS: Each question or incomplete statement is followed by several suggested answers or completions. Select the one that BEST answers the question or completes the statement. *PRINT THE LETTER OF THE CORRECT ANSWER IN THE SPACE AT THE RIGHT.*

1. Which of the following was originally a device of preven-   1.___
   tive justice that obliged persons suspected of future
   misbehavior to stipulate with and give full assurance to
   the court and the public that the apprehended offense
   would not occur?
   A. Parole   B. Bail
   C. Recognizance   D. Probation

2. Which of the following statements about parolee rights   2.___
   and parole board actions is FALSE?
   A. Inmates who become eligible for parole are not auto-
      matically entitled to parole.
   B. If a parole board imposes a special condition of
      parole, it may not be challenged on the grounds of
      the Fifth Amendment right against self-incrimination.
   C. Inmates who have been paroled and subsequently commit
      a violent act while on parole may have parole revoked
      and be returned to prison, regardless of trial or
      conviction for the new crime.
   D. Parole boards must recognize minimum-sentence provi-
      sions from sentencing judges when considering an
      inmate's parole eligibility.

3. Which of the following is an administrative procedure   3.___
   designed to furnish personal background information to a
   bonding company and law enforcement officials?
   A. Booking   B. Classification
   C. Arraignment   D. Bailment

4. Criminologists report that along the scale of age,   4.___
   offenders typically cease criminal activity at two points.
   These are the
   A. early teens and early 60s
   B. late teens and mid-30s
   C. late teens and late 40s
   D. late 20s and mid-50s

5. The legal term for a period of proving a trial or foregive-   5.___
   ness is
   A. novitio   B. assai   C. catechism D. probatio

6. Some corrections reformists argue that the privatization   6.___
   of community-based programs would improve their effectiveness. Which of the following is NOT a reason given for
   this?

A. Greater incentive to make rehabilitation work
B. Greater accountability
C. Consolidation of program control with professional corrections personnel
D. Promotion of new ideas and strategies for treatment

7. In _____ sentencing, an inmate's final release date is decided by the parole board. 7.___
   A. determinate　　　　　　B. indeterminate
   C. presumptive　　　　　　D. guidelines-based

8. What is the commonly used term for the federal statute that permits probationers, parolees, and inmates of prisons and jails to challenge the fact, length, and conditions of their confinement or placement in particular facilities or programs? 8.___
   A. *Blue Sky* laws　　　　B. Due process laws
   C. *Habeas corpus* statute　D. The exclusionary rule

9. Over the last two decades or so, federal and state legislation concerning corrections has generally produced each of the following results EXCEPT to 9.___
   A. broadening parole board authority for making early prisoner release decisions
   B. limiting the discretionary sentencing power of judges
   C. decrease the likelihood of sentence disparities
   D. increase prisoner release predictability and the certainty of incarceration

10. Generally, in order to qualify for electronic monitoring programs, candidates must 10.___
    A. seek and maintain employment
    B. be assessed as high-risk offenders
    C. have special care requirements that can only be fulfilled by family members
    D. have no more than 180 days to serve in jail

11. What is the term for a specific criminal act involving one or more victims? 11.___
    A. Felony　　　　　　B. Offense
    C. Index crime　　　　D. Incident

12. Approximately what percentage of a probation or parole officer's working time is typically made available for client supervision? 12.___
    A. 10　　　B. 30　　　C. 50　　　D. 70

13. Of the following, inmates who have committed _____ crimes are on average most likely to successfully complete a term of parole supervision. 13.___
    A. public order　　　　B. drug
    C. violent　　　　　　D. property

14. The primary distinguishing factor between standard and
    intensive supervision probation programs is the
      A. amount of consultative services offered
      B. strictness of punitive conditions
      C. amount of face-to-face contact
      D. number of agency personnel assigned to the case
    14.___

15. Which of the following statements are TRUE of the day
    fine process?
       I. The value of each day-fine unit is calculated accord-
         ing to a percentage of the offender's daily income
     II. The seriousness of the offense is determined subjec-
         tively by an appointed board
    III. The number of day-fine units is calculated according
         to offense severity
    15.___

    The CORRECT answer is:
      A. I *only*   B. I, III   C. II, III   D. III *only*

16. For most of the period between 1820 and 1900, the prevail-
    ing philosophy operating in most United States corrections
    was that of
      A. isolation   B. rehabilitation
      C. retribution   D. deterrence
    16.___

17. Which of the following is NOT an advantage associated
    with objective parole criteria?
      A. The use of composite group scores to predict parole
         success
      B. Greater discretionary power granted to parole boards
      C. Knowledge of presumptive release dates within several
         months of incarceration
      D. Time ranges for discharge are decided using fixed
         scoring systems
    17.___

18. What type of electronic monitoring device is most useful
    for monitoring multiple clients simultaneously?
      A. Call-forwarding transmitter
      B. Cellular telephone device
      C. Programmed contact device
      D. Continuous signaling transmitter
    18.___

19. The primary purpose of most prerelease programs is to
      A. provide a future parolee with skills or education
         that will facilitate reintegration
      B. evaluate the probability of a parolee's rehabilitation
      C. determine the likelihood of recidivism
      D. make reintegration a gradual process for future
         parolees
    19.___

20. Which of the following is likely to be a special, rather
    than standard, condition of probation or parole?
      A. Notifying officer before applying for a marriage
         license
      B. Avoiding association with known or suspected criminals
      C. Prohibition against the possession of a firearm
      D. Finding and maintaining legitimate employment
    20.___

21. What is the term for the official halting or suspension   21.___
of legal proceedings against a defendant after a recorded
justice system entry -- usually followed by a referral
for treatment?
   A. Diversion   B. Rehabilitation
   C. Disposition   D. Commutation

22. The commonly used term for any probation or parole   22.___
officer who works with probationers or parolees as
clients is
   A. corrector   B. caseworker
   C. chancery   D. broker

23. What is the legal term for the principle that punishment   23.___
should correspond in degree and kind with the offense?
   A. Lex talionis   B. Parens patriae
   C. Damnum absque injuria   D. Respondeat superior

24. Which of the following is regarded as *symbolic* restitu-   24.___
tion?
   A. Day-fine programs   B. Victim-offender mediation
   C. Victim reparations   D. Community service

25. A classification system is a traditional means used by   25.___
probation/parole agencies to separate offenders according
to characteristics related to the
   A. background of the offenders
   B. type of correctional treatments applied to the
      offenders in the past
   C. nature and seriousness of the offenses
   D. relative amount of correctional treatment undergone
      by the offenders

KEY (CORRECT ANSWERS)

1. C		11. D	
2. D		12. B	
3. A		13. A	
4. B		14. C	
5. D		15. B	
6. C		16. D	
7. B		17. B	
8. C		18. B	
9. A		19. D	
10. A		20. C	

21. A
22. B
23. A
24. D
25. C

TEST 2

DIRECTIONS: Each question or incomplete statement is followed by
                several suggested answers or completions. Select the
                one that BEST answers the question or completes the
                statement. *PRINT THE LETTER OF THE CORRECT ANSWER IN
                THE SPACE AT THE RIGHT.*

1. Among paroling agencies, the LEAST desirable outcome   1.___
    measure for the effectiveness of a parole program is
        A. alcohol and drug test results
        B. technical violations
        C. number of offenders employed
        D. recidivism

2. By the year _____, every state had adopted some form of   2.___
    a parole system.
        A. 1899   B. 1929   C. 1944   D. 1965

3. In some programs, regardless of what a parole officer   3.___
    might think is best, he or she may be compelled to
    collect a supervision fee from an indigent client. This
    is an example of
        A. burnout   B. role ambiguity
        C. transactional discord D. role conflict

4. An offender who is considered unlikely to commit future   4.___
    crimes is described as
        A. status   B. situational
        C. incidental   D. rehabilitated

5. In the juvenile justice system, what is the equivalent of 5.___
    a trial?
        A. Disposition   B. Adjudication
        C. Diversion   D. Petition

6. Which of the following is a highly structured nonresiden- 6.___
    tial correction program that uses supervision, sanctions,
    and services coordinated from a central location?
        A. Halfway house   B. Community work center
        C. Day reporting center   D. Halfway out-house

7. Which of the following is a manifest function of parole?   7.___
        A. Compensating for sentence disparities
        B. Offender reintegration
        C. Decreasing prison and jail overcrowding
        D. Public safety and protection

8. In certain criminal cases that are viewed as not requiring 8.___
    an immediate sentence, an indictment may be held in
    abeyance without either dismissal or final judgment.
    This procedure is known as
        A. dormancy   B. intercession
        C. dissolution   D. filing

9. One perceived drawback to the recent movement toward the   9.___
   professionalization of careers in probation and parole
   is that it
   A. is often equated with formal academic training rather
      than the acquisition of practical skills
   B. is more likely to attract people who are less able to
      deal with inmates on an interpersonal level
   C. has not yet resulted in a clear set of universal
      standards for professional contact
   D. makes it more difficult and costly for people to
      enter the field

10. What term describes the parole board decision-making   10.___
    system that emphasizes rehabilitation and early-release
    decisions made on the basis of the offender's needs?
    _____ value system.
         A. Regulator   B. Jurist
         C. Controller   D. Treater

11. The functions of most halfway houses include   11.___
       I. provisions of food and shelter
      II. rehabilitation and reintegration
     III. client-specific treatments
      IV. provision of victim or community restitution

    The CORRECT answer is:
         A. I, II, III   B. II *only*
         C. II, III, IV   D. IV *only*

12. The act of removing a conviction from official records   12.___
    is accomplished through a(n)
         A. discretionary waiver   B. nominal disposition
         C. expungement order   D. predisposition report

13. Each of the following is considered to be a function of   13.___
    a community corrections program EXCEPT
         A. making decisions about program enrollment
         B. ensuring public safety
         C. networking with other community agencies and busi-
            nesses
         D. individual and group counseling

14. The most common organizational model for juvenile   14.___
    paroling authorities is the _____ model.
         A. institutional   B. consolidation
         C. regulatory   D. autonomous

15. What is the term for the constitutional guarantee that   15.___
    no agent or instrument of government will use any proce-
    dures to arrest, prosecute, try, or punish any person
    other than those procedures prescribed by law?
         A. Burden of proof   B. Habeas corpus
         C. Corpus delecti   D. Due process

16. The majority of parole board decisions made today involve   16.___
    those who have committed _____ offenses.
        A. public order   B. drug
        C. property   D. violent

17. When a defendant enters a guilty plea with the expectation   17.___
    of receiving a more lenient sentence, he or she engages in
        A. intake screening
        B. determinate sentencing
        C. implicit plea bargaining
        D. preventive arraignment

18. A corrections department formulates a restitution program   18.___
    which focuses on compensating victims directly for their
    offenses. This program could be described as following
    the _____ model.
        A. victim reparations
        B. victim-offender mediation
        C. victim reconciliation
        D. financial-community service

19. The main difference between conditional release and   19.___
    parole release is that
        A. conditional release is largely a response to institu-
           tional overcrowding
        B. inmates are selected according to *good time*
        C. conditional release is established by statute
        D. there is no discretion involved in conditional
           release

20. Of the parolees who are returned to state prison for   20.___
    technical violations, the highest number of them
        A. leave the jurisdiction without permission
        B. are arrested on a new charge
        C. fail a drug test
        D. fail to report to the parole officer

21. The Federal Victim and Witness Protection Act of 1982   21.___
    was designed to
        A. create the Bureau of Justice Statistics
        B. require offenders to provide restitution to victims
        C. encourage the provision of alternate sentencing by
           federal judges and others
        D. increase the severity of sentencing for drug-related
           cases

22. In evaluating a parole program's effectiveness in protect-   22.___
    ing the community, the most appropriate performance
    indicator would be
        A. number of times attending treatment/work programming
        B. number of absconders during supervision
        C. extent of victim satisfaction with service and depart-
           ment
        D. timeliness of revocation and termination hearings

23. An interpersonal situation in which the likelihood of   23.___
acquiring criminal behaviors is enhanced -- such as in
the view of many a prison -- is described as a(n) _____
environment.
   A. crimogenic   B. regressive
   C. apostatic   D. recidivistic

24. The primary complaint lodged against work release   24.___
programs by their participants tends to be that
   A. the pay is too low for the support of themselves and
      their families
   B. the strict supervision does not permit the assump-
      tion of adequate responsibility
   C. they are not accorded the same rights as members of
      labor organizations
   D. the jobs available to them do not require skills that
      are useful in the real world

25. Each of the following is generally considered to be a   25.___
negative feature of indeterminate sentencing in relation
to parole EXCEPT it
   A. can be abused to punish people with unpopular political
      beliefs
   B. applies therapy indiscriminately
   C. prevents correctional authorities from being forced
      to release an offender who is clearly not ready for
      reintegration
   D. is used primarily as a means of inmate control

KEY (CORRECT ANSWERS)

1. D		11. A
2. C		12. C
3. D		13. A
4. B		14. A
5. B		15. D
6. C		16. C
7. B		17. C
8. D		18. A
9. A		19. D
10. D		20. B

21. B
22. B
23. A
24. D
25. C

TEST 3

DIRECTIONS: Each question or incomplete statement is followed by several suggested answers or completions. Select the one that BEST answers the question or completes the statement. *PRINT THE LETTER OF THE CORRECT ANSWER IN THE SPACE AT THE RIGHT.*

1. In the justice model of probation practice, the most important role of a probation officer is to
   A. strengthen offender self-esteem
   B. supervise offenders
   C. police offender activities
   D. enforce probation rules

   1.___

2. What is another term for the *civil disabilities* that follow a conviction and are not directly imposed by the sentencing court -- such as loss of the right to vote, serve on a jury, or own a firearm?
   A. Collateral consequences   B. Custodial reproach
   C. Residual punishment   D. Associated correction

   2.___

3. Which of the following is LEAST likely to be a source of stress for parole officers?
   A. Excessive paperwork
   B. Lack of collegial consortium
   C. High risk and liability exposure
   D. Role ambiguity

   3.___

4. What is the general term used to describe programs and services such as halfway houses, psychological counseling services, employment assistance, and community-based correctional agencies?
   A. Diversion   B. Releases
   C. Deterrents   D. Aftercare

   4.___

5. To a director or supervisor of a parole department, which of the following officer responsibilities would tend to take precedence over all others?
   A. One-on-one contact with and supervision of client
   B. Timely completion of reports to the court
   C. Insuring that clients know their due process rights during revocation hearings
   D. Location and referral of adequate client services

   5.___

6. In the period from about 1985 to 1995, the parolee population in the United States grew by about _____%.
   A. 35   B. 50   C. 70   D. 100

   6.___

7. Which of the following is most commonly used as an item in a paroling authority's release risk instruments?
   A. Prison infractions
   B. Current crime involving violence
   C. Age at first incarceration
   D. Length of current term

   7.___

8. Which of the following is a theory of criminal behavior   8.___
stressing the priority, duration, frequency, and intensity
of interactions with other criminals?
   A. Deterrence   B. Medical model
   C. Differential association D. Crimogenesis

9. Which of the following statements about recidivism is   9.___
generally FALSE?
   A. Parolees tend to have higher recidivism rates than
      probationers.
   B. Shock incarceration has no influence on recidivism.
   C. Drug abuse and recidivism are not related.
   D. First-offenders tend to commit more violent crimes
      than chronic offenders.

10. Which of the following Supreme Court cases was the first 10.___
to apply the *habeas corpus* rule to the actions of parole
boards?
   A. *Jones v. Cunningham* (1963)
   B. *Mempa v. Rhay* (1967)
   C. *Morrissey v. Brewer* (1972)
   D. *Gagnon v. Scarpelli* (1973)

11. The process of predicting the future behavior of offenders 11.___
based on a correctional professional's expert training
and work is known as
   A. clinical prediction   B. actuarial prediction
   C. anamnestic prediction   D. risk analysis

12. Which of the following issues involved in the parole   12.___
revocation process has thus far NOT been addressed by
the United States Supreme Court?
The
   A. cancellation of provisional release
   B. due process rights of offenders released under pre-
      parole
   C. right to appeal revocation
   D. right to counsel during a parole revocation hearing

13. Each of the following is a guideline typically used to   13.___
direct the prisoner classification systems used by most
modern correctional organizations EXCEPT
   A. the process must be applied uniformly among similarly
      situated inmates
   B. the system must provide for decentralized, inter-
      agency control over the process
   C. all inmates should be placed in the lowest custody
      level consistent with public safety
   D. inmates should be classified on the basis of objec-
      tive information and criteria

14. The Supreme Court case which established a parole offi-   14.___
cer's right to search a client's residence was
   A. *Moody v. Daggett* (1976)
   B. *United States v. Addonizio* (1979)
   C. *Martinez v. California* (1987)
   D. *Griffin v. Wisconsin* (1987)

15. The primary purpose of structured discretion in both
    sentencing and parole decisions is to
    A. eliminate sentencing disparity
    B. standardize and create greater fairness in decisions
    C. emphasize the seriousness of violent crimes over
       others
    D. impose the maximum allowable sentence on serious
       offenders

15.___

16. Which of the following would be an element of an intensive
    scheme for juvenile parole supervision?
    A. 6 face-to-face contacts per month with youth alone
    B. 1 contact with school officials
    C. 1 face-to-face contact per month with parents
    D. 4 contacts with agency officials

16.___

17. In deferred adjudication,
    A. a defendant agrees to incarceration without a trial
    B. there is no formal finding of guilt
    C. there is a reduction in the offender's prison sen-
       tence
    D. an offender is not required to enter a plea

17.___

18. Which of the following forms of intervention has generally
    proven to be LEAST effective in the treatment of street
    offenders?
    A. Service-oriented programs
    B. Self-help
    C. Psychotherapy
    D. Skill development

18.___

19. Which of the following is NOT a widely recognized benefit
    of restitution as an intermediate sanction?
    A. Integrating the rehabilitative and punitive purposes
       of the criminal law
    B. Reducing demands on the criminal justice system
    C. Reducing the likelihood of sentence disparity
    D. Reduction in the perceived need for vengeance or
       vigilantism

19.___

20. Sometimes an officer's work-role is oriented so that he
    functions as a referral service and supplies an offender/
    client with contacts and agencies that provide services.
    This role is described as a(n)
    A. agent   B. enabler   C. broker   D. enforcer

20.___

21. The first use of work release as a correctional program
    in the United States occurred in
    A. 1832, in Massachusetts   B. 1865, in Mississippi
    C. 1906, in Vermont   D. 1942, in Idaho

21.___

22. A correctional institution that emphasizes security,
    discipline, and order is conforming to the _____ model
    of corrections.
    A. institutional   B. coercive
    C. custodial   D. medical

22.___

23. In the program model of parole agency orientation, the   23.____
emphasis is most often placed on
    A. the specialization of officers in certain kinds of
       problems
    B. offender change
    C. increased accountability for service availability
    D. even distribution of caseloads among officers

24. What is the term for the finding by a grand jury that   24.____
insufficient probable cause exists to proceed against
one or more criminal defendants?
    A. Deficiency   B. No contest
    C. Dismissal   D. No true bill

25. In which of the following organizational models are   25.____
parole decisions made by a central authority that has
independent powers, but that is organizationally situated
in the overall department of corrections?
    A. Consolidation   B. Autonomous
    C. Hierarchical   D. Incorporated

___

KEY (CORRECT ANSWERS)

1. C		11. A	
2. A		12. C	
3. B		13. B	
4. D		14. D	
5. B		15. B	
6. D		16. A	
7. B		17. B	
8. C		18. C	
9. A		19. C	
10. A		20. C	

21. C
22. C
23. A
24. D
25. A

CORRECTION SCIENCE
EXAMINATION SECTION

DIRECTIONS FOR THIS SECTION:
Each question or incomplete statement is followed by several suggested answers or completions. Select the one that BEST answers the question or completes the statement. *PRINT THE LETTER OF THE CORRECT ANSWER IN THE SPACE AT THE RIGHT.*

TEST 1

1. The one of the following techniques that would NOT be helpful in a correctional program to raise the achievement level of school dropouts is to
   A. praise all work even if it is not merited
   B. encourage recognition by the peer group
   C. use money as the general reinforcer when appropriate
   D. provide programmed instruction

   1. ...

2. Test validity is BEST described as
   A. the extent to which a test measures what it was designed to measure
   B. an index of reliability determined by correlating the scores of individuals on one form of a test with their scores on another form
   C. the degree to which a test measures anything consistently
   D. a mathematical index of the extent to which examinees believe an examination to be an appropriate testing instrument

   2. ...

3. The one of the following which is NOT characteristic of traditional learning methods such as lectures, textbooks, films, television, records, and tapes is that
   A. the learner tends to be passive
   B. the learner may not get deeply involved in the learning process
   C. these methods prove invariably dull
   D. these methods are well adapted to the learning of new concepts

   3. ...

4. The one of the following which would be MOST relevant to a decision concerning whether a particular occupation should be included in a vocational training program is the
   A. number of people currently employed in the occupation
   B. growth rate of the occupation in the recent past
   C. projected average annual openings in the occupation
   D. job turnover rate in an occupation through death or retirement

   4. ...

5. Following are three statements about the use of correspondence courses for inmates:
   I. Practical courses such as agriculture, but not cultural courses, are adaptable to correspondence courses.
   II. Correspondence courses provide material for advanced courses in which too few inmates are interested to justify the organization of classes.
   III. One drawback of offering correspondence courses to inmates is that these students often do not make a proper selection of courses.
   Which one of the following *correctly* classifies the above statements?
   A. I and II are generally correct, but III is not.
   B. II and III are generally correct, but I is not.

   5. ...

1

    C. I is generally correct, but II and III are not.

    D. II is generally correct, but I and III are not.

6. The one of the following which is of LEAST value in assess- 6. ...
ing the effectiveness of a training program for staff is

    A. change in the staff's knowledge

    B. the staff's feelings about the value of the program

    C. changes in the staff's attitudes or values

    D. the degree of success with clients by staff after they have completed the program

7. The one of the following which would be the MOST important 7. ...
factor in insuring that the participants successfully complete a training program is to

    A. increase the time allowed for training

    B. carefully select the trainees

    C. be sure that the material used in the course is readily available to the participants

    D. select instructors who are familiar with the material

8. Which of the following is a CORRECT statement regarding any 8. ...
significant proposed change in correctional practices such as the introduction of work-release programs?

    A. Costs of an innovation must be equal to or less than those of the present system.

    B. Recidivism is a minor factor when planning changes in correctional programs.

    C. Evidence must be provided that public protection is not diminished by the innovation.

    D. A change affecting the entire state system must be reviewed by the federal government.

9. The one of the following statements concerning the charac- 9. ...
teristics of offenders which is CORRECT is that offenders

    A. are seldom educationally handicapped

    B. tend to have stable work records

    C. usually have little self-esteem

    D. usually have a vocational skill

10. The one of the following that would be MOST helpful to an 10. ...
offender prior to his parole to prepare him to reenter the community is

    A. attendance at prerelease classes in penitentiaries

    B. prerelease visits by parole officers to the offender in the institution

    C. assignment to half-way houses for a period of time prior to release

    D. prerelease visits by parole officers to the family of the offender

11. The selection of a vocational skill to be taught in a 11. ...
training course should be made carefully.
Of the following, the MOST important factor to consider when making the selection is the

    A. inherent interest of the program's content

    B. simplicity of the skill to be taught

    C. attitude of society toward the institution

    D. need for the skill in the community

12. The one of the following which is LEAST likely to be an 12. ...
element of a correctional training program based upon a behavior modification approach is

    A. specifying the desired final performance level

B. holding a meeting between trainer and trainee to plan an individual program

C. providing reinforcement of desired behaviors

D. including factors to motivate the trainee

13. Of all the programs for misdemeanants, the LARGEST number of *innovative* efforts are being made for those dealing with
    A. domestic problems   B. alcoholism
    C. juvenile delinquency   D. gambling
13. ...

14. Of the following, the LEAST important factor in motivating inmates of limited educational background to complete their high school education is the
    A. use of short, attainable, and measurable educational segments
    B. possibility of obtaining a high school equivalency instead of obtaining a formal diploma
    C. substantial interpersonal relationship between the teacher and the student
    D. reinforcement of learning through recognition
14. ...

15. There are several advantages in using televised videotape as a means of instruction.
Which of the following is NOT an advantage of this method of teaching?
    A. A great number of viewers, spread over a large geographical area, can be reached.
    B. A variety of instructional materials can be integrated within a single lesson.
    C. It is a completely one-way process with the instructor separated from the students.
    D. The information and instruction, on tape, is available for replay whenever desired.
15. ...

16. Which of the following statements concerning educational programs in correctional institutions is CORRECT?
    A. The costs of educational programming in the correctional setting are generally higher than in the regular educational systems.
    B. The subjects taught in correctional education programs are generally highly innovative.
    C. The status and priority established for institutional education is commensurate with today's demand for such education.
    D. Inmate teachers have rarely been used in educational programs in correctional institutions.
16. ...

17. Assume that the goal of one of your training sessions for correctional staff is to make the staff aware of how it feels to be confined in a correctional institution.
The training technique BEST suited to attain this goal is
    A. reading relevant literature   B. role playing
    C. panel discussion   D. group discussion
17. ...

18. Following are three statements concerning programmed-learning textbooks:
    I. The subject matter is arranged logically and in small steps.
    II. The texts are structured so as to demand less concentration than that required for regular methods of instruction.
18. ...

3

III. If the learner has given an incorrect answer, he is immediately made aware of it so that he may correct it before proceeding with the lesson.

Which of the following CORRECTLY classifies the above statements?
   A. I, II and III are correct.
   B. I and II are correct, but III is not.
   C. I and III are correct, but II is not.
   D. II and III are correct, but I is not.

19. For management by objectives to be successful, all of the following conditions must be fulfilled EXCEPT 19. ...
   A. continuous feedback on managerial performance
   B. constant supervision of employees by supervisors
   C. an intensive training program preceding organizational implementation
   D. superior-subordinate relationships characterized by a high degree of cooperation and mutual respect

20. Which of the following types of programs is LEAST appropriate in a correctional institution? A(n) 20. ...
   A. religious program   B. recreational program
   C. individual counseling program
   D. methadone maintenance program

TEST 2

1. In a modern "information system," there are two main categories: "standard information," consisting of the data required for operational control, and "demand information," consisting of data which, although not needed regularly or under normal circumstances, must be available when required. Following are four types of data: 1. ...
   I. Daily count at a prison
   II. Number of correctional officers who call in sick each day
   III. Number of prisoners eligible for release within the next six months in certain categories of offenses
   IV. Average number of paroles granted per year

Which of the following CORRECTLY categorizes the above types of data into those which are "standard" and those which are "demand" items?
   A. I and II are standard, but III and IV are demand.
   B. I and III are standard, but II and IV are demand.
   C. III is standard, but I, II and IV are demand.
   D. II is standard, but I, III and IV are demand.

2. The *basic* purpose of a detention home for accused juvenile delinquents should be to 2. ...
   A. serve as a shelter for dependent or neglected children who are temporarily without a home or parental supervision
   B. hold delinquent youngsters pending a court hearing or transfer to another jurisdiction or program
   C. act as a rehabilitative institution following adjudication
   D. act as a rehabilitation institution prior to adjudication

4

3. The *majority* of prisoners in jails in the United States   3. ...
   are incarcerated because
   - A. they are a serious threat to themselves and society
   - B. they are too poor to get legal assistance
   - C. it would cost the community more if they were released and committed offenses
   - D. they are too poor to furnish bail pending trial

4. In an effort to assist defendants in obtaining legal   4. ...
   counsel, the courts rely MOST heavily on
   - A. the National Association for the Advancement of Colored People
   - B. bar associations   C. lawyers' guilds
   - D. legal aid and public defender groups

5. All of the following are characteristics of minimum secu-   5. ...
   rity prisons EXCEPT
   - A. inmates work under general or intermittent supervision
   - B. they serve a therapeutic function by creating an environment based upon trust rather than strict controls
   - C. the inmates at these institutions are often engaged in public works activities
   - D. the work experiences they provide directly relate to those the prisoner will face in the real world

6. In the United States, the LARGEST group of persons held   6. ...
   in jail are those arrested for
   - A. drunkenness   B. disorderly conduct
   - C. larceny   D. drug offenses

7. The systems model of a correctional education program   7. ...
   reaches a *visible* stage when
   - A. plans are made   B. cost is estimated
   - C. a search is made for sources of funding
   - D. a funding request is granted

8. Of the following, the LOWEST stratum in prison subculture   8. ...
   is occupied by
   - A. bank robbers   B. forgers
   - C. drug addicts   D. sex offenders

9. All of the following are characteristics of most of the   9. ...
   institutions for sentenced adult prisoners in the United
   States EXCEPT that they are
   - A. architecturally antiquated   B. overcrowded
   - C. located within metropolitan areas
   - D. too large for effective management

10. A correctional program should have measurable objectives   10. ...
    so that its success can be evaluated.
    Of the following, it would be MOST difficult to measure the
    - A. change in attitude toward work and study resulting from participation in a correctional program
    - B. percentage of participants who obtain employment after release
    - C. sum of money earned in a work release program
    - D. change in reading level during an educational program

11. The one of the following which should be developed FIRST   11. ...
    in establishing a successful training program is the
    - A. content of the training program
    - B. facilities for giving training
    - C. qualification requirements for staff
    - D. agency goals and programs

12. Which of the following statements BEST describes the   12. ...
    present role of the courts in respect to rehabilitation
    in correctional institutions? The courts are
    A. ready to abandon their "hands off" policy and take a
       more active role in institutional affairs
    B. deferring to correctional administrators who have the
       expertise as well as the responsibility for care,
       custody and treatment of defendants
    C. so busy with backlogs of cases that correctional
       problems occupy a low priority
    D. assuming legal responsibility for institutions located
       in their jurisdictions
13. All of the following statements concerning the money bail 13. ...
    system are correct EXCEPT
    A. under the bail system persons may be confined for
       crimes for which they are later acquitted
    B. members of organized criminal syndicates have little
       difficulty in posting bail although they are often
       dangerous
    C. bail is recognized in the law solely as a method of
       keeping dangerous persons in jail
    D. the bail system discriminates against poor defendants
14. Daytop Village is a treatment program in the city for   14. ...
    A. drug offenders   B. sex offenders
    C. mentally retarded offenders
    D. abused children of offenders
15. In the United States, MOST dollars, manpower, and atten-   15. ...
    tion in the correctional field have been invested in
    A. traditional institutional services outside the main-
       stream of urban life
    B. innovative correctional programming at large state
       institutions
    C. programs for local jails D. community based programs
16. Which of the following is the *single* MOST important source 16. ...
    of statistics on crime in the United States today?
    A. FBI Quarterly Review
    B. Uniform Crime Reports of the FBI
    C. Journal of Police Science and Criminal Statistics
    D. Federal Report on Criminal Statistics
17. Reading materials can help correctional staff to better   17. ...
    understand the attitudes of inmates toward incarceration.
    SOUL ON ICE, a penetrating story of one man's reaction to
    California's prisons, was written by
    A. Malcolm X   B. Huey Newton
    C. Bobby Seale   D. Eldridge Cleaver
Questions 18-20.
DIRECTIONS: Answer Questions 18 through 20 SOLELY on the basis of
             the following passage:
     The basic disparity between punitive and correctional crime con-
trol should be noted. The first explicitly or implicitly assumes the
availability of choice or freedom of the will and asserts the responsibility of the individual for what he does. Thus the concept of
punishment has both a moral and practical justification. However,
correctional crime control, though also deterministic in outlook,
either explicitly or implicitly considers criminal behavior as the
result of conditions and factors present in the individual or his

environment; it does not think in terms of free choices available to
the individual and his resultant responsibility, but rather in terms
of the removal of the criminogenic conditions for which the individual
may not be responsible and over which he may not have any control.
Some efforts have been made to achieve a theoretical reconciliation
of these two rather diametrically opposed approaches but this has not
been accomplished, and their coexistence in practice remains an unre-
solved contradiction.

18. According to the "correctional" view of crime control   18. ...
    mentioned in the above passage, criminal behavior is the
    result of
    A. environmental factors for which individuals should be
       held responsible
    B. harmful environmental factors which should be eliminated
    C. an individual's choice for which he should be held re-
       sponsible and punished
    D. an individual's choice and can be corrected in a thera-
       peutic environment

19. According to the above passage, the one of the following   19. ...
    which is a *problem* in correctional practice is
    A. identifying emotionally disturbed individuals
    B. determining effective punishment for criminal behavior
    C. reconciling the punitive and correctional views of
       crime control
    D. assuming that a criminal is the product of his environ-
       ment and has no free will

20. According to the above passage, the one of the following   20. ...
    which is an *assumption* underlying the punitive crime con-
    trol viewpoint rather than the correctional viewpoint is
    that crime is caused by
    A. inherited personality traits
    B. poor socio-economic background
    C. lack of parental guidance
    D. irresponsibility on the part of the individual

TEST 3

Questions 1-6
DIRECTIONS: Answer Questions 1 through 6 SOLELY on the basis of
               the following selection:
    Man's historical approach to criminals can be conveniently sum-
marized as a succession of three R's: Revenge, Restraint, and Reformation. Revenge was the primary response prior to the first
revolution in penology in the 18th and 19th centuries. It was
replaced during that revolution by an emphasis upon restraint.
When the second revolution occurred in the late 19th and 20th
centuries, reformation became an important objective. Attention
was focused upon the mental and emotional makeup of the offender
and efforts were made to alter these as the primary sources of difficulty.
    We have now entered yet another revolution in which a fourth
concept has been added to the list of R's: Reintegration. This
has come about because students of corrections feel that a singular
focus upon reforming the offender is inadequate. Successful rehabilitation is a two-sided coin, including reformation on one side

and reintegration on the other.

It can be argued that the third revolution is premature. Society itself is still very ambivalent about the offender. It has never really replaced all vestiges of revenge or restraint, simply supplemented them. Thus, while it is unwilling to kill or lock up all offenders permanently, it is also unwilling to give full support to the search for alternatives.

1. According to the above passage, revolutions against accepted treatment of criminals have resulted in all of the following approaches to handling criminals EXCEPT
   A. revenge   B. restraint   C. reformation D. reintegration

2. According to the above passage, society *now* views the offender with
   A. uncertainty   B. hatred   C. sympathy   D. acceptance

3. According to the above passage, the second revolution directed *particular* attention to
   A. preparing the offender for his return to society
   B. making the pain of punishment exceed the pleasure of crime
   C. exploring the inner feelings of the offender
   D. restraining the offender from continuing his life of crime

4. According to the above passage, students of corrections feel that the *lack* of success of rehabilitation programs is due to
   A. the mental and emotional makeup of the offender
   B. vestiges of revenge and restraint which linger in correction programs
   C. failure to achieve reintegration together with reformation
   D. premature planning of the third revolution

5. The above passage *suggests* that the latest revolution will
   A. fail and the cycle will begin again with revenge or restraint
   B. be the last revolution
   C. not work unless correctional goals can be defined
   D. succumb to political and economic pressures

6. The one of the following titles which BEST expresses the *main* idea of the above passage is:
   A. Is Criminal Justice Enough?
   B. Approaches in the Treatment of the Criminal Offender
   C. The Three R's in Criminal Reformation
   D. Mental Disease Factors in the Criminal Correction System

Questions 7-12.

DIRECTIONS: Answer Questions 7 through 12 SOLELY on the basis of the following selection:

In a study by J. E. Cowden, an attempt was made to determine which variables would best predict institutional adjustment and recidivism in recently committed delinquent boys. The results suggested in particular that older boys, when first institutionalized, who are initially rated as being more mature and more amenable to change, will most likely adjust better than the average boy adjusts to the institution. Prediction of institutional adjustment was rendered slightly more accurate by using the variables of age and personality prognosis in combined form.

8

With reference to the prediction of recidivism, boys who committed more serious offenses showed less recidivism than average. These boys were also older than average when first committed. The variable of age accounts in part for both their more serious offenses and for their lower subsequent rate of recidivism.

The results also showed some trends suggesting that boys from higher socioeconomic backgrounds tended to commit more serious offenses leading to their institutionalization as delinquents. However, neither the ratings of socioeconomic status nor "home-environment" appeared to be significantly related to recidivism in this study.

Cowden also found an essentially linear relationship between personality prognosis and recidivism, and between institutional adjustment and recidivism. When these variables were used jointly to predict recidivism, accuracy of prediction was increased only slightly, but in general the ability to predict recidivism fell far below the ability to predict institutional adjustment.

7. According to the above passage, which one of the following   7. ...
   was NOT found to be a significant factor in predicting
   recidivism?
   A. Age   B. Personality
   C. Socioeconomic background D. Institutional adjustment
8. According to the above passage, institutional adjustment   8. ...
   was *more* accurately predicted when the variables used were
   A. socioeconomic background and recidivism
   B. recidivism and personality   C. personality and age
   D. age and socioeconomic background
9. According to the above passage, which of the following   9. ...
   were *variables* in predicting both recidivism and institutional adjustment?
   A. Age and personality   B. Family background and age
   C. Nature of offense and age D. Personality
10. Which one of the following conclusions is MOST justified   10. ...
    by the above passage?
    A. Institutional adjustment had a lower level of predic-
       tability than recidivism.
    B. Recidivism and seriousness of offense are negatively
       correlated to some degree.
    C. Institutional adjustment and personality prognosis,
       when considered together, are significantly better
       predictors of recidivism than either one alone.
    D. A delinquent boy from a lower class family background
       is more likely to have committed a serious first of-
       fense than a delinquent boy from a higher socioeconomic
       background.
11. The study discussed in the passage found that delinquent   11. ...
    boys from a higher socioeconomic background tended to
    A. commit more serious crimes
    B. commit less serious crimes
    C. show more recidivism than average
    D. show less recidivism than average
12. The *most appropriate* conclusion to be drawn from the study 12. ...
    discussed above is that
    A. delinquent boys from higher socioeconomic backgrounds
       show less institutional adjustment than average

9

    B. a high positive correlation was found between recid-
       ivism and institutional adjustment
    C. home environment, although not <u>significantly</u> related
       to recidivism, did influence institutional adjustment
    D. older boys are more likely to commit more serious
       first offenses and show less recidivism than younger
       boys

Questions 13-18.
DIRECTIONS: Answer Questions 13 to 18 SOLELY on the basis of the in-
             formation contained in the following charts and notes.

CHART I
Number of Inmates Enrolled in Libertyville's
Basic Office Skills Program

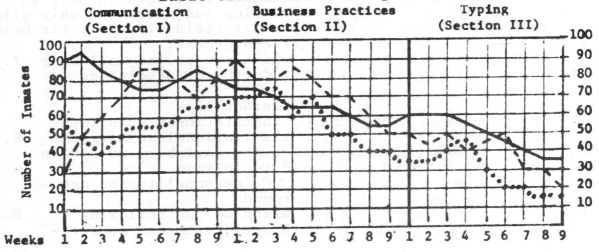

Symbol	Crime Category
——————	Victimless Crimes
– – – –	Crimes Against Property
·······	Violent Crimes

NOTES: Inmates can enter a section of the program at any point. In-
       mates can complete a section of the program at any point by
       passing an examination.
       Enrollment at the end of a section does not necessarily indi-
       cate successful completion of that section.

CHART II
Number of Inmates Who Successfully Completed
Each Section of Libertyville's
Office Skills Program

Crime Category	Completed Section I	Completed Section II	Completed Section III
Victimless Crimes	78	55	37
Crimes Against Property	43	57	28
Violent Crimes	80	50	18

10

CHART III
Percentage of Recidivism Within First Year of Parole
Among Inmates Who Successfully Completed
Various Stages of Libertyville's
Office Skills Program

Crime Category	Completed Section I	Completed Section II	Completed Section III
Victimless Crimes	40%	30%	15%
Crimes Against Property	30%	15%	5%
Violent Crimes	35%	25%	10%

13. The percentage of inmates who successfully completed   13. ...
    Section I and were recidivists is, *most nearly*,
      A. 21%   B. 35%   C. 38%   D. 47%
14. The ratio of the number of inmates who started Section   14. ...
    III the first week to the number who successfully com-
    pleted Section III is, *most nearly*,
      A. 1.5:1   B. 1.7:1   C. 2.1:1   D. 2.5:1
15. During which of the following weeks of the program was   15. ...
    the enrollment by those who committed victimless crimes
    exceeded by both those who committed crimes against
    property and by those who committed violent crimes?
      A. Week 1 of the Communication Section
      B. Week 3 of the Business Practices Section
      C. Week 9 of the Business Practices Section
      D. Week 6 of the Typing Section
16. If the average number of inmates enrolled in any stage of   16. ..
    the program is considered to be the number of inmates
    enrolled during week 5 of that Section, what is the dif-
    ference between the average number of inmates enrolled in
    Section I and in Section III?
      A. 90   B. 125   C. 190   D. 215
17. Assume that 60 percent of the inmates who completed Sec-   17. ..
    tion III of the Office Skills Program enrolled the first
    week of the program and completed all three sections of
    the program. The percent of the initial enrollees who
    completed the ENTIRE Office Skills Program was, *most nearly*,
      A. 21%   B. 28%   C. 36%   D. 49%
18. The one of the following periods which exhibits the   18. ..
    GREATEST percentage change in enrollment of inmates in
    the crimes against property category is weeks
      A. 1 to 2 in the Communication Section
      B. 2 to 4 in the Communication Section
      C. 4 to 6 in the Business Practices Section
      D. 3 to 4 in the Typing Section
19. A recent study of the bail system as it is administered   19. ..
    conducted by the Legal Aid Society, concluded that the one
    of the following factors which has the STRONGEST impact on
    an accused person's chances of being convicted is
      A. whether the person is detained or released prior to
         trial
      B. the weight of evidence against the person
      C. the type and seriousness of the alleged crime
      D. whether the person has a criminal record
20. Of the following, the *chief* DISADVANTAGE of using on-the-   20. ...
    job training is that it

11

A. is initially more costly than using other types of
   training
B. is often carried on with little or no planning
C. requires the worker to remain in the environment in
   which he will be working
D. prevents the trainee from obtaining the benefits of
   a professional's experience

KEYS (CORRECT ANSWERS)

	TEST 1				TEST 2				TEST 3		
1.	A	11.	D	1.	A	11.	D	1.	A	11.	A
2.	A	12.	B	2.	B	12.	A	2.	A	12.	D
3.	C	13.	B	3.	D	13.	C	3.	C	13.	B
4.	C	14.	B	4.	D	14.	A	4.	C	14.	B
5.	B	15.	C	5.	D	15.	A	5.	C	15.	B
6.	B	16.	A	6.	A	16.	B	6.	B	16.	A
7.	B	17.	B	7.	D	17.	D	7.	C	17.	B
8.	C	18.	C	8.	D	18.	B	8.	C	18.	A
9.	C	19.	B	9.	C	19.	C	9.	A	19.	A
10.	C	20.	D	10.	A	20.	D	10.	B	20.	B

EXAMINATION SECTION
TEST 1

DIRECTIONS: Each question or incomplete statement is followed by several suggested answers or completions. Select the one that BEST answers the question or completes the statement. *PRINT THE LETTER OF THE CORRECT ANSWER IN THE SPACE AT THE RIGHT.*

1. Which one of the following "suggestions to interviewers" should be AVOIDED?
   A. Encourage the client to verbalize his thoughts and feelings.
   B. Cover as much as possible in each interview.
   C. Don't hesitate to refer the client to someone else who might be more helpful in the situation.
   D. The problem which is presented initially, or the one which seems most obvious, often is not the real one.

1.___

2. If it seems clear that disturbance in parents' marital relationships is a major factor in causing a child to be emotionally disturbed, the counselor should
   A. point this out to the parents and tell them that for the welfare of their children, they should resolve their difficulties
   B. suggest that he will be willing to discuss their marital difficulties with them
   C. ignore this and concentrate on helping the child
   D. tactfully suggest that their marital difficulties may be playing a part in their child's disturbance and offer to refer the parents to a qualified marriage counseling service

2.___

3. The process of collecting, analyzing, synthesizing and interpreting information about the client should be
   A. completed prior to counseling
   B. completed early in the counseling process
   C. limited to counseling which is primarily diagnostic in purpose
   D. continuous throughout counseling

3.___

4. Catharsis, the "emotional unloading" of the client's feelings, has a value in the early stages of counseling because it accomplishes all BUT which one of the following goals?
   A. It relieves strong physiological tensions in the client.
   B. It increases the client's anxiety and therefore his motivation to continue counseling.
   C. It provides a verbal substitute for "acting out" the client's aggressive feelings.
   D. It releases emotional energy which the client has been using to maintain his defenses.

4.___

5. During the first interview, the counselor can expect the   5.___
   client to participate at his BEST when the counselor
   A. structures the nature of the counseling process
   B. attempts to summarize the client's problem for him
   C. allows the client to verbalize at his own pace
   D. tells the client that he understands the presenting
      problem

6. To obtain the most effective results in change of attitude   6.___
   and behavior through parent education, the leader should be
   A. thoroughly grounded in the whole field of psychology
   B. able to help members of the group look at their own
      attitudes and behavior in constructive ways
   C. completely confident as to the right solution to
      problems that may be brought up
   D. a warm, charming, friendly human being

7. A social worker's report about a client states that a   7.___
   mother has ambivalent feelings concerning her child. This
   means that the mother
   A. has contradictory emotional reactions concerning her
      child
   B. is overprotective of the child
   C. strongly rejects the child
   D. is unduly apprehensive about the child's welfare

8. A psychological report notes, "The client shows little   8.___
   effect." This means that the client
   A. did not take the test too seriously
   B. did not show emotional behavior in situations which
      normally call for such reactions
   C. did not show signs of fatigue as the testing progressed
   D. reacted to the test situation in a generally favorable
      manner

9. A psychologist's report states, in part, that a client   9.___
   exhibits some masochistic symptoms. This will be evident
   to the counselor through the client's persistent attempts at
   A. self-assertion
   B. self-effacement
   C. inflicting physical harm on others
   D. sexual molestation of others of the same sex

10. According to research studies, the type of counselor   10.___
    response that is MOST often followed by a client's
    expression of insight or illumination is
    A. clarification of feeling
    B. reflection of feeling
    C. simple acceptance
    D. exploratory question

11. Of the following, the BEST way to deal with a 12-year-old   11.___
    boy who feels inferior to his peers is to
    A. provide tasks which he can master with little difficulty
    B. show him how irrational his feelings are
    C. accept his declarations of lack of confidence
       sympathetically
    D. carefully arrange situations in which he will be obliged
       to show leadership

12. In counseling or psychotherapy, the factor which is the   12.___
    MOST important for success tends to be the
    A. counselor's theoretical orientation
    B. counselor's attitudes and feelings toward the client
    C. techniques used by the counselor
    D. amount of experience and training possessed by the
       counselor

13. Transference is an important aspect of   13.___
    A. test construction   B. grade placement
    C. anecdotal record keeping D. therapy

14. The MOST desirable way of establishing rapport with a   14.___
    client who comes to the counselor with a problem is to
    A. demonstrate sincere interest in him
    B. offer to do everything possible to solve his problem
       for him
    C. use the language of the client
    D. promise to keep his problem confidential

15. Role playing has been used as a technique in parent edu-   15.___
    cation work. Of the following, the major value is that it
    A. permits parents to express unconscious feelings and
       thereby solve conflicts
    B. tells a story in a forceful and therefore lasting way
    C. provides an opportunity for the individual to view his
       problems by standing off and looking at them through
       the eyes of someone else
    D. brings to light problems people never knew they had

16. If during a counseling situation a client expressed anger   16.___
    about a particular situation, which of the following responses
    would a non-directive counselor MOST likely make?
    A. "Why are you so angry?"
    B. "Is there any need to get so upset about this?"
    C. "This has really made you very mad, hasn't it?"
    D. "Do you feel better now that you have expressed your
       anger?"

17. In a counseling process, the counselor should usually give   17.___
    information
    A. whenever it is needed
    B. at the end of the process
    C. in the introductory interview
    D. just before the client would ordinarily request it

18. "After having recognized and clarified feelings and con-   18.___
    flicts, it is usually necessary to go beyond the stage of
    understanding and to elaborate a constructive plan for
    future action."
    Which of the following people would NOT go along with the
    above statement?
    A. Thorne   B. Robinson
    C. Williamson   D. Rogers

19. The counselor should focus his attention in the beginning   19.____
    upon
    A. the transference phenomenon
    B. evidences of hostility
    C. the unique characteristics of the particular relation-
       ship at hand
    D. indications of client aggressiveness

20. A recent guidance text that stresses the broad developments 20.____
    of our national heritage, our contemporary social setting,
    our value patterns, and also the integration into guidance
    of many disciplines - sociology, anthropology, philosophy,
    psychology - is
    A. FOUNDATIONS OF GUIDANCE - Miller
    B. GUIDANCE POLICY AND PRACTICE - Mathewson
    C. GUIDANCE IN TODAY'S SCHOOLS - Mortenson & Schmuller
    D. GUIDANCE SERVICES - Humphreys, Traxler & North

21. Which one of the following characteristics of counseling   21.____
    is inconsistent with the others?
    A. Counseling is more than advice-giving.
    B. Counseling involves something more than the solution
       to an immediate problem.
    C. Counseling concerns itself with attitudes rather than
       actions.
    D. Counseling involves intellectual rather than emotional
       attitudes as its basic raw material.

22. One approach to counseling has been labeled "non-directive". 22.____
    The word "non-directive" derives from the fact that, in
    this approach to counseling, the counselor
    A. does not tell the client what he should do
    B. makes the client responsible for the direction of the
       course of the interviews
    C. does not make judgments about the behavior of the client
    D. avoids possible areas of threat to the client

23. Of the following personality traits, which would be LEAST   23.____
    essential for an effective counselor to possess?
    A. Extroversion   B. Objectivity
    C. Security   D. Sensitivity

24. Interpretation as a therapeutic tool is considered a   24.____
    hindrance to therapy progress by
    A. orthodox Freudians   B. neo-analysts
    C. Rogerians   D. Adlerians

25. The current interpersonal behavior of the client is proba-   25.____
    bly MOST important as a therapy topic to which two analytic
    theorists?
    A. Freud and Adler   B. Adler and Rank
    C. Freud and Rank   D. Horney and Sullivan

KEY (CORRECT ANSWERS)

1. B	6. B	11. A	16. C	21. D
2. D	7. A	12. B	17. A	22. B
3. D	8. B	13. D	18. D	23. A
4. B	9. B	14. A	19. C	24. C
5. C	10. C	15. C	20. A	25. D

TEST 2

DIRECTIONS: Each question or incomplete statement is followed by several suggested answers or completions. Select the one that BEST answers the question or completes the statement. *PRINT THE LETTER OF THE CORRECT ANSWER IN THE SPACE AT THE RIGHT.*

1. When a counselor is listening to a client, it is MOST important that he be able to
   A. show interest and agreement with what the client is saying
   B. paraphrase what the client is saying
   C. understand the significance of what the client is saying
   D. differentiate between fact and fiction in what the client is saying

   1.___

2. On which one of the following is successful counseling LEAST likely to depend?
   A. The counselor's theoretical orientation
   B. The counselor's ability to bring the client's feelings and attitudes into the open
   C. The counselor's diagnostic ability
   D. The client's readiness for counseling

   2.___

3. A client is referred to you for counseling against his will and is suspicious and uncooperative. You should
   A. explain to him that you cannot help him unless he is prepared to cooperate
   B. explain that you are not taking sides and that you will be impartial
   C. show him that you know how he feels and encourage him to talk about it
   D. explain that you are on his side and will listen sympathetically to anything that he might care to bring up

   3.___

4. Which one of the following would NOT be considered a basic objective of the first interview between a client and a counselor?
   A. Beginning a sound counseling relationship
   B. Identifying the client's real problem
   C. Opening up the area of client feelings and attitudes
   D. Clarifying the nature of the counseling process for the client

   4.___

5. All of the following counselor statements or actions are appropriate techniques for ending an interview EXCEPT
   A. "Our time is nearly up. Is there something else you have in mind for today?"
   B. "Let's see now. Suppose we go over what we've accomplished today."
   C. Counselor may glance at his watch and say, "When would you like to come in again?"
   D. Counselor may shuffle papers on desk and say, "Now, let's see; when is my next appointment?"

   5.___

6. It has been recognized in recent literature that the value   6.___
   structure of the individual counselor has what kind of
   effect on the counseling process?
      A. Direct   B. Indirect
      C. Little   D. None

7. The intensive study of the same individuals over a fairly   7.___
   long period of time represents the
      A. cross-sectional approach B. longitudinal approach
      C. clinical approach   D. biographical approach

8. Of the following techniques, the one which is MOST charac-   8.___
   teristic of non-directive or client-centered therapy is
      A. encouraging transference
      B. free association
      C. reflection of feeling
      D. permissive questioning

9. In making predictions about how a client will behave in a   9.___
   given situation, a counselor
      A. should limit himself to those situations for which
         "actuarial" data are available
      B. must rely on "clinical" judgment in many situations
         but use "actuarial" data wherever possible
      C. should rely on "clinical" judgment in all situations,
         since they are more valid than "actuarial" predictions
      D. always uses "actuarial" data, but modifies them in
         light of his "clinical" impression of the client

10. A research study that establishes an hypothesis, sets up   10.___
    control groups, collects data, and generalizes from the
    data is
       A. formulative   B. diagnostic
       C. experimental   D. exploratory

11. The MOST usable single index of the social and economic   11.___
    status of all the members of any family is
       A. occupation of the father
       B. religious affiliation of the family
       C. location of the home in the community
       D. socio-economic rating by neighbors

12. When a counselor does NOT understand the meaning of a   12.___
    response that a counselee has made, the counselor usually
    should
       A. proceed to another topic
       B. admit his lack of understanding and ask for clarification
       C. act as if he understands so that the counselee's
          confidence in him is not shaken
       D. ask the counselee to choose his words more carefully

13. When the counselor makes a response which touches off a   13.___
    high degree of resistance in the counselee, he should
       A. apologize and rephrase his remark in a less threatening
          manner
       B. accept the resistance
       C. ignore the counselee's resistance
       D. recognize that little more will be accomplished in the
          interview and offer another appointment

14. Directive and non-directive counseling are two emphases in   14.___
    counseling theory and practice. From the pairs of names
    listed below, indicate the two that are representative of
    the Directive school.
    A. Thorne and Williamson   B. Rogers and Thorne
    C. Williamson and Sullivan   D. Sullivan and Rogers

15. Rogerian counseling theory is based on the assumption that   15.___
    the potential and tendency for growth toward a fully
    functioning personality is present in
    A. a few "self-actualized" persons
    B. most people of above average intelligence
    C. people whose behavior can be considered as "normal"
       and socially effective
    D. all people

16. Anecdotal records should contain which type(s) of   16.___
    information?
    A. Evaluations   B. Interpretations
    C. Factual reports   D. Prognoses

17. RESISTANCE in relation to psychological counseling typical- 17.___
    ly refers to the
    A. client's defenses against his inner conflicts
    B. counselor's unwillingness to deal with the client's
       emotional problems
    C. client's having enough ego strength so that he can
       face his problems
    D. counselor's having enough ego strength so that he can
       help the client face his problems

18. On which one of the following does the democratic leader   18.___
    specifically rely? His ability to
    A. listen and tactfully guide the discussion in the
       direction he has planned and the members' willingness
       to cooperate
    B. diagnose situations, to interpret and explain them to
       the members and their willingness to accept
    C. discern the issues which the members could profitably
       discuss and his willingness to allow them with his help
       to do so
    D. understand the meaning of the response from the member's
       frame of reference and his willingness for them to make
       decisions

19. Advisement in counseling is MOST effective when the   19.___
    counselee is in a state of
    A. perceiving his problem as related to a conflict with
       inner forces
    B. minimal conflict and of optimal readiness for action
    C. perceiving his problem as related to an external conflict
    D. feeling extremely ambivalent about his self-concept

20. Of the following, the MOST valid use of projective   20.___
    techniques is the study of the
    A. problems which an individual faces
    B. cultural effects upon an individual
    C. inner world of an individual
    D. human relationships of an individual

21. Diagnosis is NOT regarded as a helpful antecedent to   21.___
    counseling by
    A. Cottle   B. Rogers
    C. Thorne   D. Williamson

22. The beginning counselor must be alert to interferences to   22.___
    rapport. Which one of the following is NOT considered an
    intereference?
    A. Injecting the counselor's present mood
    B. Engaging in "small talk" at the start of the interview
    C. Registering surprise or dismay
    D. Emphasizing the counselor's ability

23. There is some evidence according to Rogers that counseling   23.___
    is more effective with
    A. younger adults or higher intelligence
    B. older adults of higher intelligence
    C. younger adults of lower intelligence
    D. older adults of lower intelligence

24. In assisting with the scheduling of interviews for educa-   24.___
    tional planning, the counselor should suggest that group
    instruction
    A. follow the counseling interview
    B. is not necessary when individual interviews can be
       scheduled since each case is different
    C. precede the counseling
    D. may either precede or follow the counseling interview

25. A client has requested an interview with the counselor to   25.___
    discuss a personal problem. In general, the BEST way to
    begin the interview is to
    A. come directly to the point and encourage the client
       to talk about his problem
    B. assure him that everything discussed will be confidential
    C. offer to help him in every way possible
    D. inquire whether he has discussed the problem with
       anyone else

KEY (CORRECT ANSWERS)

1.	C	11.	A
2.	A	12.	B
3.	C	13.	B
4.	B	14.	A
5.	D	15.	D
6.	A	16.	C
7.	B	17.	A
8.	C	18.	C
9.	B	19.	B
10.	C	20.	C

21.	B
22.	B
23.	A
24.	C
25.	A

EXAMINATION SECTION

TEST 1

1. The one of the following which is the BEST description of
   a properly objective investigator is one who
      A. is friendly and sensitive to the client's feelings,
   without becoming emotionally involved
      B. is distant and impersonal, remaining unaffected by
   what the client says
      C. lets personal emotions enter as far as the client's
   situation calls for them
      D. becomes emotionally involved with the client's situ-
   ation but without showing this involvement   1.____

2. The one of the following which is MOST necessary for successfully interviewing a person who belongs to a culture
   different from that of the investigator is for the investigator to
      A. have some appreciation of the other culture
      B. ignore those cultural differences which lead to bias
      C. stay away from sensitive, "touchy" issues
      D. assume the mannerisms of people in the other cultures   2.____

3. In fact-finding interviews, it is generally assumed that
   the smaller the number of interviewees, the greater the
   increase of reliability with the addition of others. The
   PROPER number of interviewees needed to insure the accuracy of information obtained *generally* depends upon the
      A. educational level of those interviewed
      B. number of people who have the required information
      C. directness of the questions asked
      D. variability of the information received   3.____

4. The one of the following which is generally MOST likely
   to be accurately described in an interview by an interviewee is
      A. the presence of a large painting in the investi-
   gator's office
      B. the number of people in the investigator's waiting
   room
      C. space relations
      D. duration of time   4.____

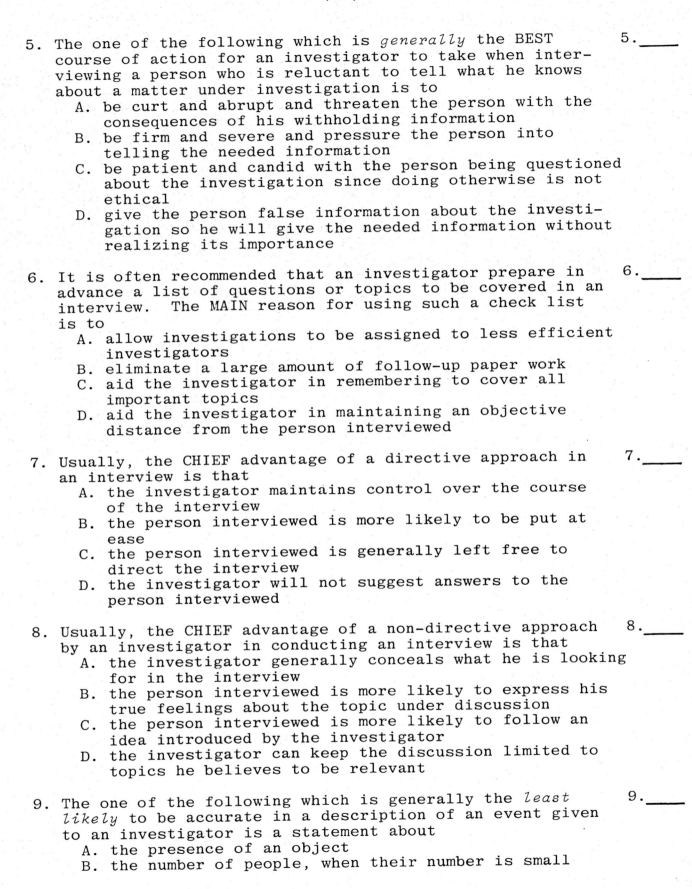

5. The one of the following which is *generally* the BEST   5.____
course of action for an investigator to take when inter-
viewing a person who is reluctant to tell what he knows
about a matter under investigation is to
   A. be curt and abrupt and threaten the person with the
      consequences of his withholding information
   B. be firm and severe and pressure the person into
      telling the needed information
   C. be patient and candid with the person being questioned
      about the investigation since doing otherwise is not
      ethical
   D. give the person false information about the investi-
      gation so he will give the needed information without
      realizing its importance

6. It is often recommended that an investigator prepare in   6.____
advance a list of questions or topics to be covered in an
interview. The MAIN reason for using such a check list
is to
   A. allow investigations to be assigned to less efficient
      investigators
   B. eliminate a large amount of follow-up paper work
   C. aid the investigator in remembering to cover all
      important topics
   D. aid the investigator in maintaining an objective
      distance from the person interviewed

7. Usually, the CHIEF advantage of a directive approach in   7.____
an interview is that
   A. the investigator maintains control over the course
      of the interview
   B. the person interviewed is more likely to be put at
      ease
   C. the person interviewed is generally left free to
      direct the interview
   D. the investigator will not suggest answers to the
      person interviewed

8. Usually, the CHIEF advantage of a non-directive approach   8.____
by an investigator in conducting an interview is that
   A. the investigator generally conceals what he is looking
      for in the interview
   B. the person interviewed is more likely to express his
      true feelings about the topic under discussion
   C. the person interviewed is more likely to follow an
      idea introduced by the investigator
   D. the investigator can keep the discussion limited to
      topics he believes to be relevant

9. The one of the following which is generally the *least*   9.____
likely to be accurate in a description of an event given
to an investigator is a statement about
   A. the presence of an object
   B. the number of people, when their number is small

    C. locations of people
    D. duration of time

10. Assume that you, an investigator, are conducting a char-   10.____
    acter investigation. In an interview, the one of the
    following character traits of the person being interviewed
    which can USUALLY be determined with a *good* degree of
    reliability is
    A. honesty
    C. forcefulness
                               B. dependability
                               D. perseverance

11. As an investigator, you have been assigned the task of   11.____
    obtaining a family's social history. The BEST place for
    you to interview members of the family while obtaining
    this social history would *generally* be in
    A. the family's home
    B. your agency's general offices
    C. the home of a friend of the family
    D. your own private office

12. You, an investigator, are checking someone's work his-   12.____
    tory. The way for you to get the MOST reliable infor-
    mation from a previous employer is to
    A. send personal letters; the employer will respond
       to the personal attention
    B. send form letters; the employer will cooperate
       readily since little time or effort is asked of him
    C. arrange a personal interview; the employer may offer
       information he would not care to put in a letter or
       speak over the phone
    D. telephone; this method is as effective as a personal
       interview and is much more convenient

13. The effect that attestation, or the formal taking of an   13.____
    oath, has on witness testimony is to
    A. decrease accuracy, since a witness under oath is
       more nervous about what is said
    B. make little difference, since the witness is not
       too swayed by an oath
    C. increase accuracy, since a witness under oath feels
       more responsibility for what is said
    D. eliminate inaccuracy unless there is deliberate per-
       jury on the part of the witness

14. If an investigator obtains testimony from persons in   14.____
    interviews by means of interrogation or asking questions
    rather than by letting the person freely relate the tes-
    timony, what is said will GENERALLY be
    A. greater in range and less accurate
    B. greater in range and more accurate
    C. about the same in range and less accurate
    D. about the same in range and more accurate

4 (#1)

15. Experienced investigators have learned to phrase their   15._____
    questions carefully in order to obtain the desired re-
    sponse. Of the following, the question which would
    usually elicit the MOST accurate answer is:
        A. "How old are you?"
        B. "What is your income?"
        C. "How are you today?"
        D. "What is the date of your birth?"

16. The one of the following questions which would *generally*   16._____
    lead to the LEAST reliable answer is
        A. "Did you see a wallet?"
        B. "Was the German Shepherd gray?"
        C. "Didn't you see the stop sign?"
        D. "Did you see the guard on duty?"

17. Some investigators may make a practice of observing de-   17._____
    tails of the surroundings when interviewing in someone's
    home or office. Such a practice is *generally* considered
        A. *undesirable*, mainly because such snooping is an un-
           warranted, unethical invasion of privacy
        B. *undesirable*, mainly because useful information is
           rarely, if ever, gained this way
        C. *desirable*, mainly because useful insights into the
           character of the person interviewed may be gained
        D. *desirable*, mainly because it is impossible to evalu-
           ate a person adequately without such observation of
           his environment

18. The one of the following questions which will MOST   18._____
    often lead to a reliable answer is:
        A. "Was his hair very dark?"
        B. "Wasn't there a clock on the wall?"
        C. "Was the automobile white or gray?"
        D. "Did you see a motorcycle?"

19. The one of the following which can MOST accurately be   19._____
    determined by an investigator by means of interviewing
    is
        A. a persons's intelligence
        B. factual information about an event
        C. a person's aptitude for a specific task
        D. a person's perceptions of his own abilities

20. The one of the following which is *most likely* to help a   20._____
    person being interviewed feel at ease is for the inves-
    tigator to
        A. let him start the conversation
        B. give him an abundance of time
        C. be relaxed himself
        D. open the interview by telling a joke

21. If the interviewee is to perceive some goal for himself   21.____
in the interview and thus be motivated to participate in
it, it is important that he clearly understand some of
the aspects of the interview. Of the following aspects,
the one the interviewee needs LEAST to understand is
    A. the purpose of the interview
    B. the mechanics of interviewing
    C. the use made of the information he contributes
    D. what will be expected of him in the interview

22. As an investigator working on a project requiring inter-   22.____
agency cooperation, you find that employees of an agency
involved in the project are constantly making it difficult
for you to obtain necessary information. Of the following,
the BEST action for you to take FIRST is to
    A. discuss the problem with your supervisor
    B. speak with your counterpart in the other agency
    C. discuss the problem with the head of the uncooperative
       agency
    D. contact the head of your agency

23. The investigator is justified in misleading the inter-   23.____
viewee only when, in the investigator's judgment, this
is clearly required by the problem being investigated.
Such practice is
    A. *necessary*; there are times when complete honesty
       will impede a successful investigation
    B. *unnecessary*; such a tactic is unethical and should
       never be employed
    C. *necessary*; an investigator must be guided by success
       rather than ethical considerations in an investigation
    D. *unnecessary*; it is clearly doubtful whether such a
       practice will help the investigator conclude the
       investigation successfully

24. Assume that, in investigating a case of possible welfare   24.____
fraud, it becomes necessary to hold an interview in the
client's home in order to observe family interaction and
conditions. Upon arriving, the investigator finds that
the client's living room is noisy and crowded, with
neighbors present and children running in and out. Of the
following, the BEST course of action for the investigator
to take is to
    A. conduct the interview in the living room after telling
       the children to behave, and asking the neighbors to
       leave
    B. tell the client that it is impossible to conduct the
       interview in the apartment, and make an appointment
       for the next day in the investigator's office
    C. suggest that they move from the living room into the
       kitchen where there is a table on which he can write
    D. try his best to conduct the interview in the noisy
       and crowded living room

25. You, an investigator, are giving testimony in court about 25._____
a matter you have investigated. An attorney is questioning you in an abrasive, badgering way, and, in an
insulting manner, calls into doubt your ability as an
investigator. You lose your temper and respond angrily,
telling the attorney to stop harassing and insulting you.
Of the following, the BEST description of such a response
is that it is *generally*
    A. *appropriate*; as a witness in court, you do not have
       to take insults from anybody, including an attorney
    B. *inappropriate*; losing your temper will show that you
       are weak and cannot be trusted as an investigator
    C. *appropriate*; a judge and jury will usually respect
       someone who responds strongly to unjust provocation
    D. *inappropriate*; such conduct is unprofessional and
       may unfavorably impress a judge and jury

_____

KEY (CORRECT ANSWERS)

1. A		11. A
2. A		12. C
3. D		13. C
4. A		14. A
5. C		15. D
6. C		16. B
7. A		17. C
8. B		18. D
9. D		19. D
10. C		20. C

21. B
22. A
23. A
24. C
25. D

_____

TEST 2

DIRECTIONS: Each question or incomplete statement is followed by several suggested answers or completions. Select the one that BEST answers the question or completes the statement. *PRINT THE LETTER OF THE CORRECT ANSWER IN THE SPACE AT THE RIGHT.*

1. The reliability of information obtained increases with the number of persons interviewed. The more the interviewees differ in their statements, the more persons it is necessary to interview to ascertain the true facts. According to this statement, the dependability of the information about an occurrence obtained from interviews is related to   1.____
    A. how many people are interviewed
    B. how soon after the occurrence an interview can be arranged
    C. the individual technique of the interviewer
    D. the interviewer's ability to detect differences in the statements of interviewees

2. An investigator interviews members of the public at his desk. The attitude of the public toward this department will probably be LEAST affected by this investigator's   2.____
    A. courtesy   B. efficiency
    C. height   D. neatness

3. The *one* of the following which is NOT effective in obtaining complete testimony from a witness during an interview is to   3.____
    A. ask questions in chronological order
    B. permit the witness to structure the interview
    C. make sure you fully understand the response to each question
    D. review questions to be asked beforehand

4. The person MOST likely to be a good interviewer is one who   4.____
    A. is able to outguess the person being interviewed
    B. tries to change the attitudes of the persons he interviews
    C. controls the interview by skillfully dominating the conversation
    D. is able to imagine himself in the position of the person being interviewed

5. When you are interviewing someone to obtain information, the BEST of the following reasons for you to repeat certain of his exact words is to   5.____
    A. *assure* him that appropriate action will be taken
    B. *encourage* him to elaborate on a point he has made
    C. *assure* him that you agree with his point of view
    D. *encourage* him to switch to another topic of discussion

6. You are interviewing a client who has just been assaulted. 6.____
   He has trouble collecting his thoughts and telling his
   story coherently. Which of the following represents the
   MOST effective method of questioning under these circum-
   stances?
   A. Ask questions which structure the client's story
      chronologically into units, each with a beginning,
      middle and end.
   B. Ask several questions at a time to structure the
      interview.
   C. Ask open-ended questions which allow the client to
      respond in a variety of ways.
   D. Begin the interview with several detailed questions
      in order to focus the client's attention on the
      situation.

7. You are conducting an initial interview with a witness 7.____
   who expresses reluctance, even hostility, to being ques-
   tioned. You feel it would be helpful to take some notes
   during the interview.
   In this situation, it would be BEST to
   A. put off note-taking until a follow-up interview,
      and concentrate on establishing rapport with the
      witness
   B. explain the necessity of note-taking, and proceed
      to take notes during the interview
   C. make notes from memory after the witness has left
   D. take notes, but as unobtrusively as possible

8. You are interviewing the owner of a stolen car about 8.____
   facts relating to the robbery. After completing his
   statement, the car owner suddenly states that some of
   the details he has just related are not correct. You
   realize that this change might be significant.
   Of the following, it would be BEST for you to
   A. ask the owner what other details he may have given
      incorrectly
   B. make a note of the discrepancy for discussion at
      a later date
   C. repeat your questioning on the details that were
      misstated until you have covered that area com-
      pletely
   D. explain to the owner that because of his change of
      testimony, you will have to repeat the entire inter-
      view

9. Assume that you have been asked to get all the pertinent 9.____
   information from an employee who claims that she wit-
   nessed a robbery.
   Which of the following questions is *least likely* to in-
   fluence the witness's response?
   A. "Can you describe the robber's hair?"
   B. "Did the robber have a lot of hair?"
   C. "Was the robber's hair black or brown?"
   D. "Was the robber's hair very dark?"

10. In order to obtain an accurate statement from a person who has witnessed a crime, it is BEST to question the witness   10.____
    A. as soon as possible after the crime was committed
    B. after the witness has discussed the crime with other witnesses
    C. after the witness has had sufficient time to reflect on events and formulate a logical statement
    D. after the witness has been advised that he is obligated to tell the whole truth

11. Assume that your superior assigns you to interview an individual who, he warns, seems to be hightly "introverted." You should be aware that, during an interview, such a person is likely to   11.____
    A. hold views which are highly controversial in nature
    B. be domineering and try to control the direction of the interview
    C. resist answering personal questions regarding his background
    D. give information which is largely fabricated

12. A young woman was stabbed in the hand in her home by her estranged boyfriend. Her mother and two sisters were at home at the time.   12.____
    Of the following, it would generally be BEST to interview the young woman in the presence of
    A. her mother *only*
    B. all members of her immediate family
    C. members of the family who actually observed the crime
    D. the official authorities

13. The one of the following statements concerning interviewing which is LEAST valid is that   13.____
    A. skill in interviewing can be improved by knowledge of the basic factors involving relations between people
    B. interviewing should become a routine and mechanical practice to the skilled and experienced interviewer
    C. genuine interest in people is essential for successful interviewing
    D. certain psychological traits characterize most people most of the time

14. The initial interview will normally be more of a problem to the interviewer than any subsequent interviews he may have with the same person because   14.____
    A. the interviewee is likely to be hostile
    B. there is too much to be accomplished in one session
    C. he has less information about the client than he will have later
    D. some information may be forgotten when later making record of this first interview

15. Continuous taking of notes during an interview is gener-   15.____
    ally
    A. *desirable* because no important facts will be for-
       gotten
    B. *undesirable* because it gives the person being inter-
       viewed a clue to the importance of the information
       being obtained from him
    C. *desirable* because the interviewer cannot write as
       fast as the person being interviewed can speak
    D. *undesirable* because it may put the person being
       interviewed ill at ease

16. "Carefully planned interviews tend to impose restrictions   16.____
    which leave little room for spontaneity." A flaw in this
    critiscism of the planned interview is that it does NOT
    take into account that
    A. a planned interview obviates the need for spontaneity
    B. even the planned interview may be flexible
    C. not all planned interviews impose restrictions
    D. restrictions that result from planning are undesirable

17. Writing up the interview into a systematic report is   17.____
    BEST done
    A. in the presence of the subject, so that mistakes
       can be corrected immediately
    B. within a reasonably short time after the interview,
       so that nothing is forgotten
    C. no sooner than several days after the interview, so
       that the interviewer will have had plenty of time
       to think about it
    D. with the help of someone not present at the inter-
       view, so that an objective view can be obtained

18. While you are conducting an interview, the telephone on   18.____
    your desk rings. Of the following, it would be BEST for
    you to
    A. ask the interviewer at the next desk to answer your
       telephone and take the message for you
    B. excuse yourself, pick up the telephone, and tell
       the person on the other end you are busy and will
       call him back later
    C. ignore the ringing telephone and continue with the
       interview
    D. use another telephone to inform the operator not
       to put calls through to you while you are conducting
       an interview

19. An interviewee is at your desk, which is quite near to   19.____
    desks where other people work. He beckons you a little
    closer and starts to talk in a low voice as though he
    does not want anyone else to hear him. Under these
    circumstances, the BEST thing for you to do is to
    A. ask him to speak a little louder so that he can be
       heard

  B. cut the interview short and not get involved in his
   problems
  C. explain that people at other desks are not eaves-
   droppers
  D. listen carefully to what he says and give it consideration

20. Of the following, the BEST way for a person to develop 20.____
  competence as an interviewer is to
  A. attend lectures on interviewing techniques
  B. practice with employees on the job
  C. conduct interviews under the supervision of an
   experienced instructor
  D. attend a training course in counseling

21. During the course of an interview, it would be LEAST 21.____
  desirable for the investigator to
  A. correct immediately any grammatical errors made by
   an interviewee
  B. express himself in such a way as to be clearly
   understood
  C. restrict the interviewee to the subject of the
   interview
  D. make notes in a way that will not disturb the interviewee

22. Suppose that you are interviewing an eleven year old boy. 22.____
  The CHIEF point among the following for you to keep in
  mind is that a child, as compared with an adult, is
  generally
  A. more likely to attempt to conceal information
  B. a person of lower intelligence
  C. more garrulous
  D. more receptive to suggestive questions

23. In interviewing a person, "suggestive questions" should 23.____
  be avoided because, among the following,
  A. the answers to leading questions are not admissible
   in evidence
  B. an investigator must be fair and impartial
  C. the interrogation of a witness must be formulated
   according to his mentality
  D. they are less apt to lead to the truth

24. Among the following, it is generally desirable to inter- 24.____
  view a person outside his home or office because
  A. the presence of relatives and friends may prevent
   him from speaking freely
  B. a person's surroundings tend to color his testimony
  C. the person will find less distraction outside his
   home or office
  D. a person tends to dominate the interview when in
   familiar surroundings

25. For the interviewing process to be MOST successful, the   25.____
    interviewer should generally
    A. remind the person being interviewed that false
       statements will constitute perjury and will be
       prosecuted as such
    B. devise a single and unvarying pattern for all inter-
       viewing situations
    C. let the individual being interviewed control the
       content of the interview but not its length
    D. vary his interviewing approach as the situation
       requires it

____

KEY (CORRECT ANSWERS)

1. A		11. C	
2. C		12. D	
3. B		13. B	
4. D		14. C	
5. B		15. D	
6. A		16. B	
7. B		17. B	
8. C		18. B	
9. A		19. D	
10. A		20. C	

21. A
22. D
23. D
24. A
25. D

____

EXAMINATION SECTION

TEST 1

DIRECTIONS: Each question or incomplete statement is followed by several suggested answers or completions. Select the one that BEST answers the question or completes the statement. *PRINT THE LETTER OF THE CORRECT ANSWER IN THE SPACE AT THE RIGHT.*

Questions 1-20.

DIRECTIONS: Questions 1 through 20 are based on the accompanying reading comprehension section which quotes a portion of the Correction Law, starting on Page 6.

1. Provisions of *Section 212* apply to
   A. parole and conditional release for all prisoners
   B. conditional release for persons sentenced to reformatories only
   C. parole or conditional release of persons serving indeterminate or reformatory sentences
   D. probation or conditional release for persons incarcerated with fixed minimum sentences

1.____

2. Which one of the following does NOT apply to both reformatory and indefinite sentences?
   A. The parole board's determinations may affect the minimum term of confinement.
   B. The prisoner is entitled to a personal interview and a notice in writing concerning determinations made in respect to his period of confinement.
   C. The board must determine within six months after confinement the minimum date for parole consideration.
   D. If the board does not grant parole at the expiration of the minimum period of confinement, review of parole determinations must be made periodically.

2.____

3. The parole board determines minimum prison sentences
   A. whenever there is an indeterminate sentence
   B. when an indeterminate sentence was imposed and the court did not fix the minimum term
   C. when, in the interests of society, a minimum term should be established
   D. when no minimum term is established for the offense in the penal code

3.____

4. In setting a minimum term, the inmate must be afforded
   A. counsel if he requests it
   B. a quasi-judicial hearing before the entire board
   C. an interview
   D. an opportunity to review the files being considered in arriving at the determination

4.____

5. All determinations by individual members of the parole
   board relating to minimum sentences
   A. must be concurred in by all the members of the board
   B. are subject to court review as provided to ascertain
      whether they are arbitrary, unreasonable, or capricious
   C. must bear the recommendation of the head of the board
      of the institution before the determination is deemed
      to be final
   D. are deemed tentative if the minimum term is more than
      one-third of the maximum sentence or more than three
      years from the date sentence commenced, whichever is
      less

6. Which one of the following is NOT a function of the
   parole board? To
   A. pass upon applications for conditional releases
   B. determine when persons serving indeterminate or
      reformatory sentences shall be eligible for parole
   C. determine when persons serving an indeterminate
      sentence with court-fixed minimum terms are eligible
      for parole
   D. review the minimum sentences prescribed by the courts
      periodically to determine whether there should be a
      reduction in such minimum term, provided that the
      minimum period shall in no case be less than one year

7. The principal purpose of *Section 212 (3)* and *(4)* is
   A. to establish a time schedule for parole considerations
   B. to establish procedures for reconsideration of
      parole determinations
   C. to establish time schedules for minimum periods of
      imprisonment
   D. all of the above

8. For persons who have received a reformatory sentence,
   A. the parole board must determine the earliest date
      prisoner is to be considered for parole
   B. the date established for determination of eligibility
      for parole is always subject to review
   C. all procedures for reformatory sentences subject to
      parole are identical with those for prisoners serving
      indeterminate sentences
   D. the principal difference between parole proceedings
      for reformatory prisoners and those incarcerated in
      prisons is that there must be court notification of
      the actions taken in respect to reformatory inmates

9. Conditional release as defined
   A. is the same as parole in respect to the rules governing
      eligibility
   B. differs from parole in that parolees' time under parole
      may be considered for credit against the term of the
      sentence if there is a revocation
   C. is the same as parole in respect to earned good behavior
      time
   D. differs from parole in that persons so released continue
      in legal custody until the expiration of their maximum
      term

10. Which one of the following is NOT accurate in respect   10.___
to conditional releases?
    A. The parole board sets the conditions of the release.
    B. With one major exception, the conditions for condi-
       tional release and parole are required to be sub-
       stantially the same.
    C. A released inmate is still under the custody of the
       State Department of Correction.
    D. After a specified minimum period, inmates must auto-
       matically be considered for conditional release.

11. The procedure governing revocation of parole or conditional 11.___
release as provided for in this statute requires
    A. a quasi-judicial hearing
    B. a finding of reasonable cause to revoke
    C. that the entire board hear the charges
    D. that the violator be given an opportunity to present
       witnesses in his defense

12. At a hearing to revoke conditional release or parole, the   12.___
person charged with violations
    A. may not have counsel
    B. must appear personally
    C. may require that the hearing be held in a place close
       to his official residence
    D. may not cross-examine the complaining witness

13. In respect to an absolute discharge, which one of the   13.___
following statements is NOT true?
    A. Such a discharge may be granted at the absolute
       discretion of the parole board.
    B. It terminates the sentence.
    C. It may be granted when the board feels it to be in
       the interest of society.
    D. It may be granted to persons serving reformatory
       sentences as provided for in the penal law.

14. Which one of the following statements is NOT true in   14.___
respect to sentences imposed prior to September, 1967?
    A. Except for persons convicted of murder one or two,
       kidnapping, felony drug violations for the third time
       or any other fourth felony offender, all prisoners
       are eligible for parole after a minimum period of
       imprisonment of eight years and four months or sooner.
    B. Eligibility for parole under minimum periods established
       is computed from date of incarceration after sentencing.
    C. Computations for concurrent and consecutive sentences
       differ.
    D. No credit is allowed for good conduct except as
       provided by the laws of 1970 or other provisions of law.

15. For prisoners sentenced prior to September, 1967, in   15.___
respect to concurrent sentences, in computing minimum time
served to ascertain eligibility for parole, the
    A. minimum time required is the sum of the minimum time
       for each sentence

B. minimum sentence requirements are met by service of the period that has the longest unexpired time to run

C. time served on any sentence is to be credited against the minimum period of all the sentences

D. minimum sentence may be ascertained by a computation of the total time encompassed in the concurrent sentences and by determining the minimum period for a term of that duration

16. In respect to parole eligibility consideration for persons sentenced prior to September, 1967, 16.__

A. there is an absolute right to be considered for parole

B. there is an absolute right to parole

C. eligibility for parole is ascertainable only by reference to the court's sentencing

D. eligibility for parole is ascertainable only by reference to the penal code

17. Which one of the following statements reflects the thrust of *Section 212-a*? 17.__

A. There is an absolute minimum time that must be served by all prisoners sentenced under the prior penal statute.

B. Depending upon the category of crime committed, there is a minimum period that a prisoner serves before he must be considered for parole.

C. Prisoners are entitled to parole within six months after they are eligible.

D. The section establishes guidelines for determining eligibility for parole, but the ultimate determinations concerning when a prisoner shall be considered eligible for parole remain with the parole board.

18. Which one of the following statements BEST reflects the guidelines established by this statute as the factors to be considered in granting parole or conditional release? 18.__

A. Good conduct in jail is indicative of conduct to be expected from a parolee and is, therefore, an important factor to be considered in determinations governing parole or conditional release.

B. There are no standards that can be established because each case is different; therefore, the determination to parole must be based upon the discretion of the board.

C. The standards that guide the board in determining whether to parole or conditionally release a prisoner are that he is not likely to be guilty of criminal behavior while at large and that he will not otherwise so conduct himself that he might endanger others.

D. Since the primary consideration in parole determinations is whether the parolee can return to society without breaking the law again, the prisoner's good conduct while in jail or efficient performance of duties assigned to him are irrelevant in making parole or conditional release determinations.

19. In making its determinations concerning the release of   19.___
    prisoners, the board
    A. must be satisfied that the prisoner will be suitably
       employed upon his release at a wage that will sustain
       him
    B. relies wholly upon reports of the prison officials
       and physical and psychiatric reports
    C. is bound by the decision of the majority of the
       members sitting on the case
    D. is bound by the *substantial evidence rule* in arriving
       at its determination after it examines the record
       as a whole

20. In establishing conditions for parole, the board   20.___
    A. must provide that the parolee remain within the state
       unless he is given prior approval for travel by the
       parole officer
    B. may not provide that parole is conditioned upon the
       parolee's making restitution of monies or goods
       stolen
    C. may be so general that the parolee is subject to the
       dictates of standards of conduct established not by
       the board but solely by the parole officer
    D. may incorporate both specific rules in regard to the
       particular parolee as well as rules of general
       applicability respecting parolees

CORRECTION LAW

§ 212. Parole and conditional release under indeterminate and reformatory sentences.

1. The provisions of this section shall govern, to the exclusion of, other provisions of this article, the duties and powers of the board of parole and the procedures with respect to parole and conditional release and the revocation thereof where an indeterminate or reformatory sentence has been imposed pursuant to the provisions of the penal law as enacted by chapter ten hundred thirty of the laws of nineteen hundred sixty-five, as amended. Matters not expressly covered herein or covered in such penal law shall be governed by such other provisions of law as may be applicable.

2. In any case where a person is received in an institution under the jurisdiction of the state department of correction with an indeterminate sentence, and the court has not fixed the minimum period of imprisonment, the board shall cause to be brought before one or more members not sooner than nine months or later than one year from the date the term of such sentence commenced all information with regard to such person referred to in section two hundred eleven and such of the information specified in subdivision four of section two hundred fourteen of this chapter as may have been compiled. The member or members receiving such information shall study same and shall personally interview the sentenced person. Upon conclusion of the interview, such member or members shall make a determination as to the minimum period of imprisonment to be served prior to parole consideration. Such determination shall have the same force and effect as a minimum period fixed by a court, except that the board may at any time make subsequent determinations reducing such minimum period provided that the period shall in no case be reduced to less than one year. Notification of the determination and of any subsequent determination shall be furnished in writing to the sentenced person and to the person in charge of the institution as soon as practicable.
In any case where the minimum period of imprisonment is fixed pursuant to this subdivision, at more than one-third of the maximum term, or at more than three years from the date the sentence commenced whichever is less, such determination shall be deemed tentative and shall be reviewed by the entire board as soon as practicable. Upon any such review, it shall not be necessary for the board members to personally interview the sentenced person, and the decision of a majority of the board shall constitute the determination.

3. At least one month prior to the expiration of the minimum period or periods of imprisonment fixed by the court, or fixed as provided in subdivision two of this section, the board shall determine whether a person serving an indeterminate sentence of imprisonment should be paroled at the expiration of the minimum period or periods. Such determination shall be made in accordance with sections two hundred thirteen and two hundred fourteen of this chapter insofar as consistent with this section. If the board does not grant parole at such time, it shall specify a date not more than twenty-four months from the date of such determination for reconsideration, and the procedures to be followed upon reconsideration shall be the same.

4.   In any case where a person is received in an institution under the jurisdiction of the state department of correction with a reformatory sentence, the board shall fix a minimum date for parole consideration within six months from the date the period of such sentence commenced and shall make a determination as to whether parole shall be granted not later than the expiration of such date.   The procedures specified in subdivisions two and three of this section shall apply insofar as consistent, except that the initial decision shall be reviewed by the board if the minimum date is fixed at more than eighteen months from the date the term commenced, and reconsiderations of parole determinations shall be at eighteen month intervals.

5.   All requests for conditional release under paragraph (b) of subdivision one of section 70.40 of the penal law shall be made in writing to the board of parole on forms prescribed by the board and furnished by the division of parole.   Within one month from the date any such application is received by the board, if it appears that the applicant is eligible for conditional release, or will be eligible for conditional release during such month, the conditions of release shall be fixed in accordance with rules and regulations prescribed by the board.   Such conditions shall be substantially the same as the conditions imposed upon parolees, except that time spent under conditional release shall not be credited against the term of the sentence.   No person shall be conditionally released unless he has agreed, in writing, to the conditions of release, and any such agreement shall contain the following clause printed immediately above the signature line: I understand and agree that if I am returned to an institution under the jurisdiction of the state department of correction for violation of any of the above conditions, the time spent under conditional release will not be credited against the term of my sentence and that the good behavior time earned by me prior to the date of my conditional release cannot be used as a basis for requesting any subsequent release.   I further understand that if I am so returned, I may, however, subsequently receive time allowances against the remaining portion of my maximum or aggregate maximum term not to exceed in the aggregate one-third of such portion provided such remaining portion of my maximum or aggregate maximum term is more than one year and that I shall not again earn any good behavior time against the remaining portion of my sentence if such remaining portion of my sentence is one year or less.

6.   Persons paroled and conditionally released from institutions under the jurisdiction of the state department of correction shall, while on parole or conditional release, be in the legal custody of the board of parole until expiration of the maximum term or period of the sentence, or expiration of the period of supervision, or return to such an institution, as the case may be.

7.   Whenever there is reasonable cause to believe that a person who is on parole or conditional release has violated the conditions thereof, the board of parole, as soon as practicable, shall declare such person to be delinquent.   Thereafter, the board shall at the first available opportunity permit the alleged violator to appear personally, but not through counsel or others, before a panel of three members and explain the alleged violation.   Such appearance shall be either at an institution under the jurisdiction of the state department of correction or at such other place as may be designated pursuant

to rules and regulations of the board. The board shall within a reasonable time make a determination on any such declaration of delinquency either by dismissing the declaration or revoking the parole or conditional release. If the board dismisses the declaration, the interruptions specified in subdivision three of section 70.40 of the penal law shall not apply, but the time spent in custody in any state or local correctional institution by a person who is on conditional release shall be credited against the term of his sentence in accordance with the rules specified in paragraph (c) of that subdivision.

Revocation of parole or of conditional release shall not prevent re-parole, or re-release provided such re-parole, or re-release is not inconsistent with any other provisions of law.

8. If the board of parole is satisfied that an absolute discharge from parole or from conditional release is in the best interest of society, the board may grant such a discharge prior to expiration of the full maximum term to any indeterminate sentence parolee who has been on unrevoked parole for at least five consecutive years or to any person who has been on unrevoked conditional release for at least two consecutive years. Discharge of persons under a reformatory sentence may be granted at any time, as provided in the penal law.

A discharge granted under this section shall constitute a termination of the sentence with respect to which it was granted.

9. The provisions of sections sixty-six, two hundred fifteen, two hundred sixteen, two hundred seventeen, two hundred twenty-one, two hundred twenty-two, two hundred twenty-four, two hundred twenty-four-a, two hundred twenty-five, and two hundred eighty-three of this chapter shall apply to parole and conditional release insofar as consistent with this section.

10. The board of parole shall promulgate rules and regulations for the procedures to be followed in carrying out its duties and the duties of the division of parole under this section. Any action taken by the board pursuant to this article shall be deemed a judicial function and shall not be reviewable if done in accordance with law.

11. In any case where a person is entitled to jail time credit under the provisions of paragraph (c) of subdivision three of section 70.40 of the penal law, it shall be the duty of the board of parole, or of such officer as may be designated by the board, to certify to the commissioner of correction the amount of such credit. Formerly § 805, amended L.1969, c. 270, § 3; renumbered 212 and amended L.1970, c. 476, § 43, eff. on 60th day after May 8, 1970.

§ 212-a. Parole eligibility of certain inmates sentenced for crimes committed prior to September first, nineteen hundred sixty-seven.

1. The provisions of this subdivision shall apply in any case where a person is under one or more of the following sentences imposed pursuant to the penal law in effect prior to September first, nineteen hundred sixty-seven:

(a) Life imprisonment for the crime of murder in the first degree pursuant to section ten hundred forty-five or section ten hundred forty-five-a of such law;

(b) Life imprisonment for the crime of kidnapping pursuant to section twelve hundred fifty of such law; or

(c) Death commuted to life imprisonment for the crime of murder in the first degree or for the crime of kidnapping pursuant to one of the above sections.

Any such person who is not otherwise or who will not sooner become eligible for release on parole under such sentence shall be or become eligible for release on parole after service of a minimum period of imprisonment of twenty years.

2.   The provisions of this subdivision shall apply in any case where a person is under one or more of the following sentences imposed pursuant to the penal law in effect prior to September first, nineteen hundred sixty-seven:

(a) A minimum term of twenty years or more and a maximum of natural life for the crime of murder in the second degree pursuant to section ten hundred forty-eight of such law;

(b) A minimum term of twenty years or more and a maximim of natural life for the crime of kidnapping imposed pursuant to section twelve hundred fifty of such law;

(c) A minimum term of fifteen years or more and a maximum of natural life for a third conviction of a felony under laws relating to narcotic drugs pursuant to section nineteen hundred forty-one of such law; or

(d) A minimum term of fifteen years or more and a maximum of natural life for a fourth conviction of a felony pursuant to section nineteen hundred forty-two of such law.

Any such person who is not otherwise or who will not sooner become eligible for release on parole under such sentence shall be or become eligible for release on parole after service of a minimum period of imprisonment of fifteen years.

3.   The provisions of this subdivision shall apply in any case where a person is under a sentence imposed pursuant to the penal law in effect prior to September first, nineteen hundred sixty-seven, other than a sentence specified in subdivisions one and two of this section. Any person who is not otherwise or who will not sooner become eligible for release on parole shall be or become eligible for release on parole under such sentence after service of a minimum period of imprisonment of eight years and four months.

4.   In calculating time required to be served prior to eligibility for parole under the minimum periods of imprisonment established by this section, the following rules shall apply:

(a) Service of such time shall be deemed to have commenced on the day the inmate was received in an institution under the jurisdiction of the department pursuant to the sentence;

(b) Where an inmate is under more than one sentence, (i) if the sentences run concurrently, the time served under imprisonment on any of the sentences shall be credited against the minimum periods of all the concurrent sentences, and (ii) if the sentences run consecutively, the minimum periods of imprisonment shall merge in and be satisfied by service of the period that has the longest unexpired time to run;

(c) No credit shall be allowed for *good conduct and efficient and willing performance of duties*, under former section two hundred thirty of this chapter, repealed by chapter four hundred seventy-six of the laws of nineteen hundred seventy and continued in effect as to certain inmates, or under any other provision of law;

(d) Calculations with respect to *jail time*, *time served under vacated sentence*, and interruption for *escape* shall be in accordance with the provisions of subdivisions three, five, and six of section 70.30 of the penal law as enacted by chapter ten hundred thirty of the laws of nineteen hundred sixty-five, as amended.

5. The provisions of this section shall not be construed as diminishing the discretionary authority of the board of parole to determine whether or not an inmate is to be paroled. The board of parole shall establish special rules for the appearance before the board of those inmates who are or become eligible for parole by virtue of this section on the effective date of the section or within six months after such date, and no such inmate shall have the right to require the board to make a determination prior to the expiration of six months from the date he becomes eligible under this section.

§ 213. Reasons for release

Discretionary release on parole shall not be granted merely as a reward for good conduct or efficient performance of duties assigned in prison, but only if the board of parole is of opinion that there is reasonable probability that, if such prisoner is released, he will live and remain at liberty without violating the law, and that his release is not incompatible with the welfare of society. If the board of parole shall so determine, such prisoner shall be allowed to go upon parole outside of prison walls and enclosure upon such terms and conditions as the board shall prescribe and shall remain while thus on parole in the legal custody of the board of parole until the expiration of the maximum term or period of the sentence or return to an institution under the jurisdiction of the commissioner of correction.

§ 214. Method of release
* * * * *
4. In addition and with respect to all prisoners, the board of parole shall have before it a report from a warden of each prison in which such prisoner has been confined as to the prisoner's conduct in prison, with a detailed statement as to all infractions of prison rules and discipline, all punishments meted out to such prisoner and the circumstances connected therewith, as well as a report from each such warden as to the extent to which such prisoner has responded to the efforts made in prison to improve his mental and moral condition, with a statement as to the prisoner's then attitude towards society, towards the judge who sentenced him, towards the district attorney who prosecuted him, towards the policeman who arrested him, and how the prisoner then regards the crime for which he is in prison and his previous criminal career. In addition, the board shall have before it a report from the superintendent of prison industries giving the prisoner's industrial record while in prison, the average number of hours per day that he has been employed in industry, the nature of

his occupations while in prison and a recommendation as to the kind
of work he is best fitted to perform and at which he is most likely
to succeed when he leaves prison. Such board shall also have before
it the report of such physical, mental, and psychiatric examinations
as have been made of such prisoner which so far as practicable shall
have been made within two months of the time of his eligibility for
parole. The board of parole, before releasing any prisoner on parole,
shall have the prisoner appear before such board and shall personally
examine him and check up so far as possible the reports made by prison
wardens and others mentioned in this section. Such board shall reach
its own conclusions as to the desirability of releasing such prisoner
on parole. No prisoner shall be released on parole unless the board
is satisfied that he will be suitably employed in self-sustaining
employment is so released.

4. Appearance before the board pursuant to subdivision four of
this section shall mean a personal interview by at least three members
of the board at the institution in which the inmate is confined or at
such other place within the state as may be agreed upon between the
chairman of the board and the commissioner of correctional services.
Release on parole shall be determined by unanimous vote of the board
members who personally interviewed the inmate or by the vote of a
majority of the entire board of parole pursuant to rules of the board.

§ 215.   Conditions of parole

The board of parole in releasing an inmate on parole shall
specify in writing the conditions of his parole, and a copy of such
conditions shall be given to the parolee. A violation of such conditions may render the parolee liable to arrest and re-imprisonment.
The board shall adopt general rules with regard to conditions of
parole and their violation and three members of the board may make
special rules to govern particular cases. Such rules, both general
and special, may include, among other things, a requirement that the
parolee shall not leave the state without the consent of the board,
that he shall, if eligible, reside in a suitable hostel or foster
home, or that he shall, if eligible, reside in any suitable correctional facility, that he shall contribute to his own support in such
hostel, foster home, or correctional facility, that he shall contribute
to the support of his dependents, that he shall make restitution for
his crime, that he shall, if there is a record, report or other
evidence satisfactory to the board that he is addicted to the use of
narcotic drugs, take clinic or similar treatment for narcotic addiction at a hospital or other facility where such treatment is available,
that he shall abandon evil associates and ways, that he shall carry
out the instructions of his parole officer and, in general, so comport
himself as such officers shall determine.

KEY (CORRECT ANSWERS)

1. C		11. B
2. C		12. B
3. B		13. A
4. C		14. D
5. D		15. C
6. D		16. A
7. A		17. B
8. A		18. C
9. B		19. A
10. D		20. D

PREPARING WRITTEN MATERIAL
EXAMINATION SECTION
TEST 1

DIRECTIONS: Each question or incomplete statement is followed by several suggested answers or completions. Select the one that BEST answers the question or completes the statement. *PRINT THE LETTER OF THE CORRECT ANSWER IN THE SPACE AT THE RIGHT.*

1. The one of the following sentences which is LEAST acceptable from the viewpoint of correct usage is: 1.___
    A. The police thought the fugitive to be him.
    B. The criminals set a trap for whoever would fall into it.
    C. It is ten years ago since the fugitive fled from the city.
    D. The lecturer argued that criminals are usually cowards.
    E. The police removed four bucketfuls of earth from the scene of the crime.

2. The one of the following sentences which is LEAST acceptable from the viewpoint of correct usage is: 2.___
    A. The patrolman scrutinized the report with great care.
    B. Approaching the victim of the assault, two bruises were noticed by the patrolman.
    C. As soon as I had broken down the door, I stepped into the room.
    D. I observed the accused loitering near the building, which was closed at the time.
    E. The storekeeper complained that his neighbor was guilty of violating a local ordinance.

3. The one of the following sentences which is LEAST acceptable from the viewpoint of correct usage is: 3.___
    A. I realized immediately that he intended to assault the woman, so I disarmed him.
    B. It was apparent that Mr. Smith's explanation contained many inconsistencies.
    C. Despite the slippery condition of the street, he managed to stop the vehicle before injuring the child.
    D. Not a single one of them wish, despite the damage to property, to make a formal complaint.
    E. The body was found lying on the floor.

4. The one of the following sentences which contains NO error in usage is: 4.___
    A. After the robbers left, the proprietor stood tied in his chair for about two hours before help arrived.
    B. In the cellar I found the watchmans' hat and coat.
    C. The persons living in adjacent apartments stated that they had heard no unusual noises.
    D. Neither a knife or any firearms were found in the room.
    E. Walking down the street, the shouting of the crowd indicated that something was wrong.

5. The one of the following sentences which contains NO   5.___
   error in usage is:
   A. The policeman lay a firm hand on the suspect's
      shoulder.
   B. It is true that neither strength nor agility are the
      most important requirement for a good patrolman.
   C. Good citizens constantly strive to do more than
      merely comply the restraints imposed by society.
   D. No decision was made as to whom the prize should
      be awarded.
   E. Twenty years is considered a severe sentence for a
      felony.

6. Which of the following is NOT expressed in standard   6.___
   English usage?
   A. The victim reached a pay-phone booth and manages to
      call police headquarters.
   B. By the time the call was received, the assailant had
      left the scene.
   C. The victim has been a respected member of the commu-
      nity for the past eleven years.
   D. Although the lighting was bad and the shadows were
      deep, the storekeeper caught sight of the attacker.
   E. Additional street lights have since been installed,
      and the patrols have been strengthened.

7. Which of the following is NOT expressed in standard   7.___
   English usage?
   A. The judge upheld the attorney's right to question
      the witness about the missing glove.
   B. To be absolutely fair to all parties is the jury's
      chief responsibility.
   C. Having finished the report, a loud noise in the
      next room startled the sergeant.
   D. The witness obviously enjoyed having played a part
      in the proceedings.
   E. The sergeant planned to assign the case to whoever
      arrived first.

8. In which of the following is a word misused?   8.___
   A. As a matter of principle, the captain insisted that
      the suspect's partner be brought for questioning.
   B. The principle suspect had been detained at the
      station house for most of the day.
   C. The principal in the crime had no previous criminal
      record, but his closest associate had been convicted
      of felonies on two occasions.
   D. The interest payments had been made promptly, but
      the firm had been drawing upon the principal for
      these payments.
   E. The accused insisted that his high school principal
      would furnish him a character reference.

9. Which of the following statements is ambiguous?   9.___
    A. Mr. Sullivan explained why Mr. Johnson had been
       dismissed from his job.
    B. The storekeeper told the patrolman he had made a
       mistake.
    C. After waiting three hours, the patients in the
       doctor's office were sent home.
    D. The janitor's duties were to maintain the building
       in good shape and to answer tenants' complaints.
    E. The speed limit should, in my opinion, be raised to
       sixty miles an hour on that stretch of road.

10. In which of the following is the punctuation or capitali-   10.___
    zation faulty?
    A. The accident occurred at an intersection in the Kew
       Gardens section of Queens, near the bus stop.
    B. The sedan, not the convertible, was struck in the side.
    C. Before any of the patrolmen had left the police car
       received an important message from headquarters.
    D. The dog that had been stolen was returned to his
       master, John Dempsey, who lived in East Village.
    E. The letter had been sent to 12 Hillside Terrace,
       Rutland, Vermont 05701.

Questions 11-25.

DIRECTIONS: Questions 11 through 25 are to be answered in accordance
               with correct English usage; that is, standard English
               rather than nonstandard or substandard. Nonstandard
               and substandard English includes words or expressions
               usually classified as slang, dialect, illiterate, etc.,
               which are not generally accepted as correct in current
               written communication. Standard English also requires
               clarity, proper punctuation and capitalization and
               appropriate use of words. Write the letter of the
               sentence NOT expressed in standard English usage in the
               space at the right.

11. A. There were three witnesses to the accident.   11.___
    B. At least three witnesses were found to testify for the
       plaintiff.
    C. Three of the witnesses who took the stand was uncertain
       about the defendant's competence to drive.
    D. Only three witnesses came forward to testify for the
       plaintiff.
    E. The three witnesses to the accident were pedestrians.

12. A. The driver had obviously drunk too many martinis   12.___
       before leaving for home.
    B. The boy who drowned had swum in these same waters many
       times before.
    C. The petty thief had stolen a bicycle from a private
       driveway before he was apprehended.

    D. The detectives had brung in the heroin shipment they intercepted.
    E. The passengers had never ridden in a converted bus before.

13.   A. Between you and me, the new platoon plan sounds like a good idea.   13.___
      B. Money from an aunt's estate was left to his wife and he.
      C. He and I were assigned to the same patrol for the first time in two months.
      D. Either you or he should check the front door of that store.
      E. The captain himself was not sure of the witness's reliability.

14.   A. The alarm had scarcely begun to ring when the explosion occurred.   14.___
      B. Before the firemen arrived on the scene, the second story had been destroyed.
      C. Because of the dense smoke and heat, the firemen could hardly approach the now-blazing structure.
      D. According to the patrolman's report, there wasn't nobody in the store when the explosion occurred.
      E. The sergeant's suggestion was not at all unsound, but no one agreed with him.

15.   A. The driver and the passenger they were both found to be intoxicated.   15.___
      B. The driver and the passenger talked slowly and not too clearly.
      C. Neither the driver nor his passengers were able to give a coherent account of the accident.
      D. In a corner of the room sat the passenger, quietly dozing.
      E. The driver finally told a strange and unbelievable story, which the passenger contradicted.

16.   A. Under the circumstances I decided not to continue my examination of the premises.   16.___
      B. There are many difficulties now not comparable with those existing in 1960.
      C. Friends of the accused were heard to announce that the witness had better been away on the day of the trial.
      D. The two criminals escaped in the confusion that followed the explosion.
      E. The aged man was struck by the considerateness of the patrolman's offer.

17.   A. An assemblage of miscellaneous weapons lay on the table.   17.___
      B. Ample opportunities were given to the defendant to obtain counsel.

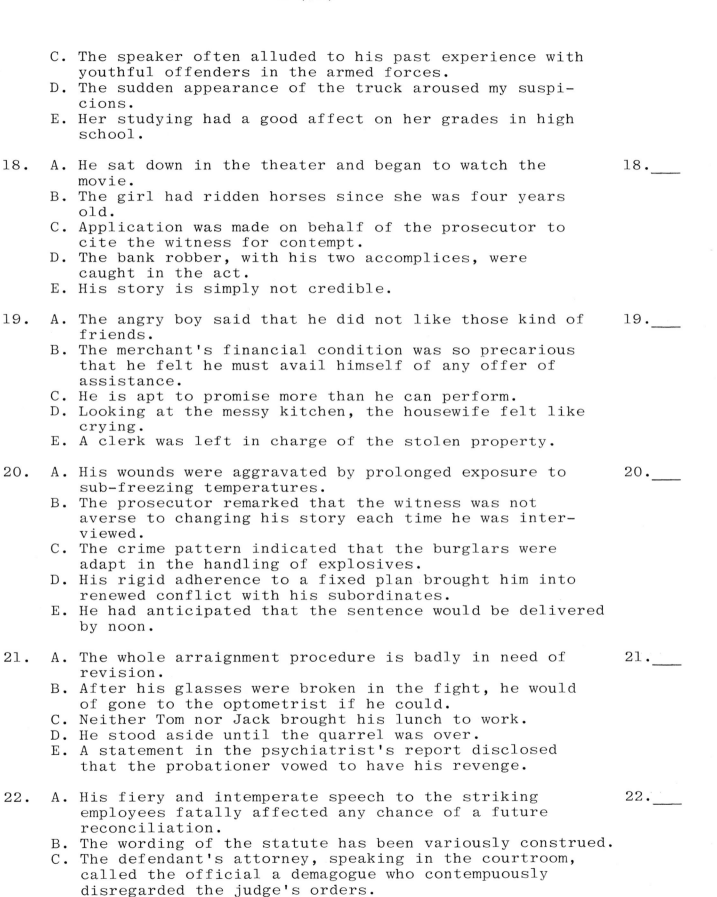

C. The speaker often alluded to his past experience with youthful offenders in the armed forces.
D. The sudden appearance of the truck aroused my suspicions.
E. Her studying had a good affect on her grades in high school.

18. A. He sat down in the theater and began to watch the movie.
    B. The girl had ridden horses since she was four years old.
    C. Application was made on behalf of the prosecutor to cite the witness for contempt.
    D. The bank robber, with his two accomplices, were caught in the act.
    E. His story is simply not credible.

18.___

19. A. The angry boy said that he did not like those kind of friends.
    B. The merchant's financial condition was so precarious that he felt he must avail himself of any offer of assistance.
    C. He is apt to promise more than he can perform.
    D. Looking at the messy kitchen, the housewife felt like crying.
    E. A clerk was left in charge of the stolen property.

19.___

20. A. His wounds were aggravated by prolonged exposure to sub-freezing temperatures.
    B. The prosecutor remarked that the witness was not averse to changing his story each time he was interviewed.
    C. The crime pattern indicated that the burglars were adapt in the handling of explosives.
    D. His rigid adherence to a fixed plan brought him into renewed conflict with his subordinates.
    E. He had anticipated that the sentence would be delivered by noon.

20.___

21. A. The whole arraignment procedure is badly in need of revision.
    B. After his glasses were broken in the fight, he would of gone to the optometrist if he could.
    C. Neither Tom nor Jack brought his lunch to work.
    D. He stood aside until the quarrel was over.
    E. A statement in the psychiatrist's report disclosed that the probationer vowed to have his revenge.

21.___

22. A. His fiery and intemperate speech to the striking employees fatally affected any chance of a future reconciliation.
    B. The wording of the statute has been variously construed.
    C. The defendant's attorney, speaking in the courtroom, called the official a demagogue who contempuously disregarded the judge's orders.

22.___

   D. The baseball game is likely to be the most exciting
      one this year.
   E. The mother divided the cookies among her two children.

23.   A. There was only a bed and a dresser in the dingy room.   23.___
      B. John is one of the few students that have protested
         the new rule.
      C. It cannot be argued that the child's testimony is
         negligible; it is, on the contrary, of the greatest
         importance.
      D. The basic criterion for clearance was so general that
         officials resolved any doubts in favor of dismissal.
      E. Having just returned from a long vacation, the
         officer found the city unbearably hot.

24.   A. The librarian ought to give more help to small   24.___
         children.
      B. The small boy was criticized by the teacher because
         he often wrote careless.
      C. It was generally doubted whether the women would permit
         the use of her apartment for intelligence operations.
      D. The probationer acts differently every time the officer
         visits him.
      E. Each of the newly appointed officers has 12 years of
         service.

25.   A. The North is the most industrialized region in the   25.___
         country.
      B. L. Patrick Gray 3d, the bureau's acting director,
         stated that, while "rehabilitation is fine" for some
         convicted criminals, "it is a useless gesture for those
         who resist every such effort."
      C. Careless driving, faulty mechanism, narrow or badly
         kept roads all play their part in causing accidents.
      D. The childrens' books were left in the bus.
      E. It was a matter of internal security; consequently,
         he felt no inclination to rescind his previous order.

KEY (CORRECT ANSWERS)

1. C	6. A	11. C	16. C	21. B
2. B	7. C	12. D	17. E	22. E
3. D	8. B	13. B	18. D	23. B
4. C	9. B	14. D	19. A	24. B
5. E	10. C	15. A	20. C	25. D

TEST 2

DIRECTIONS: Each question or incomplete statement is followed by several suggested answers or completions. Select the one that BEST answers the question or completes the statement. *PRINT THE LETTER OF THE CORRECT ANSWER IN THE SPACE AT THE RIGHT.*

Questions 1-6.

DIRECTIONS: Each of Questions 1 through 6 consists of a statement which contains a word (one of those underlined) that is either incorrectly used because it is not in keeping with the meaning the quotation is evidently intended to convey, or is misspelled. There is only one INCORRECT word in each quotation. Of the four underlined words, determine if the first one should be replaced by the word lettered A, the second replaced by the word lettered B, the third replaced by the word lettered C, or the fourth replaced by the word lettered D. *PRINT THE LETTER OF THE REPLACEMENT WORD YOU HAVE SELECTED IN THE SPACE AT THE RIGHT.*

1. Whether one depends on <u>fluorescent</u> or artificial light or both, adequate <u>standards</u> should be <u>maintained</u> by means of <u>systematic</u> tests.   1.___
   A. natural   B. safeguards
   C. established   D. routine

2. A policeman has to be <u>prepared</u> to assume his <u>knowledge</u> as a social <u>scientist</u> in the <u>community</u>.   2.___
   A. forced   B. role
   C. philosopher   D. street

3. It is <u>practically</u> impossible to <u>indicate</u> whether a sentence is <u>too</u> long simply by <u>measuring</u> its length.   3.___
   A. almost   B. tell   C. very   D. guessing

4. Strong <u>leaders</u> are <u>required</u> to organize a community for delinquency prevention and for <u>dissemination</u> of organized <u>crime</u> and drug addiction.   4.___
   A. tactics   B. important   C. control   D. meetings

5. The <u>demonstrators</u> who were taken to the Criminal Courts building in <u>Manhattan</u> (because it was large enough to <u>accommodate</u> them), contended that the arrests were <u>unwarrented</u>.   5.___
   A. demonstraters   B. Manhatten
   C. accomodate   D. unwarranted

6. They were <u>guaranteed</u> a calm <u>atmosphere</u>, free from   6.___
   <u>harrassment</u>, which would be <u>conducive</u> to quiet consideration of the <u>indictments</u>.
   A. guarenteed   B. atmospher
   C. harassment   D. inditements

Questions 7-11.

DIRECTIONS: Each of Questions 7 through 11 consists of a statement
              containing four words in capital letters. One of these
              words in capital letters is not in keeping with the
              meaning which the statement is evidently intended to
              carry. The four words in capital letters in each
              statement are reprinted after the statement. Print
              the capital letter preceding the one of the four words
              which does MOST to spoil the true meaning of the state-
              ment in the space at the right.

7. Retirement and pension systems are essential not only to   7.___
   provide employees with a means of support in the future,
   but also to prevent longevity and CHARITABLE considerations
   from UPSETTING the PROMOTIONAL opportunities for RETIRED
   members of the career service.
   A. charitable   B. upsetting
   C. promotional   D. retired

8. Within each major DIVISION in a properly set up public or   8.___
   private organization, provision is made so that each
   NECESSARY activity is CARED for and lines of authority
   and responsibility are clear-cut and INFINITE.
   A. division   B. necessary   C. cared   D. infinite

9. In public service, the scale of salaries paid must be   9.___
   INCIDENTAL to the services rendered, with due CONSIDERATION
   for the attraction of the desired MANPOWER and for the
   maintenance of a standard of living COMMENSURATE with
   the work to be performed.
   A. incidental   B. consideration
   C. manpower   D. commensurate

10. An understanding of the AIMS of an organization by the   10.___
    staff will AID greatly in increasing the DEMAND of the
    correspondence work of the office, and will to a large
    extent DETERMINE the nature of the correspondence.
    A. aims   B. aid   C. demand   D. determine

11. BECAUSE the Civil Service Commission strongly feels that   11.___
    the MERIT system is a key factor in the MAINTENANCE of
    democratic government, it has adopted as one of its
    major DEFENSES the progressive democratization of its
    own procedures in dealing with candidates for positions
    in the public service.
    A. Because   B. merit
    C. maintenance   D. defenses

Questions 12-14.

DIRECTIONS: Questions 12 through 14 consist of one sentence each. Each sentence contains an incorrectly used word. First, decide which is the incorrectly used word. Then, from among the options given, decide which word, when substituted for the incorrectly used word, makes the meaning of the sentence clear.

EXAMPLE:
The U.S. national income exhibits a pattern of long term deflection.
   A. reflection   B. subjection
   C. rejoicing   D. growth

The word *deflection* in the sentence does not convey the meaning the sentence evidently intended to convey. The word *growth* (Answer D), when substituted for the word *deflection*, makes the meaning of the sentence clear. Accordingly, the answer to the question is D.

12. The study commissioned by the joint committee fell   12.___
    compassionately short of the mark and would have to be
    redone.
       A. successfully   B. insignificantly
       C. experimentally   D. woefully

13. He will not idly exploit any violation of the provisions   13.___
    of the order.
       A. tolerate   B. refuse   C. construe   D. guard

14. The defendant refused to be virile and bitterly protested   14.___
    service.
       A. irked   B. feasible   C. docile   D. credible

Questions 15-25.

DIRECTIONS: Questions 15 through 25 consist of short paragraphs. Each paragraph contains one word which is INCORRECTLY used because it is NOT in keeping with the meaning of the paragraph. Find the word in each paragraph which is INCORRECTLY used and then select as the answer the suggested word which should be substituted for the incorrectly used word.

SAMPLE QUESTION:
In determining who is to do the work in your unit, you will have to decide just who does what from day to day. One of your lowest responsibilities is to assign work so that everybody gets a fair share and that everyone can do his part well.
   A. new   B. old   C. important   D. performance

EXPLANATION:
The word which is NOT in keeping with the meaning of the paragraph is *lowest*. This is the INCORRECTLY used word. The suggested word *important* would be in keeping with the meaning of the paragraph and should be substituted for *lowest*. Therefore, the CORRECT answer is choice C.

15. If really good practice in the elimination of preventable injuries is to be achieved and held in any establishment, top management must refuse full and definite responsibility and must apply a good share of its attention to the task.   15.___
    A. accept   B. avoidable C. duties   D. problem

16. Recording the human face for identification is by no means the only service performed by the camera in the field of investigation. When the trial of any issue takes place, a word picture is sought to be distorted to the court of incidents, occurrences, or events which are in dispute.   16.___
    A. appeals   B. description
    C. portrayed   D. deranged

17. In the collection of physical evidence, it cannot be emphasized too strongly that a haphazard systematic search at the scene of the crime is vital. Nothing must be overlooked. Often the only leads in a case will come from the results of this search.   17.___
    A. important   B. investigation
    C. proof   D. thorough

18. If an investigator has reason to suspect that the witness is mentally stable, or a habitual drunkard, he should leave no stone unturned in his investigation to determine if the witness was under the influence of liquor or drugs, or was mentally unbalanced either at the time of the occurrence to which he testified or at the time of the trial.   18.___
    A. accused   B. clue   C. deranged   D. question

19. The use of records is a valuable step in crime investigation and is the main reason every department should maintain accurate reports. Crimes are not committed through the use of departmental records alone but from the use of all records, of almost every type, wherever they may be found and whenever they give any incidental information regarding the criminal.   19.___
    A. accidental   B. necessary
    C. reported   D. solved

20. In the years since passage of the Harrison Narcotic Act of 1914, making the possession of opium amphetamines illegal in most circumstances, drug use has become a subject of considerable scientific interest and investigation. There is at present a voluminous literature on drug use of various kinds.
    A. ingestion   B. derivatives
    C. addiction   D. opiates
   20.___

21. Of course, the fact that criminal laws are extremely patterned in definition does not mean that the majority of persons who violate them are dealt with as criminals. Quite the contrary, for a great many forbidden acts are voluntarily engaged in within situations of privacy and go unobserved and unreported.
    A. symbolic   B. casual
    C. scientific   D. broad-gauged
   21.___

22. The most punitive way to study punishment is to focus attention on the pattern of punitive action: to study how a penalty is applied, to study what is done to or taken from an offender.
    A. characteristic   B. degrading
    C. objective   D. distinguished
   22.___

23. The most common forms of punishment in times past have been death, physical torture, mutilation, branding, public humiliation, fines, forfeits of property, banishment, transportation, and imprisonment. Although this list is by no means differentiated, practically every form of punishment has had several variations and applications.
    A. specific   B. simple
    C. exhaustive   D. characteristic
   23.___

24. There is another important line of inference between ordinary and professional criminals, and that is the source from which they are recruited. The professional criminal seems to be drawn from legitimate employment and, in many instances, from parallel vocations or pursuits.
    A. demarcation   B. justification
    C. superiority   D. reference
   24.___

25. He took the position that the success of the program was insidious on getting additional revenue.
    A. reputed   B. contingent
    C. failure   D. indeterminate
   25.___

KEY (CORRECT ANSWERS)

1. A	6. C	11. D	16. A	21. D
2. B	7. D	12. D	17. D	22. C
3. B	8. D	13. A	18. C	23. C
4. C	9. A	14. C	19. D	24. A
5. D	10. C	15. B	20. B	25. B

TEST 3

DIRECTIONS: Each question or incomplete statement is followed by
               several suggested answers or completions. Select the
               one that BEST answers the question or completes the
               statement. *PRINT THE LETTER OF THE CORRECT ANSWER IN
               THE SPACE AT THE RIGHT.*

Questions 1-5.

DIRECTIONS: Question 1 through 5 are to be answered on the basis
               of the following:

     You are a supervising officer in an investigative unit. Earlier
in the day, you directed Detectives Tom Dixon and Sal Mayo to investigate a reported assault and robbery in a liquor store within your
area of jurisdiction.

     Detective Dixon has submitted to you a preliminary investigative
report containing the following information:

  - At 1630 hours on 2/20, arrived at Joe's Liquor Store at 350
    SW Avenue with Detective Mayo to investigate A & R.
  - At store interviewed Rob Ladd, store manager, who stated
    that he and Joe Brown (store owner) had been stuck up about
    ten minutes prior to our arrival.
  - Ladd described the robbers as male whites in their late teens
    or early twenties. Further stated that one of the robbers
    displayed what appeared to be an automatic pistol as he
    entered the store, and said, *Give us the money or we'll kill
    you.* Ladd stated that Brown then reached under the counter
    where he kept a loaded .38 caliber pistol. Several shots
    followed, and Ladd threw himself to the floor.
  - The robbers fled, and Ladd didn't know if any money had been
    taken.
  - At this point, Ladd realized that Brown was unconscious on
    the floor and bleeding from a head wound.
  - Ambulance called by Ladd, and Brown was removed by same to
    General Hospital.
  - Personally interviewed John White, 382 Dartmouth Place, who
    stated he was inside store at the time of occurrence. White
    states that he hid behind a wine display upon hearing someone
    say, *Give us the money.* He then heard shots and saw two young
    men run from the store to a yellow car parked at the curb.
    White was unable to further describe auto. States the taller
    of the two men drove the car away while the other sat on
    passenger side in front.
  - Recovered three spent .38 caliber bullets from premises and
    delivered them to Crime Lab.
  - To General Hospital at 1800 hours but unable to interview
    Brown, who was under sedation and suffering from shock and a
    laceration of the head.
  - Alarm #12487 transmitted for car and occupants.
  - Case Active.

Based solely on the contents of the preliminary investigation submitted by Detective Dixon, select one sentence from the following groups of sentences which is MOST accurate and is grammatically correct.

1. A. Both robbers were armed.
   B. Each of the robbers were described as a male white.
   C. Neither robber was armed.
   D. Mr. Ladd stated that one of the robbers was armed.

1.___

2. A. Mr. Brown fired three shots from his revolver.
   B. Mr. Brown was shot in the head by one of the robbers.
   C. Mr. Brown suffered a gunshot wound of the head during the course of the robbery.
   D. Mr. Brown was taken to General Hospital by ambulance.

2.___

3. A. Shots were fired after one of the robbers said, *Give us the money or we'll kill you.*
   B. After one of the robbers demanded the money from Mr. Brown, he fired a shot.
   C. The preliminary investigation indicated that although Mr. Brown did not have a license for the gun, he was justified in using deadly physical force.
   D. Mr. Brown was interviewed at General Hospital.

3.___

4. A. Each of the witnesses were customers in the store at the time of occurrence.
   B. Neither of the witnesses interviewed was the owner of the liquor store.
   C. Neither of the witnesses interviewed were the owner of the store.
   D. Neither of the witnesses was employed by Mr. Brown.

4.___

5. A. Mr. Brown arrived at General Hospital at about 5:00 P.M.
   B. Neither of the robbers was injured during the robbery.
   C. The robbery occurred at 3:30 P.M. on February 10.
   D. One of the witnesses called the ambulance.

5.___

Questions 6-10.

DIRECTIONS: Each of Questions 6 through 10 consists of information given in outline form and four sentences labelled A, B, C, and D. For each question, choose the one sentence which CORRECTLY expresses the information given in outline form and which also displays PROPER English usage.

6. Client's Name - Joanna Jones
   Number of Children - 3
   Client's Income - None
   Client's Marital Status - Single
   A. Joanna Jones is an unmarried client with three children who have no income.
   B. Joanna Jones, who is single and has no income, a client she has three children.

6.___

    C. Joanna Jones, whose three children are clients, is single and has no income.
    D. Joanna Jones, who has three children, is an unmarried client with no income.

7.   Client's Name - Bertha Smith   7.___
Number of Children - 2
Client's Rent - $105 per month
Number of Rooms - 4
    A. Bertha Smith, a client, pays $105 per month for her four rooms with two children.
    B. Client Bertha Smith has two children and pays $105 per month for four rooms.
    C. Client Bertha Smith is paying $105 per month for two children with four rooms.
    D. For four rooms and two children client Bertha Smith pays $105 per month.

8.   Name of Employee - Cynthia Dawes   8.___
Number of Cases Assigned - 9
Date Cases were Assigned - 12/16
Number of Assigned Cases Completed - 8
    A. On December 16, employee Cynthia Dawes was assigned nine cases; she has completed eight of these cases.
    B. Cynthia Dawes, employee on December 16, assigned nine cases, completed eight.
    C. Being employed on December 16, Cynthia Dawes completed eight of nine assigned cases.
    D. Employee Cynthia Dawes, she was assigned nine cases and completed eight, on December 16.

9.   Place of Audit - Broadway Center   9.___
Names of Auditors - Paul Cahn, Raymond Perez
Date of Audit - 11/20
Number of Cases Audited - 41
    A. On November 20, at the Broadway Center 41 cases was audited by auditors Paul Cahn and Raymond Perez.
    B. Auditors Raymond Perez and Paul Cahn has audited 41 cases at the Broadway Center on November 20.
    C. At the Broadway Center, on November 20, auditors Paul Cahn and Raymond Perez audited 41 cases.
    D. Auditors Paul Cahn and Raymond Perez at the Broadway Center, on November 20, is auditing 41 cases.

10. Name of Client - Barbra Levine   10.___
Client's Monthly Income - $210
Client's Monthly Expenses - $452
    A. Barbra Levine is a client, her monthly income is $210 and her monthly expenses is $452.
    B. Barbra Levine's monthly income is $210 and she is a client, with whose monthly expenses are $452.
    C. Barbra Levine is a client whose monthly income is $210 and whose monthly expenses are $452.
    D. Barbra Levine, a client, is with a monthly income which is $210 and monthly expenses which are $452.

Questions 11-13.

DIRECTIONS: Questions 11 through 13 involve several statements of fact presented in a very simple way. These statements of fact are followed by 4 choices which attempt to incorporate all of the facts into one logical sentence which is properly constructed and grammatically correct.

11.   I. Mr. Brown was sweeping the sidewalk in front of his house.   11.___
   II. He was sweeping it because it was dirty.
  III. He swept the refuse into the street
   IV. Police Officer Green gave him a ticket.

Which one of the following BEST presents the information given above?
  A. Because his sidewalk was dirty, Mr. Brown received a ticket from Officer Green when he swept the refuse into the street.
  B. Police Officer Green gave Mr. Brown a ticket because his sidewalk was dirty and he swept the refuse into the street.
  C. Police Officer Green gave Mr. Brown a ticket for sweeping refuse into the street because his sidewalk was dirty.
  D. Mr. Brown, who was sweeping refuse from his dirty sidewalk into the street, was given a ticket by Police Officer Green.

12.   I. Sergeant Smith radioed for help.   12.___
   II. The sergeant did so because the crowd was getting larger.
  III. It was 10:00 A.M. when he made his call.
   IV. Sergeant Smith was not in uniform at the time of occurrence.

Which one of the following BEST presents the information given above?
  A. Sergeant Smith, although not on duty at the time, radioed for help at 10 o'clock because the crowd was getting uglier.
  B. Although not in uniform, Sergeant Smith called for help at 10:00 A.M. because the crowd was getting uglier.
  C. Sergeant Smith radioed for help at 10:00 A.M. because the crowd was getting larger.
  D. Although he was not in uniform, Sergeant Smith radioed for help at 10:00 A.M. because the crowd was getting larger.

13.   I. The payroll office is open on Fridays.   13.___
    II. Paychecks are distributed from 9:00 A.M. to 12 Noon.
  III. The office is open on Fridays because that's the
       only day the payroll staff is available.
   IV. It is open for the specified hours in order to
       permit employees to cash checks at the bank during
       lunch hour.

The choice below which MOST clearly and accurately
presents the above idea is:
   A. Because the payroll office is open on Fridays from
      9:00 A.M. to 12 Noon, employees can cash their checks
      when the payroll staff is available.
   B. Because the payroll staff is only available on
      Fridays until noon, employees can cash their checks
      during their lunch hour.
   C. Because the payroll staff is available only on
      Fridays, the office is open from 9:00 A.M. to 12 Noon
      to allow employees to cash their checks.
   D. Because of payroll staff availability, the payroll
      office is open on Fridays. It is open from 9:00 A.M.
      to 12 Noon so that distributed paychecks can be
      cashed at the bank while employees are on their lunch
      hour.

Questions 14-16.

DIRECTIONS: In each of Questions 14 through 16, the four sentences
                are from a paragraph in a report. They are not in the
                right order. Which of the following arrangements is
                the BEST one?

14.   I. An executive may answer a letter by writing his   14.___
       reply on the face of the letter itself instead of
       having a return letter typed.
    II. This procedure is efficient because it saves the
       executive's time, the typist's time, and saves
       office file space.
  III. Copying machines are used in small offices as well
       as large offices to save time and money in making
       brief replies to business letters.
   IV. A copy is made on a copying machine to go into the
       company files, while the original is mailed back to
       the sender.

The CORRECT answer is:
   A. I, II, IV, III   B. I, IV, II, III
   C. III, I, IV, II   D. III, IV, II, I

15.   I. Most organizations favor one of the types but always   15.___
include the others to a lesser degree.
  II. However, we can detect a definite trend toward
greater use of symbolic control.
 III. We suggest that our local police agencies are today
primarily utilizing material control.
  IV. Control can be classified into three types: physical,
material, and symbolic.

The CORRECT answer is:
A. IV, II, III, I   B. II, I, IV, III
C. III, IV, II, I   D. IV, I, III, II

16.   I. They can and do take advantage of ancient political   16.___
and geographical boundaries, which often give them
sanctuary from effective police activity.
  II. This country is essentially a country of small police
forces, each operating independently within the
limits of its jurisdiction.
 III. The boundaries that define and limit police operations do not hinder the movement of criminals, of
course.
  IV. The machinery of law enforcement in America is
fragmented, complicated, and frequently overlapping.

The CORRECT answer is:
A. III, I, II, IV   B. II, IV, I, III
C. IV, II, III, I   D. IV, III, II, I

17. Examine the following sentence, and then choose from   17.___
below the words which should be inserted in the blank
spaces to produce the best sentence.
The unit has exceeded _____ goals and the employees
are satisfied with _____ accomplishments.
A. their, it's   B. it's, it's
C. its, there   D. its, their

18. Examine the following sentence, and then choose from   18.___
below the words which should be inserted in the blank
spaces to produce the best sentence.
Research indicates that employees who _____ no opportunity
for close social relationships often find their work
unsatisfying, and this _____ of satisfaction often reflects
itself in low production.
A. have, lack   B. have, excess
C. has, lack   D. has, excess

19. Words in a sentence must be arranged properly to make   19.___
sure that the intended meaning of the sentence is clear.
The sentence below that does NOT make sense because a
clause has been separated from the word on which its
meaning depends is:
A. To be a good writer, clarity is necessary.
B. To be a good writer, you must write clearly.
C. You must write clearly to be a good writer.
D. Clarity is necessary to good writing.

Questions 20-21.

DIRECTIONS: Each of Questions 20 and 21 consists of a statement
which contains a word (one of those underlined) that
is either incorrectly used because it is not in keeping
with the meaning the quotation is evidently intended to
convey, or is misspelled. There is only one INCORRECT
word in each quotation. Of the four underlined words,
determine if the first one should be replaced by the
word lettered A, the second one replaced by the word
lettered B, the third one replaced by the word lettered
C, or the fourth one replaced by the word lettered D.
*PRINT THE LETTER OF THE REPLACEMENT WORD YOU HAVE
SELECTED IN THE SPACE AT THE RIGHT.*

20.   The alleged killer was occasionally permitted to   20.___
excercise in the corridor.
    A. alledged   B. ocasionally
    C. permited   D. exercise

21.   Defense counsel stated, in affect, that their conduct   21.___
was permissible under the First Amendment.
    A. council   B. effect
    C. there   D. permissable

Question 22.

DIRECTIONS: Question 22 consists of one sentence. This sentence
contains an incorrectly used word. First, decide which
is the incorrectly used word. Then, from among the
options given, decide which word, when substituted for
the incorrectly used word, makes the meaning of the
sentence clear.

22.   As today's violence has no single cause, so its causes   22.___
have no single scheme.
    A. deference B. cure   C. flaw   D. relevance

23.   In the sentence, *A man in a light-grey suit waited thirty-*   23.___
five minutes in the ante-room for the all-important
document, the word IMPROPERLY hyphenated is
    A. light-grey   B. thirty-five
    C. ante-room   D. all-important

24.   In the sentence, *The candidate wants to file his applica-*   24.___
tion for preference before it is too late, the word *before*
is used as a(n)
    A. preposition   B. subordinating conjunction
    C. pronoun   D. adverb

25.   In the sentence, *The perpetrators ran from the scene*, the   25.___
word *from* is a
    A. preposition   B. pronoun
    C. verb   D. conjunction

KEY (CORRECT ANSWERS)

1. D		11. D	
2. D		12. D	
3. A		13. D	
4. B		14. C	
5. D		15. D	
6. D		16. C	
7. B		17. D	
8. A		18. A	
9. C		19. A	
10. C		20. D	

21. B
22. B
23. C
24. B
25. A

———

PREPARING WRITTEN MATERIAL

PARAGRAPH REARRANGEMENT

COMMENTARY

The sentences which follow are in scrambled order. You are to rearrange them in proper order and indicate the letter choice containing the correct answer at the space at the right.

Each group of sentences in this section is actually a paragraph presented in scrambled order. Each sentence in the group has a place in that paragraph; no sentence is to be left out. You are to read each group of sentences and decide upon the best order in which to put the sentences so as to form as well-organized paragraph.

The questions in this section measure the ability to solve a problem when all the facts relevant to its solution are not given.

More specifically, certain positions of responsibility and authority require the employee to discover connections between events sometimes, apparently, unrelated. In order to do this, the employee will find it necessary to correctly infer that unspecified events have probably occurred or are likely to occur. This ability becomes especially important when action must be taken on incomplete information.

Accordingly, these questions require competitors to choose among several suggested alternatives, each of which presents a different sequential arrangement of the events. Competitors must choose the MOST logical of the suggested sequences.

In order to do so, they may be required to draw on general knowledge to infer missing concepts or events that are essential to sequencing the given events. Competitors should be careful to infer only what is essential to the sequence. The plausibility of the wrong alternatives will always require the inclusion of unlikely events or of additional chains of events which are NOT essential to sequencing the given events.

It's very important to remember that you are looking for the best of the four possible choices, and that the best choice of all may not even be one of the answers you're given to choose from.

There is no one right way to these problems. Many people have found it helpful to first write out the order of the sentences, as they would have arranged them, on their scrap paper before looking at the possible answers. If their optimum answer is there, this can save them some time. If it isn't, this method can still give insight into solving the problem. Others find it most helpful to just go through each of the possible choices, contrasting each as they go along. You should use whatever method feels comfortable, and works, for you.

While most of these types of questions are not that difficult, we've added a higher percentage of the difficult type, just to give you more practice. Usually there are only one or two questions on this section that contain such subtle distinctions that you're unable to answer confidently, and you then may find yourself stuck deciding between two possible choices, neither of which you're sure about.

———

EXAMINATION SECTION

DIRECTIONS: Each question consists of several sentences which can be arranged in a logical sequence. For each question, select the choice which places the numbered sentences in the MOST logical sequence. *PRINT THE LETTER OF THE CORRECT ANSWER IN THE SPACE AT THE RIGHT.*

1.   I. A body was found in the woods.
  II. A man proclaimed innocence.
 III. The owner of a gun was located.
  IV. A gun was traced.
   V. The owner of a gun was questioned.

1.____

The CORRECT answer is:
  A. IV, III, V, II, I
  C. I, IV, III, V, II
  E. I, II, IV, III, V
  B. II, I, IV, III, V
  D. I, III, V, II, IV

2.   I. A man was in a hunting accident.
  II. A man fell down a flight of steps.
 III. A man lost his vision in one eye.
  IV. A man broke his leg.
   V. A man had to walk with a cane.

2.____

The CORRECT answer is:
  A. II, IV, V, I, III
  C. III, I, IV, V, II
  E. I, III, II, IV, V
  B. IV, V, I, III, II
  D. I, III, V, II, IV

3.   I. A man is offered a new job.
  II. A woman is offered a new job.
 III. A man works as a waiter.
  IV. A woman works as a waitress.
   V. A woman gives notice.

3.____

The CORRECT answer is:
  A. IV, II, V, III, I
  C. II, IV, V, III, I
  E. IV, III, II, V, I
  B. IV, II, V, I, III
  D. III, I, IV, II, V

4.   I. A train left the station late.
  II. A man was late for work.
 III. A man lost his job.
  IV. Many people complained because the train was late.
   V. There was a traffic jam.

4.____

The CORRECT answer is:
  A. V, II, I, IV, III
  C. V, I, II, IV, III
  E. II, I, IV, V, III
  B. V, I, IV, II, III
  D. I, V, IV, II, III

5. I. The burden of proof as to each issue is determined before trial and remains upon the same party through-out the trial.
   II. The jury is at liberty to believe one witness' testi-mony as against a number of contradictory witnesses.
  III. In a civil case, the party bearing the burden of proof is required to prove his contention by a fair prepon-derance of the evidence.
   IV. However, it must be noted that a fair preponderance of evidence does not necessarily mean a greater number of witnesses.
    V. The burden of proof is the burden which rests upon one of the parties to an action to persuade the trier of the facts, generally the jury, that a proposition he asserts is true.
   VI. If the evidence is equally balanced, or if it leaves the jury in such doubt as to be unable to decide the controversy either way, judgment must be given against the party upon whom the burden of proof rests.

5.___

The CORRECT answer is:
  A. III, II, V, IV, I, VI   B. I, II, VI, V, III, IV
  C. III, IV, V, I, II, VI   D. V, I, III, VI, IV, II
  E. I, V, III, VI, IV, II

6. I. If a parent is without assets and is unemployed, he cannot be convicted of the crime of non-support of a child.
   II. The term *sufficient ability* has been held to mean sufficient financial ability.
  III. It does not matter if his unemployment is by choice or unavoidable circumstances.
   IV. If he fails to take any steps at all, he may be liable to prosecution for endangering the welfare of a child.
    V. Under the penal law, a parent is responsible for the support of his minor child only if the parent is *of sufficient ability*.
   VI. An indigent parent may meet his obligation by borrow-ing money or by seeking aid under the provisions of the Social Welfare Law.

6.___

The CORRECT answer is:
  A. VI, I, V, III, II, IV   B. I, III, V, II, IV, VI
  C. V, II, I, III, VI, IV   D. I, VI, IV, V, II, III
  E. II, V, I, III, VI, IV

7. I. Consider, for example, the case of a rabble rouser who urges a group of twenty people to go out and break the windows of a nearby factory.
   II. Therefore, the law fills the indicated gap with the crime of *inciting to riot*.
  III. A person is considered guilty of inciting to riot when he urges ten or more persons to engage in tumultuous and violent conduct of a kind likely to create public alarm.

7.___

IV. However, if he has not obtained the cooperation of at least four people, he cannot be charged with unlawful assembly.

V. The charge of inciting to riot was added to the law to cover types of conduct which cannot be classified as either the crime of *riot* or the crime of *unlawful assembly*.

VI. If he acquires the acquiescence of at least four of them, he is guilty of unlawful assembly even if the project does not materialize.

The CORRECT answer is:
A. III, V, I, VI, IV, II   B. V, I, IV, VI, II, III
C. III, IV, I, V, II, VI   D. V, I, IV, VI, III, II
E. V, III, I, VI, IV, II

8.   I. If, however, the rebuttal evidence presents an issue of credibility, it is for the jury to determine whether the presumption has, in fact, been destroyed.

   II. Once sufficient evidence to the contrary is introduced, the presumption disappears from the trial.

  III. The effect of a presumption is to place the burden upon the adversary to come forward with evidence to rebut the presumption.

  IV. When a presumption is overcome and ceases to exist in the case, the fact or facts which gave rise to the presumption still remain.

   V. Whether a presumption has been overcome is ordinarily a question for the court.

  VI. Such information may furnish a basis for a logical inference.

8.___

The CORRECT answer is:
A. IV, VI, II, V, I, III   B. III, II, V, I, IV, VI
C. V, III, VI, IV, II, I   D. V, IV, I, II, VI, III
E. II, III, V, I, IV, VI

9.   I. An executive may answer a letter by writing his reply on the face of the letter itself instead of having a return letter typed.

   II. This procedure is efficient because it saves the executive's time, the typist's time, and saves office file space.

  III. Copying machines are used in small offices as well as large offices to save time and money in making brief replies to business letters.

  IV. A copy is made on a copying machine to go into the company files, while the original is mailed back to the sender.

9.___

The CORRECT answer is:
A. I, II, IV, III   B. I, IV, II, III
C. III, I, IV, II   D. III, IV, II, I

10. I. Most organizations favor one of the types but always 10.___
    include the others to a lesser degree.
  II. However, we can detect a definite trend toward
    greater use of symbolic control.
 III. We suggest that our local police agencies are today
    primarily utilizing material control.
  IV. Control can be classified into three types: physical,
    material, and symbolic.

The CORRECT answer is:
 A. IV, II, III, I   B. II, I, IV, III
 C. III, IV, II, I   D. IV, I, III, II

11. I. Project residents had first claim to this use, 11.___
    followed by surrounding neighborhood children.
  II. By contrast, recreation space within the project's
    interior was found to be used more often by both
    groups.
 III. Studies of the use of project grounds in many cities
    showed grounds left open for public use were neglected
    and unused, both by residents and by members of the
    surrounding community.
  IV. Project residents had clearly laid claim to the play
    spaces, setting up and enforcing unwritten rules for
    use.
  V. Each group, by experience, found their activities
    easily disrupted by other groups, and their claim to
    the use of space for recreation difficult to enforce.

The CORRECT answer is:
 A. IV, V, I, II, III   B. V, II, IV, III, I
 C. I, IV, III, II, V   D. III, V, II, IV, I

12. I. They do not consider the problems correctable within 12.___
    the existing subsidy formula and social policy of
    accepting all eligible applicants regardless of
    social behavior and lifestyle.
  II. A recent survey, however, indicated that tenants
    believe these problems correctable by local housing
    authorities and management within the existing
    financial formula.
 III. Many of the problems and complaints concerning public
    housing management and design have created resentment
    between the tenant and the landlord.
  IV. This same survey indicated that administrators and
    managers do not agree with the tenants.

The CORRECT answer is:
 A. II, I, III, IV   B. I, III, IV, II
 C. III, II, IV, I   D. IV, II, I, III

13.   I. In single-family residences, there is usually enough   13.___
distance between tenants to prevent occupants from
annoying one another.
   II. For example, a certain small percentage of tenant
families has one or more members addicted to alcohol.
 III. While managers believe in the right of individuals
to live as they choose, the manager becomes concerned
when the pattern of living jeopardizes others' rights.
  IV. Still others turn night into day, staging lusty enter-
tainments which carry on into the hours when most
tenants are trying to sleep.
   V. In apartment buildings, however, tenants live so
closely together that any misbehavior can result in
unpleasant living conditions.
  VI. Other families engage in violent argument.

The CORRECT answer is:
  A. III, II, V, IV, VI, I   B. I, V, II, VI, IV, III
  C. II, V, IV, I, III, VI   D. IV, II, V, VI, III, I

14.   I. Congress made the commitment explicit in the Housing   14.___
Act of 1949, establishing as a national goal the
realization of *a decent home and suitable environment for every American family*.
   II. The result has been that the goal of decent home and
suitable environment is still as far distant as ever
for the disadvantaged urban family.
 III. In spite of this action by Congress, federal housing
programs have continued to be fragmented and grossly
underfunded.
  IV. The passage of the National Housing Act signalled a
new federal commitment to provide housing for the
nation's citizens.

The CORRECT answer is:
  A. I, IV, III, II   B. IV, I, III, II
  C. IV, I, II, III   D. II, IV, I, III

15.   I. The greater expense does not necessarily involve   15.___
exploitation, but it is often perceived as exploi-
tative and unfair by those who are aware of the
price differences involved, but unaware of operating
costs.
   II. Ghetto residents believe they are *exploited* by local
merchants, and evidence substantiates some of these
beliefs.
 III. However, stores in low-income areas were more likely
to be small independents, which could not achieve the
economies available to supermarket chains and were,
therefore, more likely to charge higher prices, and
the customers were more likely to buy smaller-sized
packages which are more expensive per unit of
measure.
  IV. A study conducted in one city showed that distinctly
higher prices were charged for goods sold in ghetto
stores than in other areas.

The CORRECT answer is:
A. IV, II, I, III   B. IV, I, III, II
C. II, IV, III, I   D. II, III, IV, I

———

KEY (CORRECT ANSWERS)

1.	C	6.	C	11.	D
2.	E	7.	A	12.	C
3.	B	8.	B	13.	B
4.	D	9.	C	14.	B
5.	D	10.	D	15.	C

———

REPORT WRITING
EXAMINATION SECTION

DIRECTIONS FOR THIS SECTION:
Each question or incomplete statement is followed by several suggested answers or completions. Select the one that BEST answers the question or completes the statement. *PRINT THE LETTER OF THE CORRECT ANSWER IN THE SPACE AT THE RIGHT.*

TEST 1

Questions 1-3.
DIRECTIONS: Questions 1 to 3 are based on the following example of a report. The report consists of ten numbered sentences, some of which are *not* consistent with the principles of good report writing.

(1) On the evening of February 24, 1992, Roscoe and Leroy, two members of the "Red Devils," were entering with a bottle of wine in their hands. (2) It was unusually good wine for these boys to buy. (3) I told them to give me the bottle and they refused, and added that they wouldn't let anyone "put them out." (4) I told them they were entitled to have a good time, but they could not do it the way they wanted; there were certain rules they had to observe. (5) At this point, Roscoe said he had seen me box at camp and suggested that Leroy not accept my offer. (6) Then I said firmly that the 25-cent admission fee did not give them the authority to tell me what to do. (7) I also told them that, if they thought I would fight them over such a matter, they were sadly mistaken. (8) I added, however, that we could go to the gym right now and settle it another way if they wished. (9) Leroy immediately said that he was sorry, he had not understood the rules, and he did not want his quarter back. (10) On the other hand, they would not give up their bottle either, so they left the premises.

1. Only material that is relevant to the main thought of a report should be included.
   Which of the following sentences from the report contains material which is LEAST relevant to this report? Sentence
   A. 2   B. 3   C. 8   D. 9   1. ...

2. A good report should be arranged in logical order.   2. ...
   Which of the following sentences from the report does NOT appear in its proper sequence in the report? Sentence
   A. 3   B. 5   C. 7   D. 9

3. Reports should include all essential information.   3. ...
   Of the following, the MOST important fact that is *missing* from this report is:
   A. Who was involved in the incident
   B. How the incident was resolved
   C. When the incident took place
   D. Where the incident took place

4. The MOST serious of the following faults *commonly* found   4. ...
   in explanatory reports is
   A. the use of slang terms   B. excessive details
   C. personal bias   D. redundancy

5. In reviewing a report he has prepared to submit to his   5. ...
   superiors, a supervisor finds that his paragraphs are a typewritten page long and decides to make some revisions.
   Of the following, the MOST important question he should ask about each paragraph is:
   A. Are the words too lengthy?
   B. Is the idea under **discussion** too abstract?

C. Is more than one central thought being expressed?

D. Are the sentences too long?

6. The summary or findings of a long management report in-   6. ...
   tended for the typical manager should, *generally*, appear
     A. at the very beginning of the report
     B. at the end of the report   C. throughout the report
     D. in the middle of the report

7. In preparing a report that includes several tables, if not   7. ...
   otherwise instructed, the typist should *most properly* include a list of tables
     A. in the introductory part of the report
     B. at the end of each chapter in the body of the report
     C. in the supplementary part of the report as an appendix
     D. in the supplementary part of the report as a part of
        the index

8. When typing a preliminary draft of a report, the one of   8. ...
   the following which you should *generally* NOT do is to
     A. erase typing errors and deletions rather than "X"ing
        them out
     B. leave plenty of room at the top, bottom and sides of
        each page
     C. make only the number of copies that you are asked to
        make
     D. type double or triple space

9. When you determine the methods of emphasis you will use in   9. ...
   typing the titles, headings and subheadings of a report,
   the one of the following which it is MOST important to
   keep in mind is that
     A. all headings of the same rank should be typed in the
        same way
     B. all headings should be typed in the single style which
        is most pleasing to the eye
     C. headings should not take up more than one third of the
        page width
     D. only one method should be used for all headings, what-
        ever their rank

10. The one of the following ways in which inter-office memo-   10. ...
    randa *differ* from long formal reports is that they, *generally*,
      A. are written as if the reader is familiar with the
         vocabulary and technical background of the writer
      B. do not have a "subject line" which describes the
         major topic covered in the text
      C. include a listing of reference materials which sup-
         port the memo writer's conclusions
      D. require that a letter of transmittal be attached

11. It is *preferable* to print information on a field report   11. ...
    rather than write it out longhand MAINLY because
      A. printing takes less time to write than writing longhand
      B. printing is usually easier to read than longhand writing
      C. longhand writing on field reports is not acceptable in
         court cases
      D. printing occupies less space on a report than longhand
         writing

12. Of the following characteristics of a written report, the   12. ...
    one that is MOST important is its
      A. length   B. accuracy   C. organization D. grammar

13. A written report to your superior contains many spelling   13. ...
    errors.
    Of the following statements relating to spelling errors,
    the one that is *most nearly* correct is that
    A. this is unimportant as long as the meaning of the
       report is clear
    B. readers of the report will ignore the many spelling
       errors
    C. readers of the report will get a poor opinion of the
       writer of the report
    D. spelling errors are unimportant as long as the grammar
       is correct

14. Written reports to your superior should have the same   14. ...
    general arrangement and layout.
    The BEST reason for this requirement is that the
    A. report will be more accurate
    B. report will be more complete
    C. person who reads the report will know what the subject
       of the report is
    D. person who reads the report will know where to look
       for information in the report

15. The first paragraph of a report usually contains detailed 15. ...
    information on the subject of the report.
    Of the following, the BEST reason for this requirement is
    to enable the
    A. reader to quickly find the subject of the report
    B. typist to immediately determine the subject of the
       report so that she will understand what she is typing
    C. clerk to determine to whom copies of the report shall
       be routed
    D. typist to quickly determine how many copies of the
       report will be needed

16. Of the following statements concerning reports, the one   16. ...
    which is LEAST valid is:
    A. A case report should contain factual material to
       support conclusions made.
    B. An extremely detailed report may be of less value
       than a brief report giving the essential facts.
    C. Highly technical language should be avoided as far
       as possible in preparing a report to be used at a
       court trial.
    D. The position of the important facts in a report does
       not influence the emphasis placed on them by the
       reader.

17. Suppose that you realize that you have made an error in   17. ...
    a report that has been forwarded to another unit. You
    know that this error is not likely to be discovered for
    some time.
    Of the following, the MOST advisable course of action for
    you to take is to
    A. approach the supervisor of the other unit on an in-
       formal basis, and ask him to correct the error
    B. say nothing about it since most likely one error
       will not invalidate the entire report
    C. tell your supervisor immediately that you have made
       an error so that it may be corrected, if necessary

3

      D. wait until the error is discovered and then admit
         that you had made it

18. In a report, words in a sentence must be arranged proper-   18. ...
ly to make sure that the intended meaning of the sentence
is clear.
The sentence below that does NOT make sense because a
clause has been separated from the word on which its meaning depends is:
    A. To be a good writer, clarity is necessary.
    B. To be a good writer, you must write clearly.
    C. You must write clearly to be a good writer.
    D. Clarity is necessary to good writing.

19. The use of a graph to show statistical data in a report   19. ...
is *superior* to a table because it
    A. emphasizes approximations
    B. emphasizes facts and relationships more dramatically
    C. presents data more accurately
    D. is easily understood by the average reader

20. Of the following, the degree of formality required of a   20. ...
written report is, *most likely*, to depend on the
    A. subject matter of the report
    B. frequency of its occurrence
    C. amount of time available for its preparation
    D. audience for whom the report is intended

Questions 21-25.

DIRECTIONS: Questions 21 through 25 consist of sets of four sentences
lettered A, B, C, and D. For each question, choose the sentence which
is grammatically and stylistically *most appropriate* for use in a *formal*
WRITTEN REPORT.

21. A. It is recommended, therefore, that the impasse panel   21. ...
      hearings are to be convened on September 30.
    B. It is therefore recommended that the impasse panel
      hearings be convened on September 30.
    C. Therefore, it is recommended to convene the impasse
      panel hearings on September 30.
    D. It is recommended that the impasse panel hearings
      therefore should be convened on September 30.

22. A. Penalties have been assessed for violating the Taylor   22. ...
      Law by several unions.
    B. When they violated provisions of the Taylor Law,
      several unions were later penalized.
    C. Several unions have been penalized for violating pro-
      visions of the Taylor Law.
    D. Several unions' violating provisions of the Taylor Law
      resulted in them being penalized.

23. A. The number of disputes settled through mediation has   23. ...
      increased significantly over the past two years.
    B. The number of disputes settled through mediation are
      increasing significantly over two-year periods.
    C. Over the past two years, through mediation, the number
      of disputes settled increased significantly.
    D. There is a significant increase over the past two years
      of the number of disputes settled through mediation.

24. A. The union members will vote to determine if the con-   24. ...
      tract is to be approved.

B. It is not yet known whether the union members will ratify the proposed contract.

C. When the union members vote, that will determine the new contract.

D. Whether the union members will ratify the proposed contract, it is not yet known.

25. A. The parties agreed to an increase in fringe benefits in return for greater work productivity.

    B. Greater productivity was agreed to be provided in return for increased fringe benefits.

    C. Productivity and fringe benefits are interrelated; the higher the former, the more the latter grows.

    D. The contract now provides that the amount of fringe benefits will depend upon the level of output by the workers.

25. ...

TEST 2

Questions 1-4.

DIRECTIONS: Answer Questions 1 through 4 on the basis of the following report which was prepared by a supervisor for inclusion in his agency's annual report.

Line
#

1	On Oct. 13, 1985, I was assigned to study the salaries paid
2	to clerical employees in various titles by the city and by
3	private industry in the area.
4	In order to get the data I needed, I called Mr. Johnson at
5	the Bureau of the Budget and the payroll officers at X Corp. -
6	a brokerage house, Y Co. - an insurance company, and Z Inc. -
7	a publishing firm. None of them was available and I had to call
8	all of them again the next day.
9	When I finally got the information I needed, I drew up a
10	chart, which is attached. Note that not all of the companies I
11	contacted employed people at all the different levels used in the
12	city service.
13	The conclusions I draw from analyzing this information is
14	as follows: The city's entry-level salary is about average for
15	the region; middle-level salaries are generally higher in the
16	city government than in private industry; but salaries at the
17	highest levels in private industry are better than city em-
18	ployees' pay.

1. Which of the following *criticisms* about the style in which this report is written is MOST valid?

   A. It is too informal.   B. It is too concise.

   C. It is too choppy.   D. The syntax is too complex.

1. ...

2. Judging from the statements made in the report, the method followed by this employee in performing his research was

   A. *good;* he contacted a representative sample of businesses in the area

   B. *poor;* he should have drawn more definite conclusions

   C. *good;* he was persistent in collecting information

   D. *poor;* he did not make a thorough study

2. ...

3. One sentence in this report contains a grammatical error. This sentence *begins* on line number

3. ...

A. 4   B. 7   C. 10   D. 13

4. The type of information given in this report which should   4. ...
be presented in footnotes or in an appendix, is the
    A. purpose of the study
    B. specifics about the businesses contacted
    C. reference to the chart
    D. conclusions drawn by the author

5. Of the following, a DISTINGUISHING characteristic of a   5. ...
written report intended for the head of your agency as
compared to a report prepared for a lower-echelon staff
member is that the report for the agency head should,
usually, include
    A. considerably more detail, especially statistical data
    B. the essential details in an abbreviated form
    C. all available source material
    D. an annotated bibliography

6. Assume that you are asked to write a lengthy report for   6. ...
use by the administrator of your agency, the subject of
which is "The Impact of Proposed New Data Processing Operations on Line Personnel" in your agency. You decide that
the *most appropriate* type of report for you to prepare is
an analytical report, including recommendations.
The MAIN reason for your decision is that
    A. the subject of the report is extremely complex
    B. large sums of money are involved
    C. the report is being prepared for the administrator
    D. you intend to include charts and graphs

7. Assume that you are preparing a report based on a survey   7. ...
dealing with the attitudes of employees in Division X regarding proposed new changes in compensating employees for
working overtime. Three percent of the respondents to the
survey voluntarily offer an unfavorable opinion on the
method of assigning overtime work, a question not specifically asked of the employees.
On the basis of this information, the MOST appropriate and
significant of the following comments for you to make in
the report with regard to employees' attitudes on assigning
overtime work is that
    A. an insignificant percentage of employees dislike the
       method of assigning overtime work
    B. three percent of the employees in Division X dislike
       the method of assigning overtime work
    C. three percent of the sample selected for the survey
       voiced an unfavorable opinion on the method of as-
       signing overtime work
    D. some employees voluntarily voiced negative feelings
       about the method of assigning overtime work, making
       it impossible to determine the extent of this attitude

8. Assume that you have been asked to prepare a narrative   8. ...
summary of the monthly reports submitted by employees in
your division.
In preparing your summary of this month's reports, the
FIRST step to take is to
    A. read through the reports, noting their general content
       and any unusual features

6

    B. decide how many typewritten pages your summary should contain

    C. make a written summary of each separate report, so that you will not have to go back to the original reports again

    D. ask each employee which points he would prefer to see emphasized in your summary

9. Assume that an administrative officer is writing a brief report to his superior outlining the advantages of matrix organization.
Of the following, it would be INCORRECT to state that   9. ...

    A. in matrix organization, a project is emphasized by designating one individual as the focal point for all matters pertaining to it

    B. utilization of manpower can be flexible in matrix organization because a reservoir of specialists is maintained in the line operations

    C. the usual line-staff management is generally reversed in matrix organization

    D. in matrix organization, responsiveness to project needs is generally faster due to establishing needed communication lines and decision points

10. Written reports dealing with inspections of work and installations SHOULD be   10. ...

    A. as long and detailed as practicable

    B. phrased with personal interpretations

    C. limited to the important facts of the inspection

    D. technically phrased to create an impression on superiors

11. It is important to use definite, exact words in preparing a descriptive report and to avoid, as much as possible, nouns that have vague meanings and, possibly, a different meaning for the reader than for the author.
Which of the following sentences contains *only* nouns that are *definite* and *exact*?   11. ...

    A. The free enterprise system should be vigorously encouraged in the United States.

    B. Arley Swopes climbed Mount Everest three times last year.

    C. Beauty is a characteristic of all the women at the party.

    D. Gil Noble asserts that he is a real democrat.

12. One way of shortening an unnecessarlly long report is to reduce sentence length by eliminating the use of several words where a single one that does not alter the meaning will do.
Which of the following sentences CANNOT be shortened without losing some of its information content?   12. ...

    A. After being polished, the steel ball bearings ran at maximum speed.

    B. After the close of the war, John Taylor was made the recipient of a pension.

    C. In this day and age, you can call anyone up on the telephone.

    D. She is attractive in appearance, but she is a rather selfish person.

13. Employees are required to submit **written reports** of all   13. ...
    unusual occurrences promptly. The BEST reason for such
    promptness is that the
    A. report may be too long if made at one's convenience
    B. employee will not be so likely to forget to make the
       report
    C. report will tend to be more accurate as to facts
    D. employee is likely to make a better report under
       pressure

14. In making a report, it is POOR practice to erase informa-   14. ...
    tion on the report in order to make a change because
    A. there may be a question of what was changed and why
       it was changed
    B. you are likely to erase through the paper and tear
       the report
    C. the report will no longer look neat and presentable
    D. the duplicate copies will be smudged

15. The one of the following which BEST describes a periodic   15. ...
    report is that it
    A. provides a record of accomplishments for a given time
       span and a comparison with similar time spans in the
       past
    B. covers the progress made in a project that has been
       postponed
    C. integrates, summarizes, and, perhaps, interprets pub-
       lished data on technical or scientific material
    D. describes a decision, advocates a policy or action,
       and presents facts in support of the writer's position

16. The PRIMARY purpose of including pictorial illustrations   16. ...
    in a formal report is *usually* to
    A. amplify information which has been adequately treated
       verbally
    B. present details that are difficult to describe verbally
    C. provide the reader with a pleasant, momentary distrac-
       tion
    D. present supplementary information incidental to the
       main ideas developed in the report

KEYS (CORRECT ANSWERS)

TEST 1				TEST 2			
1.	A	11.	B	1.	A	9.	C
2.	B	12.	B	2.	D	10.	C
3.	D	13.	C	3.	D	11.	B
4.	C	14.	D	4.	B	12.	A
5.	C	15.	A	5.	B	13.	C
6.	A	16.	D	6.	A	14.	A
7.	A	17.	C	7.	D	15.	A
8.	A	18.	A	8.	A	16.	B
9.	A	19.	B				
10.	A	20.	D				
		21.	B				
		22.	C				
		23.	A				
		24.	B				
		25.	A				

SENTENCING AND THE PAROLE PROCESS

CONTENTS

Page

Part I—Interrelationships of Legislatures, Courts, and
Parole Boards in the Sentence-Fixing Process____   1

Part II—Types of Sentence- and Parole-Fixing Power_____   11

Part III—The Model Penal Code and the Model Sentencing
Act_____   21

SENTENCING AND THE PAROLE PROCESS

PART I—INTERRELATIONSHIPS OF LEGISLATURES, COURTS, AND PAROLE BOARDS IN THE SENTENCE-FIXING PROCESS

Determining the nature and extent of an offender's sentence is a divided task. Part of this job is assumed by the legislature, when it sets upper and lower limits to the sentences which a court may impose for each offense. Another part is done by the courts, in their separate decisions on each case. The parole board can only exercise discretion in whatever leeway is left it when the legislature and the courts are through. This range for parole decision varies greatly from one jurisdiction to the next.

The Criminal Sentence as a Product of Legislatures and Courts

American Government evolved from a series of efforts to reduce the extent to which any single individual controlled the liberty of another. Legislatures first developed to restrain the power of kings, but their checking function now is mainly directed at elected officials and their appointees. Legislatures also serve the ideal of "a government of laws, not men" by setting statutory limits on the discretion which judges, boards, and administrators may exercise.

Because of unhappy experiences with judges in colonial days, early American State legislatures severely restricted judicial discretion in sentencing. The law frequently specified the penalty for each offense, so that the judge served mainly to preside over trial proceedings. When a man was found guilty of a particular crime, he generally had to serve the penalty prescribed by statute for that crime.

Having a single sentence for each offense poses many problems. Most manifest are the diverse types of behavior which can be classified as a single type of offense, and the variation in the personal character of offenders. For example, the act called "murder" may sometimes be an honorable man's overly vigorous expression of justifiable anger at being terribly wronged, sometimes a first offender's panicky effort to suppress someone's scream which would expose and disgrace him for committing an indiscretion, or sometimes a carefully planned and coldblooded assault by a hardened criminal in order to gain unjust personal advantages.

There are two ways in which the law commonly permits the courts to provide diversity of sentence for each offense, in order to take varieties of behavior and character into account. One method is to try to specify all variations of crime and criminals in the statutes. Thus "murder" may become several varieties of "homicide," including

1

"murder," "manslaughter," and "homicide by negligence or recklessness." Often several "degrees" are distinguished for each major offense. Some times severer penalties are specified when the offender has a prior criminal record, and the type of sentence permitted sometimes depends upon the age and sex of the offender.

The alternative method of making sentences vary is to allow the judge to determine sentence according to his own judgment in each case. The law may specify the upper and lower limits within which the judge may make his determination, but it does not lay down detailed rules for sentence-fixing within these limits. Usually, these two methods are combined, with many categories of each offense distinguished in the law and a separate range of penalties allowed for each. Also, there are informal processes of adjustment, to be discussed later, whereby a man clearly guilty of one offense is allowed to plead guilty instead to a lesser charge, thus permitting the judge to impose a shorter sentence than would otherwise be mandatory.

The argument for legislative authority in fixing the minimum sentence for an offense, usually presumes that some penalty would have a deterrent effect on the offender or on others. The statutory minimum provides the law's promise that anyone convicted of an offense will receive punishment of at least a minimum severity. Deterrence presumably depends upon the predictability of the punishment. A statutory minimum severity of penalty contributes to predictability, but only in part; the remaining parts are certainty of apprehension and conviction, both of which may vary independently of each other and of the severity.

Predictability is reduced by giving the judge authority to set a minimum term of imprisonment, rather than having it fixed entirely by law. However, it may be argued that the judge's observations at the time of the trial make him best qualified to assess the deterrent needed for each individual case, considering both the history of the offender, and the character of others in the community to be deterred. One may also argue that the dimensions of the offense enter into this effectiveness of a minimum penalty as a deterrent, since a criminal presumably would risk a greater penalty for a $100,000 burglary than for a $10 burglary.

A somewhat different concern with retribution justifies legislative and court fixing of maximum limits to confinement. The classical notion of 18th and early 19th century legal philosophy, still inherent in our statutes, is that the pain imposed by punishment should exceed only moderately the suffering of others from the offense. This led to a decline in use of capital punishment for minor offenses in the 19th century, and it still restricts the extent to which we hold the State justified in depriving a man of his liberty. The legislatures and the courts are said to reflect public opinion in holding that the upper

2

limit of a penalty should have some relationship to the magnitude of the damage done by the offender. An additional reason for imposing an upper limit on confinement of even the worst offenders is knowledge that humans often err in judging men to be forever beyond reform.

By setting limits to the sentence which a court may impose for any particular crime, the legislature creates restraints upon a judge's power to negate the deterrent effect intended by the law, or to deprive persons of their liberty. At the same time, the range between statutory limits allows the court flexibility to cope with variations of behavior included within a single category of crime, and variations in the character of the criminals who commit the crime. However, this does not solve all problems which arise from legislatively fixed sentences, and it creates several new problems. These result from the human and political aspects of judicial operations.

Illogical Disparities of Sentence

A single jurisdiction frequently has several judges. They are bound to differ considerably from each other in the standards which they apply to the evaluation of crimes and criminals, in their mental habits in reaching decisions, in their intelligence, and in their personal character. As a consequence, wherever the statutes allow judges much range of discretion in determining the sentence, similar crimes by similar offenders may result in vastly different sentences, if different judges are involved. It can be demonstrated statistically that judges within a single jurisdiction will vary markedly in the average sentence they impose, and in the type and severity of their sentences, even where cases are assigned in rotation, so they all receive a similar cross section.[1] Sentencing disparity contributes to the maxim of criminal law practice, that the best way to serve a client who is a criminal is to study the judges, not the law.

[1] Frederick J. Gaudet, "The Sentencing Behavior of Judges," in V. C. Branham and S. B. Kutash, *Encyclopedia of Criminology*, New York: Philosophical Press, 1949; Harold E. Lane, "Illogical Variations in Sentences of Felons Committed to Massachusetts State Prison," *Journal of Criminal Law and Criminology*, vol. 32, No. 2 (July–August 1941), pp. 171–190; Morris Ploscowe, "The Court and the Correctional System," in Paul W. Tappan, editor, *Contemporary Corrections*, New York: McGraw-Hill, 1951, pp. 51–60; Rudolph W. Dvorak, "Determinate Sentences in Illinois," *Criminal Justice*, No. 72 (May 1945), pp. 21–24; Coe Lanpher, "Length of Sentence and Duration of Sentence of Federal Prisoners," *Federal Probation*, vol. 9, No. 2 (1945), p. 13; R. Clyde White, "Sentencing and the Treatment of the Criminal," *Social Service Review*, vol. 11, No. 2 (June 1937), pp. 234–246; W. A. Lunden, *The Courts and Criminal Justice in Iowa*, Ames, Iowa: Iowa State University, 1957, pp. 41–53. See also the annual reviews of crime statistics in Cook County published by the Chicago Crime Commission in *Criminal Justice* and other publications, which give averages and other statistics on the sentences of each judge in the Criminal Court of Cook County.

It is possible for the judicial system itself to provide some remedy for this variation in judges, while still allowing discretion in sentencing for each crime. This remedy is provided by appellate review of sentences. In our military court martial cases, in the courts of Europe, and elsewhere, sentences for serious crimes are reviewed automatically by a higher court or other authority. The reviewing authority imposes some uniformity within a judicial system by reducing sentences which seem to be unusually severe. Usually these reviewing authorities cannot impose a severer sentence than that prescribed by the trial court.

Most jurisdictions in the United States also provide some review of sentences by a higher court, but only if the defendant appeals for a review, and only if the appeal questions the legality of the sentence, rather than its wisdom. Two States, however, Massachusetts and Connecticut, permit appeals on the grounds that a sentence is unwise, even if there is no question of its legality. The court hearing these appeals can increase the severity of the sentence as well as decrease it. A convicted person, therefore, is not likely to appeal unless he has some confidence in his case.[2] It has been argued that the mere possibility of a reviewing action makes the courts cautious to avoid giving clearly inappropriate sentences.[3]

For most American courts it still is true that "we are the only country in the free world where a single judge may, without being subjected to any review of his determination on the merits, decide absolutely the minimum period of time during which a convicted offender must remain in prison."[4]

Informal Sentence-Fixing Processes Within the Courts

Pressures on the prosecuting attorneys to get the work of their office completed rapidly and successfully, as well as pressures on judges to complete the handling of many cases awaiting trial, often make the determination of sentence in the courts much different from what one would envision in studying the statutes. These pressures lead to compromises completely at variance with legislative intention or public expectation as to the penalties which particular criminal acts will incur. Such compromises develop regardless of what types of law are passed with respect to judicial discretion in sentencing, although they take a different form under different types of law.

---

[2] "Appellate Review of Primary Sentencing Decisions: A Connecticut Case Study," *Yale Law Journal*, vol. 69, No. 8 (July 1960), pp. 1453–1478.

[3] Simon E. Sobeloff, "The Sentence of the Court: Should There Be Appellate Review?" *American Bar Association Journal*, vol. 41, No. 1 (January 1955), pp. 13–17.

[4] B. J. George, Jr., "Comparative Sentencing Techniques," *Federal Probation*, vol. 23, No. 1 (March 1959), pp. 27–31 (original italicized).

When the law orders a specific sentence or range of sentences for each type of offense, the accused criminal is motivated to try to have his crime defined as a type which receives the smallest specific or maximum penalty. Since charges generally are drafted by the prosecuting attorney, their determination might appear to be something beyond the influence of the criminal or his defense counsel. However, a prosecutor, like other humans, usually wants to expedite his work. Also, if he is elected, if he has ambitions for other offices, or simply by personal choice, he usually is anxious to achieve a high percentage of convictions. It is on these prosecutor interests that the defense often bases its tactics.

The manner in which a criminal's defense is conducted can greatly affect the amount of work involved in the prosecutor's job, and the prospects that the work will result in a conviction. Taking these considerations into account, defense counsel may successfully offer to have his client plead guilty to a lesser offense, if the prosecutor will drop the charges which could bring a severer penalty. Conversely, the defense may seek a maximum number of continuances, challenge jurors, and engage in other legal procedures not for the reasons they assert in doing these things, but primarily as a means of delaying the trial to the point where the prosecutor will be willing to accept its offer, simply to get the case concluded quickly. Often the prosecutor takes the initiative in suggesting that he will drop some charges, if the accused will plead guilty to others. Of course, the strength of the evidence that the prosecutor and the defense counsel think they can present enters into their willingness to compromise, in the course of this bargaining.

Bargaining frequently occurs with the full knowledge of the judge. Indeed, once charges are filed, the judge may have to authorize having them dropped, and he may also be a party to the bargaining, because he shares the prosecutor's interest in expediting cases. In this event, the bargain may include an explicit or implicit promise of a lesser sentence if the accused pleads guilty, and the threat of a severer sentence if he has to be tried to be found guilty.[5]

---

[5] Donald J. Newman, "Pleading Guilty for Considerations: A Study of Bargain Justice." *Journal of Criminal Law, Criminology, and Police Science*, vol. 46, No. 6 (March–April 1956), pp. 780–790; Arthur L. Wood, "Informal Relations in the Practice of Criminal Law," *American Journal of Sociology*, vol. 62, No. 1 (July 1956), pp. 48–55; Lloyd E. Ohlin and Frank J. Remington, "Sentencing Structure: Its Effect Upon Systems for the Administration of Criminal Justice," *Law and Contemporary Problems*, vol. 23, No. 3 (summer 1958), pp. 495–507; opinion by Chief Judge Campbell in *U.S. v. Wiley*, 184 F. Supp. 679 (N.D. Ill. 1960), quoted in Richard C. Donnelly, Joseph Goldstein, and Richard D. Schwartz, *Criminal Law*, New York: Free Press of Glencoe, 1962, pp. 48–54. The effects of bargaining on the quality of judicial decisions, and proposals for preventing the unfavorable effects, are well discussed in Sol Rubin, *The Law of Criminal Correction*, St. Paul: West Publishing Co., 1963, pp. 64–72.

From such bargaining we often find that what seems to be the trial of a deliberate murder is concluded by a plea of guilty to a manslaughter charge. Similar processes result in acts that are clearly burglary, or even armed robbery, emerging from the courts as larceny. This is one of the reasons why, in most jurisdictions, from 80 to over 90 percent of criminal cases are concluded with the defense not contesting the charges on which the accused is convicted. Bargaining is especially frequent in crowded metropolitan courts.

When legislators do not anticipate the effects of these informal bargaining processes in the courts, laws which they pass in order to achieve one effect may actually have quite the opposite effect. This is dramatically illustrated by the experience of the last few decades in Illinois. Prior to 1943, Illinois law directed the courts to impose minimum and maximum sentences which gave wide latitude to the parole board. For example, all persons convicted of burglary or of armed robbery received a minimum sentence of 1 year and a maximum sentence of life imprisonment, all persons convicted of auto larceny received a minimum of 1 year and a maximum of 20 years, and all persons convicted of larceny received a minimum of 1 year and a maximum of 10 years. Under this system, several newspapers claimed that the parole board was releasing men too early. On the presumption that they would be corrected by giving more authority to the judges, the law was amended in 1943 to permit the courts to fix any minimum and maximum sentences they desired, within the statutory ranges of the old law.

Offenders convicted under the old Illinois law frequently bargained to be charged with larceny, regardless of their offense. After 1943, however, they bargained for a low maximum sentence, under any charge. Because of this process, the maximum sentence imposed in many cases became less than the period of imprisonment which the parole board previously had almost always insisted upon before considering such cases for parole. Also, the disparity between average maximum sentences for first offenders and the average for recidivists became negligible under some State's attorneys; this reflects the tendency of first offenders to confess their crimes and plead guilty without bargaining, while experienced criminals utilize their bargaining strengths before agreeing to plead guilty. Regardless of whether or not one approves of the longer confinement terms imposed by the Illinois board before 1943, it was clear that the bargaining process made the 1943 amendment have consequences for length of confinement opposite from those intended.[6]

---

[6] Donald T. Blackiston, "The Inadequacies of the Sentence and Parole Act of 1943," *Criminal Justice*, No. 77 (January 1950), pp. 24-28; Donald T. Blackiston, "The Judge, the Defendant, and Criminal Law Administration," (University of Chicago, Ph. D. dissertation, 1952).

6

We have seen that the statutory directives for a court's sentencing operations do not specify all of the procedures which may actually determine the sentence that a man receives. Informal bargaining processes in the courts may alter both the designation of an offense and the penalty which is imposed. However, the predominant pattern of court procedure depends greatly on the manner in which sentence-fixing authority has been divided between the legislature, the courts, and the parole board. What variations are there in this division? Where may each pattern be found, and what are its apparent consequences?

PART II—TYPES OF SENTENCE AND PAROLE-FIXING POWER

Superimposed on all variations of court-sentencing authority are diverse powers given to parole boards to alter the length of a prisoner's confinement. As indicated earlier, one of the latent functions of parole is to compensate for illogical disparities in court sentences. There are several ways of accomplishing this.

The Traditional Dichotomy

The most commonly made distinction between systems for specifying parole board authority is that between the definite and the indeterminate sentence. These labels provide a useful starting point for further distinctions, but they are somewhat misleading, since parole can occur even under a definite sentence, and thus the effects of the sentence are not fully definite or determinate when it is imposed.

An indeterminate sentence, as the term is ordinarily used, is one in which the court specifies two periods of confinement for each case, one being the minimum and the other the maximum. Thus, indeterminate sentences may be for 1 year to life, for 1 to 5 years, for 10 to 20 years, or for any other combination of a minimum and a maximum. A prisoner with an indeterminate sentence is eligible for parole at any time after completion of the minimum, and he must be discharged from his sentence at completion of the maximum. In some jurisdictions, time may be taken off the minimum sentence for good behavior, elsewhere it may be taken off the maximum, and sometimes it is taken from both. In some systems, the statutes specify what the minimum and maximum shall be for each offense, and in others they give discretion to the judge, in fixing one or both of these limits. In the preceding section we described both of those systems in Illinois, before and after 1943.

Under a definite sentence system, the court imposes a sentence for a given number of years, within statutory limits, but the parole board may release a prisoner on parole after a portion of this sentence has been served in prison. Usually this portion is set as a fraction of the sentence, such as one-third, but it may be a given number of months or years. This system is also referred to as a "fixed," "flat," or "general" sentence system.

Because the freedom of the parole board to alter the period of confinement often is greater under definite, than under indeterminate sentencing, these traditional labels are not very useful. When the

9

judge has authority to fix both minimum and maximum for each offender, he can make the difference between the two very small, for example, an 8 to 10 year sentence. The indeterminate sentence then becomes much more rigidly fixed than a definite sentence of 8, 9, or 10 years, on which parole can occur when one-third is completed.

The bargaining process in the courts frequently takes parole possibilities into account. An experienced criminal usually likes to have his term as predictable as possible, and will bargain for a low maximum sentence, rather than accept a low minimum with a high maximum and take his chances on early parole.[7] Conversely, the prosecutor may persuade a novice offender that if he cooperates by pleading guilty he will get a low minimum sentence and will have good prospects for an early parole.

Varieties of Sentencing Structure

Because of the diversity of practice under both the indeterminate and the definite sentence systems, other types of classification may define more clearly the various ways in which length of imprisonment is determined.

We shall indicate here the most distinctive combinations of statutory arrangement, and the judicial systems in which they are employed. It should be noted, however, that many jurisdictions have different types of sentencing structures for different offenses, or even give the court a choice of alternative types of sentencing in a given case. Therefore, our reference to a particular pattern existing in a jurisdiction may not mean that it is the only pattern found there. The following attempt at a classification within these limits is an expansion of categories developed in a previous survey by the *Columbia Law Review*.[8]

1. *Both Maximum and Minimum Term Fixed by the Court (Within Upper Limit for Maximum and Lower Limit for Minimum Set by the Law for Each Offense).* Parole eligibility under this system occurs at completion of the minimum term, or the minimum less time off for good behavior. With this system, there usually is great dis-

---

[7] Ohlin and Remington, *op. cit.* There is a decision that it is a reversible error in court proceeding for a prosecutor openly to refer to a defendant's chances for parole, and probable time before parole, if found guilty. This was held prejudicial to the accused as suggesting to the jury that they could pass on to the parole board some of the responsibility they assume in deciding on guilt. See *Shoemaker* v. *State*, 228 Md. 462, 180 A. 2d 482 (1961).

[8] Note, "Statutory Structures for Sentencing Felons to Prison," *Columbia Law Review*, vol. 60, No. 8 (December 1960), pp. 1134–1172. We have found a few apparent discrepancies in this and in every other compilation we have encountered, and some errors may also exist in our compilation, but it has been checked with statutes, cases, articles, and personal reports by parole board members.

parity—within the range permitted by statute—in the minimum, in the maximum, and in the span between the two, since judges have much discretion in varying each. This system is found in 14 States, and is used exclusively or almost exclusively in 9 States: New Hampshire, Vermont, Massachusetts, New Jersey, Kentucky, Georgia, Arizona, Colorado, and Wyoming. It is also prescribed for most offenses in Illinois, Nebraska, North Carolina, and South Carolina, and is an option in Arkansas and in the Federal system.

States using this system vary greatly in the proportion of their prisoners who are paroled. In 1961, among the States using this system exclusively, this proportion ranged from 100 percent of first releases being by parole in New Hampshire, 97 percent in Colorado, and 88 percent in New Jersey, to only 18 percent in Vermont, 27 percent in Wyoming, and 36 percent in Georgia. The average time imprisoned before first release in 1960 ranged from a low of 12 months in Vermont and 16 months in Wyoming, to a high of 29 months in New Hampshire and Georgia. This means none was appreciably above the national average of 28 months.[9]

2. *Both Maximum and Minimum Term Fixed by the Court (Within Limits Set by Law), But Minimum Not To Exceed a Fraction of Maximum.* This system guarantees the possibility of a certain maximum relationship of the parole period to the term of confinement. In Montana and North Carolina the minimum cannot be above one-fourth of the maximum imposed, in the District of Columbia and in Alaska the minimum may not exceed one-third of the maximum imposed, in Pennsylvania its upper limit is one-half of the maximum imposed, and in New York and Maine it may not exceed one-half of the statutory maximum. Under the latter arrangement, in New York and Maine, it is possible for the minimum to be nearly as high as the maximum, if the maximum imposed is about half the statutory maximum.

Six of these seven jurisdictions paroled about 9 out of 10 of their first releases in 1961; North Carolina paroled one-third. These States varied greatly in time confined before first release in 1960, from a low of 18 months in Montana and 19 months in Maine, to a high of 37 months in New York and Pennsylvania and 40 months in the District of Columbia.

---

[9] All figures on percent paroled reported in this chapter are from *National Prisoner Statistics*, "Prisoners in State and Federal Institutions 1961," Washington, D.C.: U.S. Bureau of Prisons, August 1962.

All figures on average duration of imprisonment before first release are from *National Prisoner Statistics*. "Prisoners Released from State and Federal Institutions 1960," Washington, D.C.: U.S. Bureau of Prisons, 1963.

Percentages have been rounded to the nearest whole percentage, instead of being presented with decimals.

3. *Maximum Term Fixed by the Court (Within Limits Set by Law), Minimum Fixed by Law.* This is the court-imposed variety of the definite sentence system. Effectively, the minimum is the period before parole eligibility, although it is not called a minimum sentence. Sometimes this period is a fraction of the sentence, sometimes it is a specific period of time such as 1 year, and sometimes it is either a fraction or a given number of years, whichever is least. There has been some contention that prison terms tend to be shortest in jurisdictions having this definite sentence system.[10] However, the differences are not consistent or extreme, and it has been argued that these differences occur because the jurisdictions with this system least often use probation; they impose short prison terms in cases which elsewhere would receive probation.[11]

This system is used exclusively or almost exclusively in 12 States. In 6 (Mississippi, Alabama, Louisiana, Oklahoma, Texas, and Rhode Island) and in the Federal system, a prisoner is eligible for parole at one-third of his definite term (except that in Alabama the period before parole eligibility cannot exceed 10 years). In Virginia, eligibility occurs at one-fourth of the sentence or 12 years, whichever is less, and in Delaware a prisoner can only be paroled after he serves half his sentence. In Florida, the parole board can release anyone after 6 months' confinement; in Connecticut, after 1 year for most offenses; and in Wisconsin, after half the sentence or 2 years, whichever is less. In Tennessee, the minimum varies more with the offense. This type of sentence is also used for some offenses in Arkansas, Idaho, Illinois, and South Carolina, where parole eligibility on definite sentences occurs at one-third of the sentence; in North Carolina, where eligibility occurs at one-fourth of the sentence; and in Indiana, where parole can occur after 1 year is served.

On the whole, States predominantly employing this system parole a smaller proportion of their prison inmates than do most other States, but they vary greatly in this respect. Of the States using this system exclusively, Connecticut paroled 92 percent of its first releases from prison in 1961, Wisconsin 82 percent, Louisiana 72 percent, Texas 53 percent, Rhode Island 42 percent, Florida 40 percent, Virginia 37 percent, Alabama 33 percent, Delaware 32 percent, Mississippi and Tennessee 31 percent, and Oklahoma only 18 percent. However, all except Mississippi have shorter than average sentences, and half are below the national average in the average time served by first releasees.

4. *Maximum Term Fixed by Law for Each Offense, But Minimum Term Fixed by the Court.* This is the system in Hawaii and Mich-

[10] Sol Rubin, "Long Prison Terms and the Form of Sentence," *National Probation and Parole Association Journal*, vol. 2, No. 4 (October 1956), pp. 337–351.
[11] Paul W. Tappan, "Sentencing Under the Model Penal Code," *Law and Contemporary Problems*, vol. 23, No. 3 (summer 1958), pp. 528–543, at page 537.

12

igan. In Hawaii, a convicted person automatically receives the statutory maximum sentence for his offense, and is then sent to prison, where he receives a parole board hearing within 3 months. This is for the purpose of recommending a minimum sentence to the court. The court has final discretion as to what the minimum sentence will be, and the prisoner is eligible for parole upon completion of this minimum.

In Michigan, the court fixes the minimum at the time of trial and the maximum is imposed automatically by law. Theoretically, this permits the court to fix the minimum close to the maximum, but in practice this rarely occurs. This system encourages bargaining for a charge carrying a low maximum. For example, in Michigan, the offense of burglary in the night carries a heavier maximum penalty than plain burglary, so offenders resisting prosecution under the former charge are frequently allowed to plead guilty to plain burglary even when their offense occurred after 10 o'clock at night.

In 1961, Hawaii paroled 84 percent of its prisoners at their first release and Michigan paroled 90 percent. The average time served before first release in 1960 was 26 months in Michigan and 38 months in Hawaii.

5. *Maximum and Minimum Sentence Fixed by Law for Each Offense.* Under this system, the court has no formal part in selecting a sentence once it finds a man guilty, although informally, the court's interest in the sentence may determine the charge on which a man is convicted. This system is used exclusively or predominantly in eight States: Ohio, West Virginia, Indiana, Kansas, North and South Dakota, New Mexico, and Nevada. It is also used under some circumstances in Maryland and in South Carolina.

The proportion paroled varies somewhat for these States. In 1961, Ohio paroled 96 percent of first releases, West Virginia 89 percent, Indiana 87 percent, while South Carolina paroled only 13 percent and Nevada 15 percent. These States also were diverse, but generally below the national average, in the average duration of confinement before first release in 1960, ranging from a low of 17 months in South Dakota and 22 months in Kansas, North Dakota, and Nevada, to a high of 34 months in Indiana, 33 months in West Virginia, and 31 months in Ohio.

6. *Maximum Terms Fixed by Law for Each Offense, No Minimum Sentence, But Minimum Term Set by Parole Board at an Early Hearing Is Equivalent to Minimum Sentence.* This is known as the "administrative sentencing" or "sentencing tribunal" system. It is used in California, Washington, Utah, and Iowa, and is optional in the Federal system. It is also used in Maryland for females and for males under 26 sentenced to the reformatory. In Washington, the parole agency appropriately is called the "Board of Prison Terms

and Paroles." [12]   Under this system the court may recommend a specific period of incarceration, but this recommendation is not binding on the board. When, as in California and Washington, the board reaches a decision in the first few months of a prisoner's confinement as to the minimum period before a regular hearing for parole consideration can be held, this period is, in effect, the minimum sentence. This decision on the minimum period may be reviewed on petition or complaint, and may be changed upward or downward, but usually it remains unaltered.

Sometimes the initial term-fixing decision tends to be interpreted as a promise to parole at the end of the term unless the prisoner's behavior is extremely unsatisfactory during this period. This decreases the strength of the argument for parole as a means of deferring decision on duration of confinement. States with this system usually also have a minimum imprisonment period fixed by law for a few of the more heinous offenses.

Washington paroled over 98 percent of their prisoners on first release from prison in 1961, California paroled 93 percent, Utah paroled 67 percent, and Iowa paroled 56 percent. These are all States which confine their prisoners for a relatively longer period before first release; the average duration of such confinement in 1960 was 30 months in California, Washington, and Utah, and 36 months in Iowa.

7. *Maximum Sentence Fixed by Court, No Minimum Sentence.* When the court sets a high maximum sentence, such as almost guarantees that the first release will be by parole, this system approximates administrative sentencing in the extent to which the parole board determines the effective sentence. This system is found exclusively in Oregon, Missouri, and Minnesota, and it predominates in Idaho. Minnesota, with 78 percent, was the highest of these four States in proportion of first releases by parole during 1961; Missouri had only 30 percent and Oregon 37 percent, while Idaho had 59 percent. Minnesota is a State of high confinement before first release from prison, their average in 1960 being 37 months, while the other States confine somewhat more briefly than most, the 1960 average being 25 months in Missouri, 22 months in Oregon, and 20 months in Idaho.

8. *Law Fixes Minimum Sentence, Maximum Period Before First Parole, and Maximum Sentence.* This describes the Youth Correction Act sentencing option in Federal courts, under which offenders below age 26 may receive a 6-year sentence from which they are eligible for parole after 60 days, and from which they must be paroled once before 4 years. The parole board also may discharge them from their sentence before 6 years. This is modeled on the British Borstal sentence. This system guarantees that all first releases are by parole.

---

[12] Norman Hayner, "Sentencing by an Administrative Board," *Law and Contemporary Problems*, vol. 23, No. 32 (summer 1958), pp. 477–494.

14

9. *Law Prescribes That Inmate Shall Be Under Correctional Supervision Until He Reaches a Given Age, Unless Discharged from the Sentence Earlier, and May Be Paroled at Any Time.* The California Youth Authority and the Minnesota Youth Conservation Commission may receive any offender under 21 years of age and subject to more than 90 days' confinement, and they maintain authority over these persons until age 25. Such inmates may be paroled immediately, but in practice, 60 days or more is likely to elapse before they have been observed adequately to permit a decision to parole them, and almost all have their first release by parole. Therefore, this sentence, in its effects, is very similar to the Federal Youth Correction Act.

This ninth type of sentence is analogous to the system under which juvenile delinquents are committed to training, reform, or industrial schools from juvenile courts in most of our States and under the Federal Juvenile Delinquency Act. They usually cannot be committed for acts done after a specified age (generally 18), but they can be confined to age 21, and may be paroled at any time before then. In terms of legal status, however, these juveniles are neither convicted nor sentenced—they are adjudged delinquent and made wards of the State—although in practice the court may ascribe criminal acts to them and commit them to a correctional institution.

PART III—THE MODEL PENAL CODE AND THE MODEL SENTENCING ACT

In characterizing the results of sentencing processes employed in the United States today, there is considerable agreement among most legal and correctional experts that sentences generally are too long and irrational criteria are used in individualizing sentences. There is also widespread agreement on the need for increased use of community (nonprison) dispositions for offenders. However, there is less consensus about the proper allocation of authority between the legislature, judiciary, and administrative boards. In addition, differences over basic policy on sentencing and the function of parole are encountered. These differences are well illustrated by two recent legislative proposals.[13]

The American Law Institute (ALI) and the Advisory Council of Judges of the National Council on Crime and Delinquency (NCCD) have formulated model legislation which has a significant impact on the parole function. The ALI's Model Penal Code and NCCD's Model Sentencing Act promise to exert considerable influence in States concerned with revision of their criminal law. A discussion of their major features concerning the sentencing structure and the parole function is of interest because of the difference of approach as well as a glimpse of possible future trends.

The Model Penal Code [14]

The Model Penal Code probably is the most ambitious legislative undertaking in the history of American criminal law. Its four major divisions deal with general principles, definitions of specific crimes, treatment and correction, and organization of correction. The code's approach to sentencing and correction is understandable only when significant features from other sections are articulated.

---

[13] See, for example, Herbert Wechsler. "Sentencing, Correction, and the Model Penal Code," *University of Pennsylvania Law Review*, vol. 109 (1961) pp. 465–469; Sol Rubin, "Sentencing and Correctional Treatment Under the Law Institute's Model Penal Code," *American Bar Association Journal*, vol. 46 (1960), p. 994.

[14] Unless otherwise noted, all references are to ALI, Model Penal Code (proposed official draft, May 4, 1962). Hereinafter referred to as the code.

The code states that its provisions on sentencing and treatment of offenders are designed to prevent crimes, promote correction and rehabilitation of offenders, safeguard offenders against excessive, disproportionate or arbitrary punishment, give fair warning of possible sentences, obtain just individualization among offenders, and advance the use of scientific methods and knowledge.[15] To help achieve these goals, the code redefines and reclassifies offenses for purposes of criminal responsibility and sentencing.

All the major crimes are distributed among three degrees of felony.[16] Lesser offenses are divided into misdemeanors and petty misdemeanors.[17] The code is premised on the assumption that the length and nature of the authorized sentence must rest in large measure on the seriousness of the crime. Rejected is the notion that sentencing must rest solely on the character of the offender.[18]

The sentencing judge is urged to give strong consideration to the granting of probation.[19] He may impose a fine, suspend the imposition of sentence, or combinations of these, or impose a term of imprisonment.[20]

The basic sentencing structure of the code requires that all convicted felons, not otherwise disposed of, receive a term of imprisonment the minimum of which is a term of 1 year or more and the maximum imposed by law. While the sentencing judge has no discretion on the maximum terms and must impose at least a 1-year minimum term, he may increase the minimum within the limits seen in the following table:

---

[15] ALI, code § 1.02(2). This section also includes the goals of harmonizing the functions of courts and administrative agencies and integration of the correctional system into a single department or agency.

[16] ALI, code §§ 1.04, 6.01. Only the most serious felonies are of the first degree. However, aggravating circumstances may move an offense into a higher degree of felony. For example, forcible rape is a felony, second degree. If serious bodily injury is inflicted or the actor had no prior sexual relationship with the victim then the offense is a felony, first degree. Burglary is a felony, third degree, unless perpetrated in the dwelling of another at night, or bodily injury is attempted or inflicted, or the felon is armed with explosives or a deadly weapon. In the latter event, burglary becomes a felony, second degree.

[17] ALI, code § 1.04. There is still another category, denominated a violation, for which the gravest sanction is a fine and which carries with it no stigma of criminality. *Ibid.*

[18] See commentary, ALI, Code § 6.01 (tentative draft No. 2, 1954).

[19] ALI, code § 7.01 which also identifies specific criteria to be used in granting probation. Persons convicted of murder receive either death, § 210.6, or life imprisonment, § 6.01.

[20] ALI, code § 6.02. The court may impose a 30-day term of imprisonment as a condition of probation.

	Minimum	Maximum
Felony, first degree	Not less than 1, nor more than 10	life
Felony, second degree	Not less than 1, nor more than 3	10
Felony, third degree	Not less than 1, nor more than 2	5

The drafters of the code believe that the judge should have some control of the minimum mainly for deterrent purposes. They believe the deterrent factor looms largest at the time of sentencing, and the judge is in the best position to evaluate the deterrent possibilities of a required minimum term of imprisonment.[22] The rationale given for at least a 1-year minimum in any case is that such a period, less any "good time," is necessary for the prison's program of classification, brief treatment, and parole preparation.[23]

The fixed maximum seeks to eliminate inequality in court-imposed sentences, reflect the moral condemnation for a particular offense, and maintain some kind of balance between the *a priori* legislative decision, court decision, and correctional decision.

To accommodate the critics of the fixed maximum sentence, the ALI council has approved an alternate provision under which the court would be empowered to set shorter maxima within the same statutory limits as described in the above table. However, the minimum may not be longer than one-half the maximum, or, when the maximum is life imprisonment, longer than 10 years.[24]

For years penologists have been concerned with devising a legal sentencing structure which separates sensibly the dangerous from the nondangerous offender. Lengthy terms of imprisonment based exclusively on the offense, or even the number of offenses, have not been satisfactory. The code expresses the view that a distinction should be drawn between ordinary and extended terms for the same crime based on the character of the offender.[25] However, the offender's character largely is determined by past criminality.

---

[21] ALI, code § 6.06. A "Huber law" approach is available to misdemeanants § 303.9.

[22] Commentary, ALI, code § 6.07 (tentative draft No. 2, 1954). See footnote 47, *infra* for a comment on the judge as an evaluator of the offender's blameworthiness.

[23] See Herbert Wechsler, "Sentencing, Correction, and the Model Penal Code," *op, cit.*; Paul Tappan, "Sentencing Under the Model Penal Code," *op. cit.*

[24] ALI, code section alternate 6.06. Sec. 6.12 gives the court discretion, having regard to the characteristics of the offense and the offender, to enter a judgment of conviction for a lesser degree of felony or for a misdemeanor and impose sentence accordingly. If judges are not reluctant to use this section, it may provide the flexibility lacking in the basic sentencing structure.

[25] Commentary, ALI, code § 6.07 (tentative draft No. 2, 1954).

Extended terms of imprisonment may be imposed if the offender is over 21 and a "persistent offender" or a "professional criminal" whose extended imprisonment is necessary for protection of the public. In addition, an extended term may be imposed on one who psychiatrically is diagnosed as a "dangerous, mentally abnormal person." [26] A "multiple offender whose criminality was so extensive" that an extended term is warranted may be so sentenced without regard to age (although he must be above juvenile court age), or a finding of danger to the public.[27]

Imposition of an extended term is discretionary with the judge and subject to specific criteria which must be incorporated in the record. The sentencing alternatives available as extended terms are as follows:

Felony, Extended Term [28]

Minimum

Felony, first degree	Not less than 5 years, nor more than 10 years.
Felony, second degree	Not less than 1 year, nor more than 5 years.
Felony, third degree	Not less than 1 year, nor more than 3 years.

Maximum

Felony, first degree	Life.
Felony, second degree	Not less than 10 years, nor more than 20 years.
Felony, third degree	Not less than 5 years, nor more than 10 years.

A presentence investigation and report are required in nearly all cases and the court must disclose the factual contents and conclusions to the defendant or his counsel before imposing sentence.[29] The judge may delay imposing sentence, if additional information is required; up to 1 year after imposing sentence, he may resentence, if he feels he misapprehended the defendant's character.[30]

At present the parole board's power to make the parole decision depends on the leeway left after the court has acted within legis-

---

[26] ALI, code § 7.03. The psychiatric conclusions must indicate he is mentally abnormal; that his criminal conduct has been characterized by a pattern of repetitive or compulsive behavior or by persistent aggressive behavior with heedless indifference to consequence; and that such condition makes him a serious danger to others. This section apparently could include the sociopath who is excluded from a successful insanity defense by the code's definition. See code § 4.01(2) "As used in this article, the terms 'mental disease or defect' do not include an abnormality manifested only by repeated criminal or otherwise anti-social conduct."

[27] ALI, code § 7.03. This section should be consulted for the detailed criteria applicable to each type of offender. Misdemeanors, not discussed here, are subject to extend terms under §§ 6.09, 7.04.

The court may not impose an extended term unless on written notice and after a hearing. § 7.07(6).

[28] ALI, code § 6.07.

[29] ALI, code § 7.07.

[30] ALI, code § 7.08.

latively defined limits. In some States parole is absolutely prohibited for persons sentenced for specified felonies or to a life term.[31] Generally, parole eligibility occurs when some fraction of the maximum term is served—one-third or one-half—or at the end of the minimum, sometimes less good time.

Uniformly, under existing law, the maximum term of imprisonment is the key to determining the length of imprisonment, the time within which parole must be granted, if at all, and the duration of parole and reconfinement after violation of parole. There, of course, are variations among the States but the maximum term is a fundamental part of our traditional frame of reference on all these issues. A clean break with this tradition occurs in the code by the creation of two separate terms: (1) a term of imprisonment; (2) a term of parole.

Under the code, the prison term determines the minimum period that must be served and the maximum period that may be served in prison prior to parole (or conditional release).[32] Every felony sentence of imprisonment includes a separate term of parole or recommitment for violation of parole. It is this term, not the original maximum imposed, which governs the duration of parole or recommitment. The minimum of such term is 1 year and the maximum is 5 years.[33]

An important objective to the drafters of the code is the requirement that the first release of all felony offenders be on parole.[34] Since the parole term is distinct from the prison term, some modification of the traditional definition of parole is required. Under the code, parole describes the possible release and supervision of an offender from a correctional institution prior to the maximum permissible term of confinement and the required period of supervision for all persons who are released even at the expiration of their maximum term of confinement. What the code terms parole, appears to be a blend of traditional parole

[31] See Sol Rubin *et al. The Law of Criminal Correction, op. cit.,* chapter 15. Only 14 jurisdictions in the United States establish no statutory exclusion on parole eligibility. Commentary, ALI, code § 305.10 (tentative draft No. 5. 1956).

[32] See commentary ALI, code § 6.09A (tentative draft No. 5, 1956). The term "conditional release" actually is used in the sense described in the above text, and that which follows.

[33] ALI, code § 6.10(2). There is considerable difference in the final draft and the first draft which keyed parole duration to time actually served in prison. This allowed for a considerably longer period of potential control. See ALI, code § 6.09A (tentative draft No. 5, 1956). For a critique of the earlier proposal, see Will Turnbladh, "A Critique of the Model Penal Code Sentencing Proposals," *Law and Contemporary Problems,* vol. 23 (1958), pp. 544–551.

[34] ALI, code § 6.10. It is conceivable that one convicted of a felony, second degree, could serve 10 years in prison and 5 years on parole.

and conditional release on "good time" credits.[35] The significant difference with ordinary conditional release is the absence of a relationship to the maximum term of confinement in determining the potential duration of parole or recommitment.

An example may clarify the code's approach to parole. A person convicted for a felony, second degree, sentenced under the ordinary terms, could receive a 2-year minimum and must receive a 10-year maximum. Parole may be granted after 2 years, less any earned good time,[36] and we shall assume parole is granted after actual imprisonment of 3 years. After 2 years on parole, the parolee is revoked for violation of conditions of parole.[37] The question is, how long may this person be required to remain in prison?

Section 305.17 states he "shall be recommitted for the remainder of his maximum parole term, after credit thereon for the period served on parole prior to the violation and for reductions for good behavior earned while on parole."[38] We must consider the term of imprisonment and term of parole as entirely separate provisions, and thus the unexpired 7 years of the original term of imprisonment is of no consequence in determining the duration of recommitment. Therefore, the maximum unexpired parole term which will govern the duration of commitment is 3 years, less approximately 5 months' good time which may have been earned and not forfeited, or 2 years and 7 months.[39] To round out the picture, and without accounting for good-time credits, it is conceivable that this person could serve 10 years in prison and 5 years under parole supervision.

The Model Sentencing Act [40]

The Model Sentencing Act is limited to the appropriate disposition of the offender. There is no attempt to redefine general principles of criminal law or specific offenses, or to suggest the appropriate organiza-

---

[35] In several jurisdictions, notably the Federal jurisdiction, a prisoner released on good-time credits must remain under supervision and on conditions as though on parole. See Sol Rubin *et al.*, *The Law of Criminal Correction, op. cit.*, p. 312.

[36] ALI, code § 305.1.

[37] See ALI, code § 305.15 for detailed procedures on revocation of parole.

[38] ALI code § 305.2 provides that, for good conduct while on parole, the parole term shall be reduced by 6 days for each month of such parole term. This is deducted from the minimum and maximum parole term. Sec. 305.4(2) provides that reductions of parole terms for good behavior may be forfeited, withheld, and restored by the board of parole.

[39] The code provides special treatment for young adult (16 to 21) offenders. This will not be discussed. See ALI, code § 6.05.

[40] All references are to the official draft of the Model Sentencing Act, hereinafter referred to as the act, printed, with comments, in *Crime and Delinquency*, vol. 9 (1963), 345 *et seq*. The Model Sentencing Act has also been published by NCCD in a separate pamphlet.

tion of correctional systems.[41]   It is anticipated that application of the act will cause improvement in existing systems.[42]

For purposes of sentencing, the act identifies first degree murder, felonies, dangerous offenders, youthful offenders and, in an optional section, atrocious crimes.   Misdemeanors are not included.[43]

The Model Sentencing Act states that persons convicted of crime shall be dealt with in accordance with their individual characteristics, circumstances, needs and potentialities as revealed by case studies.[44] Dangerous offenders are to be correctively treated for long terms as needed and other offenders treated otherwise than by institutional confinement, subject to a balancing of the individual's needs and the public safety.[45]   Thus a conscious preference for probation, suspended sentence, or fines is stated and institutionalization becomes a secondary technique.

In general, the act seeks to avoid the traditionally intimate relationship between the specific definition of the offense and the sentencing or parole decision.   The exceptions are the persons who commit murder and are to be committed for a term of life and the optional section on atrocious crimes, declared to be a contradiction to the act's philosophy of sentencing the offender. which identifies serious felonies for extended terms of imprisonment.[46]

Upon a verdict or plea of guilty, the court may, with the defendant's consent, grant probation without entering an adjudication of guilt. Upon fulfillment of the terms of probation, the defendant is discharged and thus the stigma of criminality may be avoided in a proper case.[47]

If a term of imprisonment is to be imposed for an ordinary felony (i.e., not dangerous as defined by the act), the court imposes a maxi-

[41] NCCD, and its predecessor organization, National Probation and Parole Association, have formulated model legislation in related areas.   See, for example, Annulment of a Conviction of Crime (A Model Act), Standard Family Court Act, Standard Juvenile Court Act, and Standard Probation and Parole Act. In progress is a Standard Act for State Correctional Services described in *Current Projects in the Prevention, Control, and Treatment of Crime and Delinquency*, vol. IV (1963–64), p. 112.

[42] See Sol Rubin, "The Model Sentencing Act," *New York University Law Review* (April 1964), pp. 251–262.

[43] In order to parallel the coverage given the Model Penal Code, misdemeanants and youthful offenders will not further be discussed.   Atrocious crimes are: murder, second degree; arson; forcible rape; armed robbery; mayhem; and bombing of an airplane, vehicle, vessel, building or other structure.

[44] NCCD, act § 1.

[45] Criteria for determining dangerous offenders are set out in § 5.

[46] See comments to NCCD, act, optional § 8.

[47] NCCD, act § 9.   This applies to "felonies generally."   The court may enter judgment, suspend the sentence and release defendant with or without probationary supervision.   There is no comparable provision in the code.

mum term not to exceed 5 years with no minimum term.[48] If the optional section on atrocious crimes is adopted, then the court may impose a term of years not to exceed 10. Again, no minimum term is fixed. The court has the option to commit the defendant to a local correctional facility for a term of 1 year or less.[49]

The act creates a separate category for identifying and sentencing the dangerous offender. Such an offender may be sentenced to a term of imprisonment up to 30 years, with no minimum sentence, if: (1) he is convicted of a felony (except murder in the first degree); and (2) the court finds extended confinement is necessary to protect the public and the further finding is made that: (a) the felony involved the infliction or attempt to inflict serious bodily injury and he is suffering from a severe personality disorder indicating a propensity toward crime; or (b) the defendant has committed a crime which seriously endangered another's life or safety, he has a prior conviction for any crime, and he is suffering from a severe personality disorder indicating a propensity toward crime; or (c) the defendant is being sentenced for the crime of extortion, compulsory prostitution, trafficking in narcotics, or other felony, committed as part of a continuing criminal activity with others.[50]

The dangerous recidivist or the assaultive single offender may be sentenced to prolonged imprisonment if a serious mental disorder is demonstrated by a psychiatric diagnosis at the hearing on the sentence. This finding, and the finding of professional criminality, must be incorporated in the record and would be subject to appellate review. The recidivist who has not seriously endangered anyone's life or safety must be sentenced as an ordinary felon.

The act has excluded from the possibility of receiving extended terms of imprisonment persons who commit such offenses as theft, embezzlement, burglary, or forgery. Persons who commit these offenses—without regard to frequency, extent of loss or personality characteristics—are to be handled as ordinary felons. The optional section on atrocious crimes, with the exception of arson, is keyed only to acts which threaten or impose serious bodily harm.

The act requires the extensive use of presentence investigations and reports.[51] The judge may disclose the report, or parts of it, to the defendant if the sentencing is for felonies generally, and he must if

---

[48] NCCD, act § 9.

[49] *Ibid.* The comments suggest a "Huber law" approach for such commitments to enable the person to leave the institution and seek and pursue employment, education, medical treatment or attend to domestic duties. See ALI, code § 303.9, for a similar arrangement available only to misdemeanants.

[50] NCCD, act § 5.

[51] NCCD, act §§ 2, 3, and 4.

24

the sentencing is for first degree murder or under the dangerous offender section.[52]

A sentence may be reduced by the court within 90 days after it is imposed.[53] Material newly discovered by the court services or the institution may influence the judge to reassess his prior determination.

The Model Sentencing Act permits the parole board to grant parole for any offender at any time.[54] One of the major purposes of the act is to create a legal structure that does not infringe on or limit the discretion of the parole board.[55] Relatively few States permit release of offenders anytime after they begin their terms.[56] Thus the act represents a clean break with parole laws in most jurisdictions.

This position is a departure from NPPA's Standard Probation and Parole Act of 1955. That act provided for parole eligibility "after service of the minimum term of sentence, less such work and good behavior credits as have been earned—or, where such term was not imposed, at any time . . ."[57]

The act does not specify the length of time a person may be kept under parole supervision, when the authorities may dispense with supervision or when the board may discharge. It is reasonable to assume that the parole authority may be exercised until expiration of the maximum term of imprisonment and that the extent and duration of supervision is deemed a discretionary matter for the parole authority.[58]

Variations in the Code and Act

Both proposals seek to bring humanistic and rational techniques to the problem of sentencing criminal offenders. Since common agreement on the basic goals of criminal law often is lacking, one would not expect agreement on the implementation of goals. The preceding discussion of the proper legal structure for sentencing and the responsibilities of the legislature, judiciary and administrative boards has demonstrated that these issues are subject to a variety of opinions among even the experts.

---

[52] NCCD, act § 4. Disclosure undoubtedly would be made to counsel and the defendant.

[53] NCCD, act § 11.

[54] NCCD, act § 13.

[55] NCCD, act comments to §§ 1 and 13.

[56] Georgia, Idaho, Iowa, Minnesota, Oregon, Missouri, and Utah. See commentary, ALI, code § 305.10 (tentative draft No. 5, 1956).

[57] NPPA, Standard Probation and Parole Act, § 18. Of course, as the text indicates, if no minimum term is imposed—the scheme of the act—then parole eligibility occurs anytime.

[58] NPPA, Standard Probation and Parole Act § 27 provides that the board may not discharge from parole within a period of less than 1 year after release unless the sentence expires in that time.

The area of sentencing alternatives and their consequent impact on parole illustrates the different approaches of the code and the act. The following are the more fundamental differences:

1. The act permits probation on a plea or finding of guilt without an adjudication of guilt by the court.[59]

2. The act is committed to somewhat shorter terms of imprisonment and supervision.[60]

3. The act does not provide for a minimum term of imprisonment while the code requires a 1-year minimum term or more for felonies.[61]

4. The code proposes a fixed maximum term of imprisonment for each of the three degrees of felony. Under the act, the court imposes a maximum term only within the statutory maximum.

5. The act more emphatically is committed to psychiatric evaluations before an extended term of imprisonment may be imposed on a dangerous offender.[62]

6. The act excludes from the possibility of extended terms of imprisonment those persons who commit offenses against property which neither threaten or impose bodily injury. Arson, under the optional section on atrocious crimes, is the exception.

7. The code requires that the first release of all offenders shall be by parole. The act would impose no parole supervision when release occurs upon expiration of the maximum term.

8. Under the code all terms of imprisonment include a separate term of parole. That is, the parole term is not carved from the term of imprisonment, and its only relationship to the traditionally important maximum term of imprisonment is to determine when a person must be released from prison.

---

[59] NCCD, act § 9. See ALI, code § 301.5 where, under given conditions, a judge who suspends sentence or grants probation, may provide that the conviction shall not result in any disqualification or disabiilty. Also see § 301.6.

[60] See Will Turnbladh, "A Critique of the Model Penal Code Sentencing Proposals," *op. cit.* Much of this criticism is nullified by subsequent changes in the code's final draft.

[61] Under the code, the judge has limited flexibility in setting the minimum, and undoubtedly he may use it to reflect his evaluation of the defendant and his conduct.

[62] Compare NCCD, act § 1.5 with ALI, code § 7.03. See code § 6.13 allowing for civil commitment of certain minor offenders in lieu of prosecution or sentence.

PERSONAL CHARACTERISTICS AND PAROLE OUTCOME

PART I.—INTRODUCTION

One of the principal roles of a parole board member is that of evaluator. He collects a large variety of information about an offender, and from this he must determine the risks in paroling that individual. What aspects of the case are favorable for parole outcome? What features are unfavorable? What other information is desirable? How can all the pros and cons best be combined into a single overall evaluation of each man?

When discussing the evaluation of a parolee's postrelease prospects, frequent references are made to statistics on the relative "success" or "failure" rates of various types of parolees. Since there are many objectives in parole, there can be numerous standards from which to assess parole "success." However, at this point we shall use somewhat broad criteria of parole outcome.

Parole is applied to persons who have committed crimes serious enough to justify the State's taking measures to confine them. Since parole is a conditional release from this confinement, the primary index of parole "success" used here will be negative, that the parolee's behavior does not provide State action to revoke his parole and again to confine him.

Statistics will be presented on the relationship of various characteristics of parolees to their post-release success. These statistics will be drawn from several different jurisdictions. However, it should be noted that overall parole success rates vary from one State to the next as a result of many characteristics of parole policy. For example, in States which parole only a small proportion of their prisoners, just the best risks may be paroled, so one expects that their violation rates will be lower than those of States which parole nearly all prisoners. Similarly, if the parole period is long or parole supervision is close, one expects that officials will know of more violations than would be reported under the opposite conditions.

In addition, there are many issues involved in the definition of parole violation. One agency might well return more parolees to institutions as violators than another, but because of a vigorous supervision program, proportionately fewer of those returned have committed new crimes. Differences between systems regarding the action taken in the cases of absconders or parolees given jail terms are also examples of variations in policy which can account for significant differences in "violation rates" when, in fact, the rates may be quite similar or even reversed.

1

Variations, like the above, should be borne in mind in examining the data presented here. Consequently, the statistics presented *cannot be employed to compare accurately overall violation rates between jurisdictions*, but only violation rate trends in different categories of parolees within the jurisdictions cited. For example, we can probe whether the younger parolees have higher violation rates than older ones or whether intelligence is related to parole violations citing data from several systems.

The following is a brief description of the principal sources of statistical data presented. Each is given below the title by which it will be cited:

1. *Wisconsin Parolees:* This information consists of separately tabulated data on 2,255 adult males, 206 adult females, 1,037 juvenile males, and 453 juvenile females who comprise all persons released on parole from Wisconsin's Division of Corrections from January 1, 1952, through December 31, 1954. The violation rate is based on every person whose parole was revoked, or who was again committed to a Wisconsin penal institution or placed on probation following discharge from parole, within 2 years of his release on parole. These tabulations were made available to us by the late John W. Mannering, Chief of the Bureau of Research of the Wisconsin Department of Public Welfare.

2. *New York Adult Parolees:* This information consists of separately tabulated data on 7,636 males and 738 females who comprise all parolees released on original parole by the New York Division of Parole in 1958 and 1959. The violation rate is based on those prisoners in this group who were declared "delinquent" on their parole during 1958, 1959, or 1960. These tabulations are published in the *Thirty-Second Annual Report of the Division of Parole of the Executive Department*, New York Legislative Department, 1962, No. 11, pp. 65–93.

3. *Minnesota Adult Male Parolees:* These data cover 525 men paroled from the Minnesota State Prison during 1957 and 1958. The violation rates are based on the number whose parole was rescinded within 1 year of release. These tabulations are reported in Robert Bergherr, James Brusseau, William McRae, and Richard Samelian, "Parole Success and Failure: A Study of the Influence of Selected Socio-Economic and Personal Factors and Their Effect on Parole Outcome," M.S.W. Thesis, University of Minnesota, 1962. This thesis was made available to us by Dr. Nathan G. Mandel, Director of Research, and Ira Phillips, Librarian, Minnesota Division of Correction.

4. *California Youth Authority Male Parolees:* These data cover 3,046 males released on parole during 1961 from their first admission to a California Youth Authority institution. The violation rate is based on all parole revocations occurring within

15 months of release, including both those returned to the institution, and those who were discharged from parole when under suspension, because they had committed either a parole rule violation or new offense. This tabulation was made available to us by Dr. Keith S. Griffiths, Chief of Research, California Youth Authority.

5. *Federal Adult Male Releasees:* These data cover 1,015 men who comprise a 10-percent systematic sample of all adult males released from Federal prisons on a sentence of over 1 year during 1956. These include men released from prison by expiration of sentence or by mandatory release, as well as parolees. "Failure" rates are based on all men returned to prison, for a new offense or for parole or mandatory release rule violation, as well as those men convicted of a felony-type offense or wanted for parole violation but not reimprisoned, by summer of 1959. This study is reported in Daniel Glaser, *The Effectiveness of a Prison and Parole System*, Indianapolis: Bobbs-Merrill, 1963, primarily in chapters 2 and 3.

6. *Illinois Adult Parolees:* These data cover 955 men paroled from the Joliet-Stateville and Menard branches of the Illinois State Penitentiary during 1960. Violation rates are based on warrants issued through July 1, 1962. This study is reported in Illinois Department of Public Safety, Division of the Criminologist, *Bulletin of the Sociologist-Actuary*, No. 3, June 14, 1963.

7. *Illinois Youthful Male Parolees:* These data cover 2,693 men paroled from the Pontiac branch of the Illinois State Penitentiary in 1940–49. It excludes men paroled to the Armed Forces. This is an institution for "young and improvable" male offenders; these men had an average age of 24.1 years at parole. Violation rates are based on warrants issued through 1952. This study is reported fully in Daniel Glaser, "A Reformulation and Testing of Parole Prediction Factors," Ph.D. Thesis, University of Chicago, 1954, and more briefly in articles by the same author appearing in the *American Sociological Review* in 1954 and 1955.

8. *Washington Adult Parolees:* These data cover 1,731 persons who comprise all prisoners paroled from Washington State penal facilities from July 1957 through June 1959. Only 53 were women and data for this group were not tabulated separately. Violation rates are based on all persons whose parole was suspended for absconding, technical violation, or being in custody on a felony charge, between the date of their release and December 31, 1959. This study is reported in Washington State Board of Prison Terms and Paroles, *Adult Parolee Study*, August 1960.

Each table presented includes data from every one of the above studies which had information on the topic covered. However, the only topic on which every one of these studies had some information was the relationship between type of offense and postrelease violation, summarized in table 4. Whenever there are no cases in a particular category of our tables from one of the studies, this is indicated by a line in the violation rate column; whenever there are some cases, but no violators (usually because there were very few cases), this is indicated by the entry "0%."

4

PART II.—GROSS PERSONAL CHARACTERISTICS AND PAROLE OUTCOME

The first information available on prisoners is that which most immediately identifies them. These are facts which generally can be learned quickly, such as sex, race, age, offense, prior criminal record, intelligence, and body dimensions. Some of these attributes, for example, the offense and criminal record, may actually have intricate variations. However, we shall first consider them as broad categories into which inmates may be classified soon after they reach the prison. This chapter is concerned with the parole prognosis value of this gross information by which prisoners may be divided into the young and the old, the thieves and the murderers, the first offenders and the repeaters, and so forth.

Age

One of the most firmly established pieces of statistical knowledge about criminals is that the older a man is when he is released from prison, the less likely he is to return to crime. By no means should it be inferred that all old prisoners are good risks or all youngsters poor risks. Nevertheless, as table 1 shows, for all parolees taken collectively, the older they are at release the less likely they are to fail on parole.

Table 1 indicates that the parole violation rate predominantly decreases as the age at parole increases, although there is some deviation from perfect consistency in this relationship. Such findings have been reported for many decades, and in numerous jurisdictions, both in the United States and abroad.[1] A related finding is that, as age at release increases, it is increasingly likely that if any further criminality occurs, it will be a misdemeanor rather than a felony.[2]

The easiest interpretation of this finding is that people become less criminal as they become more mature. Such an interpretation only has much validity if the word "mature" is used primarily in

---

[1] Thorsten Sellin, "Recidivism and Maturation," *National Probation and Parole Association Journal*, Vol. 4, No. 3 (July 1958), pp. 241–250; Barbara Wooton, *Social Science and Social Pathology*, New York: Macmillan, 1959, chapter 5.

[2] California Director of Corrections and Adult Authority, *California Male Prisoners Released on Parole 1946–49*, p. 23 and p. 46 (tables 7 and 31). These tables indicate felony and misdemeanor violations separately, for first paroles and for reparoles, by year of birth.

Table 1.—Postrelease Violation Rates in Relation to Age at Release

Wisconsin parolees

Age at release	Juvenile		Age at release	Adult	
	Males	Females		Males	Females
	Percent	Percent		Percent	Percent
12 to 13	78	67	Under 20	31	40
14	54	58	20 to 24	37	26
15	58	40	25 to 29	41	13
16	50	33	30 to 34	40	23
17	44	40	35 to 39	34	29
18 and over	41	34	40 to 49	29	14
			50 to 59	28	50
			60 and over	21	---------
Rates for all cases	50	39		36	23
Number of cases	1,037	453		2,255	206

New York adult parolees / Federal adult male releasees

Age at release	Males	Females	Age at release	Failure rate
	Percent	Percent		Percent
20 years or less	36	43	18 to 19	51
21 to 25	38	54	20 to 21	46
26 to 30	41	48	22 to 23	42
31 to 35	39	41	24 to 25	38
36 to 40	38	26	26 to 30	36
41 to 45	29	22	31 to 35	30
46 to 50	32	---------	36 to 40	28
51 to 55	25	17	41 to 49	25
55 and over	18	9	50 and over	29
Rates for all cases	37	43		35
Number of cases	7,626	738		1,015

Note: The violation rates shown in this table, as in all other tables, are based on the number of "failures on parole" for all reasons. For example, the following are included in these rates: new commitments, serious violations of parole rules such as absconding, and preventive actions on the part of parole authorities such as warrants issued for failure by individuals to abide by stipulated parole conditions.

a nonbiological sense. Criminals generally are at least as well developed physically as the average person of their age. They can only be considered immature by defining normal maturation as change from delinquent youth to noncriminal adulthood.

It will suffice at this point to observe that the age group which has the highest crime rates in most industrialized societies is the vaguely defined one which is in transition between childhood and adulthood. These are the people we call "adolescents." For them to become adults, in the sense that others treat them as adults, requires not just physical maturation, but the acquisition of a self-sufficient position in the adult economic and social world. Prisoners tend to be persons who have failed in the past and may be handicapped in the future in achieving this transition, although most of them eventually do become self-sufficient in a legitimate adult life.

These data have two important general implications for parole policy in dealing with youthful offenders.

First is the emphasis on change. It is the consensus of both statistical analysis and personal impressions of experienced officials that youth are the least predictable of all prisoners. Although they have high rates of return to crime, this rate diminishes as they mature, and it is hard to predict when their criminal careers may end. They are in a period in which old associates and points of view may suddenly be dropped, and new ones gained. Innumerable cases can be cited where marriage, new employment, or other incidents marked a turning point which was followed by the complete metamorphosis of such offenders. Many individuals with long histories of juvenile crime, including acts of violence and drug addiction, are now leading respectable and law-abiding lives.[3]

The second implication is that youth are particularly in need of new paths to follow toward a secure and satisfying life. Frequently, they have only had gratification in delinquent pursuits, and have only felt at ease and important in a delinquent social world. Simply to release such a youth unconditionally, to give him "another chance" with no prospect that he will enter a new social and occupational world, is likely to be futile. Placing such a youth where he may have new and satisfying legitimate achievements which contribute to his self-sufficiency, and new types of contacts among his peers, is much preferable to merely "giving him a buck" by parole. A feasible school or work program, or a combination of the two, and a home in which the youth feels "at home," are ideal ingredients for rehabilitating a youthful criminal. While it is easy to state these desirable resources, their procurement is difficult. Frequently, relatives of youth make rash promises for parole placement which they do not intend to keep, or for which neither they nor the youth are adequately prepared. This includes both home and job arrangement.

Even where ideal placement seems to be guaranteed, success is never certain. Invariably, some youth will not perceive a work or school program as feasible for them, in comparison to illegal pursuits with which they are familiar, or about which they have illusions. Similarly, new homes which seem ideal to officials may be distinctly uncomfortable or even frightening to youth from another background who have had little gratifying personal experience in new relationships. For these reasons, testing parole placement in advance of complete release is particularly desirable for youth. Both for staff information and to aid the youth's adjustment, intensive

[3] A variety of examples are illustrated by case histories in Daniel Glaser, *The Effectiveness of a Prison and Parole System*, Indianapolis: Bobbs-Merrill, 1963, chapter 4.

7

counseling should be concomitant with the early placement experience. Minimal tests of a prospective parole home may be provided by furloughs from the institution in advance of parole. An optimum program involves transfer of the youth several months before parole to release guidance centers, in the community where parole will occur.

The Criminal Record

The extent to which a person has devoted himself to crime is not easily measured. We only know of the offenses for which he was apprehended, or which he will admit, and he may have been involved in considerable criminality not revealed to us. Nevertheless, that which can be learned about prior criminality often is the most valuable information that a parole board has about a prisoner.

At first inspection of a man's file, we usually learn only the events which appear on the FBI's list of his fingerprint reports. This is sometimes called his "rap sheet." It has a wealth of valuable information, but is often difficult to interpret. One problem in using these records is that a criminal commonly is fingerprinted several times on each major offense, and each fingerprinting leads to a new line on this report. First, the prisoner may be reported by the police who arrested him, then by the sheriff who operated the jail in which the prisoner was confined, then by each prison to which he may have been committed. Each of these separate lines on the FBI sheet should not be confused with those for a new offense. Of course, this problem will not confront a parole board if it receives a casework report which summarizes the criminal record in a simpler and clearer manner than that of the original record.

During the intervals in which he was free, between his major offenses, a prisoner often will have had numerous arrests not resulting in conviction. While a man must legally be presumed innocent of any charge for which he was not convicted, such arrests suggest that the person with whom we are dealing frequented places, had associates, or kept hours which got him into difficulties with the law. These could also interfere with his fulfillment of parole requirements. Minimally, these arrests may suggest that the prisoner's reputation with the police in his home community is not conducive to his parole success there. Even where there is a possibility that this was police harassment due to his earlier behavior, the prospect of its continuing should be taken into account.

Ideally, inquiry and investigation of gaps in the criminal record and of other matters, should begin in the presentence study by the probation officer. Of course, such studies are not always made, or are not reported to the board. Remaining issues should be probed by the prison caseworker, by interview and by correspondence, so that adequate information is available when the parole board member confronts the prisoner. By directing appropriate questions to the case-workers on gaps or errors in information available at the parole board hearing, the parole board may promote improvements in the material prepared for its case.

There are so many standpoints from which criminal records can be analyzed, that we cannot exhaust all of the possibilities here. Instead we shall focus on three principal types of information for which this record is our primary or our initial source. These are: the *duration* of the prisoner's prior involvement in crime, his *prior experience with government agencies dealing with crime* (police, courts, prisons, etc.), *and the types of offense* he has committed.

Duration of Prior Criminality

The duration of prior criminality can be estimated imperfectly from several types of evidence. For example, offenders can be differentiated according to the age at which they were first arrested, first adjudicated, first committed to a correctional institution, or first reported in any type of difficulty for delinquent activity. Presumably, among offenders of approximately the same age, the earlier they first have any of these experiences, the longer is the span of their prior involvement in crime, and the more likely they are to continue in crime. This is indicated by table 2.

The foregoing conclusion has occasionally been challenged by a theory that all offenders have approximately the same period of delinquency and crime to go through, so that the earlier they start this period, the younger they will be when they conclude it. This is suggested by the finding that many older chronic offenders have no juvenile delinquency or youth crime record.[4]

Nevertheless, the predominance of evidence is against this conclusion. Despite some deviations, the overall generalization indicated by table 2 is that at any age, the longer the span of prior criminality, the more likely it is that it will be extended in the future. Unfortunately, not many cross tabulations of violation rates are available which relate age at release to age of first arrest or other index of first criminality, as does table 2.

The few rather persistent types of crime characteristically starting at a later age than the majority of offenses provide exceptions to the foregoing generalization that early onset means more persistence in crime. These late starting offenses consist of some crimes associated with alcoholism, especially check forgery, and some offenses that also seem to occur as an abnormal adjustment to senility. These include a petty theft and vagrancy combination, and certain sexual indecency offenses. The old and persistent criminals who do not have a criminal record which goes back to juvenile days, or have a long gap between youth and old age offenses, are not sufficiently numerous to contradict

---

[4] Wooton, *op. cit.*

Table 2.—Postrelease Failure Rates of Federal Adult Male Prisoners According to Both Age at Release and Indices of Duration of Prior Criminality

[Number of cases is indicated in parentheses]

Index of duration of prior involvement in crime	All cases	Age at release from prison			
		18 to 21	22 to 25	26 to 35	36 and over
Age at first arrest:					
16 and under_____percent__	46	53	43	43	40
	(304)	(94)	(68)	(106)	(35)
17 to 20_____percent__	38	37	45	41	28
	(316)	(49)	(73)	(116)	(78)
21 and over_____percent__	24	----------	24	24	24
	(395)	----------	(37)	(184)	(174)
Number of prior sentences for felony-like offenses:					
None_____percent__	25	44	31	21	11
	(423)	(78)	(98)	(151)	(96)
1_____percent__	37	52	46	34	25
	(221)	(31)	(37)	(105)	(48)
2_____percent__	44	57	52	45	28
	(154)	(23)	(27)	(64)	(40)
3 or more_____percent__	46	45	63	48	42
	(217)	(11)	(16)	(86)	(104)
All cases_____percent__	35	48	40	34	27
	(1,015)	(143)	(178)	(406)	(288)

the overall generalization that the younger a person was when his crime began, the more likely he is to persist in it.

The number of prior felony convictions is only a rough indication of the duration of prior criminality. Of course, what we know about a man's criminal record generally is limited to that which was recorded by government agencies which dealt with him. Therefore, the duration past criminality often can be roughly estimated from many types of available records on a person's experience with agents of the law.

Prior Police, Court, and Correctional Experience

Since there are many ways of classifying a criminal's record of previous experience with government agencies, it is often difficult to compare statistical tabulations from different jurisdictions. A variety of ways of classifying the data are illustrated in table 3.

These tabulations indicate, on the whole, that no matter how one counts the volume of previous experience with police, court, or correctional agencies, the overall trend is for the parole failure rate to increase as the magnitude of this prior experience increases. This trend, however, is offset by the influence of age: one or more commitments as a juvenile seems to be more unfavorable as a prognostic sign than the same number of commitments later. In general, the increase in violation rate with increasing number of prior commitments becomes progressively less, or halts completely, after a few

10

terms of imprisonment, or even of successive felony convictions. However, table 2 indicated quite clearly that this decrease in failure rate simply reflects the crime-diminishing effect of older age at release for those with three or more prior felony convictions. Possibly the reduced rate of return to crime with each successive commitment also reflects some rehabilitative or deterrent influence of imprisonment. It is clear, at any rate, that we cannot conclude with certainty that everyone in any category of prior criminal record will persist in crime indefinitely into the future.

Table 3 (Part One).—Postrelease Violation Rates in Relation to Various Classifications of Prior Contact with Agencies of the Law

California Youth Authority male parolees

Prior contacts	Violation rate
	Percent
None	24
1 or 2 contacts for delinquency, no commitment	37
3, 4, or 5 contacts for delinquency, no commitment	44
6 or more contacts for delinquency, no commitment	44
1 or 2 contacts and one commitment	49
3, 4, or 5 contacts and one commitment	46
6 or more contacts and one commitment	45
2 or more prior commitments	50
Violation rate for all cases	44
Number of cases	3,046

New York adult parolees

Number of prior arrests	Violation rate	
	Males	Females
	Percent	*Percent*
None	21	36
1	27	45
2	35	50
3	35	53
4 or more	46	46
Rates for all cases	37	43
Number of cases	7,636	738

Washington adult parolees

Prior felony conviction	Violation rate
	Percent
None	23
1	33
2	40
3 or more	50
Rates for all cases	38
Number of cases	1,731

The Wisconsin data in table 3 show that prison commitments alone may not be as unfavorable for parole prognosis as combinations of prison and lesser commitments. This unfavorable prognosis is in terms of overall violation rate only; it ignores type of violation. Persons habitually in minor difficulty with the law, such as drunks and vagrants, may not be as serious a problem to parole boards as persons less likely to violate, but more likely to commit serious new

11

Table 3 (Part Two).—Postrelease Violation Rates in Relation to Various Classifications of Prior Contact With Agencies of the Law

Federal adult male releasees

Most serious prior contact	Violation rate
	Percent
No prior contact	15
Arrests or fines only	25
Jail and/or probation	31
Training, reform, or industrial school	55
Reformatory or prison	43
Rate for all cases	35
Number of cases	1,015

Illinois youthful male parolees

Most serious prior contact	Violation rate
	Percent
No prior contact	24
Arrests or fines only	35
Jail and/or probation	40
Training, reform, or industrial school	54
Reformatory or prison	39
Rate for all cases	39
Number of cases	2,693

Wisconsin parolees

Type of prior contacts	Juveniles Males	Juveniles Females	Adults Males	Adults Females
Most serious prior commitments:	*Percent*	*Percent*	*Percent*	*Percent*
No prior commitment	46	40	27	13
Juvenile detention, jail, or probation	61	41	42	26
1 prison only			45	50
Prison plus lesser commitments			59	33
2 prison only			36	
2 prison plus lesser commitments			53	
3 prison			50	
4 or more prison			70	
Prior releases on present commitment:				
None	48	38	34	23
1	53	41	51	25
2 or more	52	41	55	40
Rates for all cases	50	39	36	23
Number of cases	1,037	453	2,255	206

offenses if they do. This observation, of course, brings out the over-simplification we are employing in most of this discussion by not distinguishing different types of violation. Some correction of this deficiency will be made in considering offense as a factor in parole prognosis.

Types of Offense

Still another aspect of the vital information provided to parole boards by the criminal record is the type of offense for which a prisoner is currently committed, or in which he was previously involved. It is appropriate therefore to provide an overall view of the many types of offense, and to compare their significance in predicting continuation of criminality.

12

The most persistent types of common crime are those in which offenders obtain someone else's money without use of violence. These crimes can be divided into two major categories: illegal service and predatory crimes.

Illegal service crimes consist of economically motivated offenses in which there is no person who clearly considers himself a victim; instead, the persons with whom the criminals deal are his customers. Examples of such crimes are the sale of illicit alcoholic beverages ("moonshine"), narcotics and stolen goods, and the provision of illegal gambling and prostitution services. Only a minute proportion of these offenses lead to arrest and prosecution. Also, conviction on some of these charges, such as gambling and prostitution, seldom leads to imprisonment, so parole boards seldom confront such criminals. Because these criminal services are both more profitable and safer than most other offenses, one can reasonably speculate that they may be the most frequently committed clearly criminal acts, even though this is not confirmed by complaint or arrest statistics.

The crimes usually encountered by parole boards are predatory crimes. As indicated in table 4, on the whole, these offenses usually fall into three main clusters, from the standpoint of violation rates. The offenses usually associated with the highest violation rates involve taking somebody else's property by stealth or by deceit. Notable here are the crimes of theft, burglary, and forgery.

Theft, which older criminal codes usually call "larceny," consists simply of taking somebody else's property. Both in the law and in statistical tabulations, the crime of auto theft usually is treated separately. Auto thieves have the highest rates of parole violation in most jurisdictions, possibly because they generally are the youngest parolees. Their crime usually is committed for the temporary enjoyment of transportation rather than for long-term economic gains. For this reason, in approximately 90 percent of auto thefts the vehicle is recovered intact, even though the thieves usually are not caught. However, in some auto thefts the cars are stripped, and some older auto thieves are in gangs which falsify ownership papers and sell stolen cars.

Other types of theft include shoplifting, removing objects from parked cars, picking pockets, taking goods from places of employment, and many more varieties of "stealing." Most of the separate crimes are small, frequently they are not immediately discovered by the victim, and probably a major portion are never reported to the police. Only a small proportion of theft reported to the police, other than auto theft, is solved by recovery of the stolen goods, or conviction of the offenders. Furthermore, the small value of the property taken in separate offenses frequently results in a convicted person receiving only a minor penalty, so that most of the time they never go to prison or receive only a short sentence. Probably the persistence of these

Table 4 (Part 1).—Postrelease Violation Rates in Relation to Offense

Offense	Wisconsin parolees				New York adult parolees	
	Juveniles [a]		Adults			
	Males	Females	Males	Females	Males	Females
Highest violations:	*Percent*	*Percent*	*Percent*	*Percent*	*Percent*	*Percent*
Auto theft	50	20	47	60		
Other theft	51	42	34	25		[c] 27
Burglary			39	20	42	36
Forgery and fraud			48	32	46	5
Intermediate and inconsistent:						
Robbery			38	12	37	38
Narcotics						
Lowest violations:						
Rape and assault to rape			31		19	
Other sex offenses	33	37	21	16	24	
Felonious assault			31	17	33	29
Homicide			16	20	19	28
All others	44	41	35	25	38	19
Rates for all cases	50	39	36	23	38	36
Number of cases	1,037	453	2,255	206	[b] 5,929	[b] 329

[a] Offenses for juveniles were tabulated by Wisconsin officials separately for 3 major offenses—theft, auto theft, and sex offenses—plus purely juvenile offenses like truancy, plus all combinations of these several categories. The above tabulations are based on all parolees charged with any of these 3 offenses, alone or in combination. The few multiple-major-offense cases are included under each of their offenses.

[b] Felonies only; excludes cases tabulated as "misdemeanors" and "youthful adjudications."

[c] Auto theft and all other thefts are compiled as 1 offense—grand larceny—in New York.

Table 4 (Part 2).—Postrelease Violation Rates in Return to Offense

Offense	Minnesota adult male parolees	California Youth Authority parolees	Federal adult male releasees	Illinois adult male parolees	Illinois youthful male parolees	Washington adult parolees
Highest violations:	*Percent*	*Percent*	*Percent*	*Percent*	*Percent*	*Percent*
Auto theft	58	49	47		50	52
Other theft	57	54	38	[c] 36	39	40
Burglary	41	42		42	48	38
Forgery and fraud	54	43	30	55	42	50
Intermediates and inconsistent:						
Robbery	47	29	28	42	31	31
Narcotics		41	30	14		
Lowest violations:						
Rape and assault to rape		41				21
Other sex offenses	22	32		[a] 14	[a] 13	16
Felonious assault	41	28	[a] [b] 18			36
Homicide	21	18		14	[d] 20	21
All others	38	48	25	44	35	34
Rates for all cases	44	44	35	37	39	38
Number of offenses	525	3,046	1,015	955	2,693	1,731

[a] Includes "rape."

[b] Includes "homicide."

[c] Includes "auto and stolen property."

[d] Includes "assault."

14

criminals is due in large part to the fact that they cannot readily be given certain or severe penalties.

Burglary consists of breaking and entering for the purpose of committing a felonious act, and it sometimes is designated in the law as "breaking" or "breaking and entering." Usually it is committed in conjunction with larceny at the place entered. However, burglary almost always causes a more severe penalty than larceny alone, so the offenders usually are prosecuted only for burglary. However, some State laws make "burglary and larceny" a single compound offense. A majority of persons arrested for burglary are under 19 years of age, but an appreciable number of the burglars who are encountered in prison populations are older. These often include those for whom burglary has become a profession in which they work closely with dealers in stolen goods ("fences").

Another kind of recurrent economic offense not involving violence is the crime of forgery. Forgers differ from most criminals in the extent to which they commit their crimes alone, and in being relatively older. Petty or naive forgery is notably associated with chronic alcoholism. Perhaps because cashing a fraudulent check requires a certain amount of facility at writing, and an appearance of success, forgers are also distinctive in generally having more education and less often coming from an impoverished home than most prisoners. Other types of fraud, often called "confidence games" or "bunko games," are less often associated with alcoholism than simple check forgery, and are more frequently persistent criminal professions. Embezzlement is a special kind of fraud, frequently involving violation of trust by a prominent and presumably trustworthy citizen, so that he is placed in a government or business position where he handles much money. These offenders generally are good risks as far as prospects for violation are concerned, but their parole poses special public relations problems.

The selling of narcotics has already been mentioned as an illegal service crime. Other narcotic offenses include illegal possession, use, and purchase of narcotic drugs. Evidence on the relative risk of these narcotic offenders, as parolees is inconsistent. There is some indication that they have very high violation rates when they are paroled to neighborhoods where narcotics usage is extensive, but that they have average or below average violation rates elsewhere.

Robbery is different from the economically motivated crimes described earlier, in that robbery involves the use or threat of violence in order to procure someone else's property. Like narcotics offenses, it is associated with diverse violation or recidivism rates in different jurisdictions, but robbers generally seem to have about the average violation rate for their age group. However, they are of concern to parole boards because of the serious injury or death which they may cause. Robbers vary tremendously in character. They include

15

groups of adolescents in slum areas who "roll" drunks coming from taverns in the late hours of night, naive individuals who make a foolhardy effort to solve economic crises by trying to hold up a large bank (often without a working weapon), and some highly dangerous individuals who have a psychological drive to hurt their victims.

The cluster of offenses associated with the lowest violation rates on parole are crimes which least often serve as vocations. These include homicide and rape. However, the strong public demand for punishment as an expression of revenge against such offenders, plus the extreme importance of preventing recurrence of these crimes, makes parole boards exceptionally cautious in paroling those who commit these offenses.

One of the least favorable crimes, from the standpoint of parole violation probability, is the crime of escape from prison. In some States, notably California, offenders sentenced for this offense have the highest violation rate of any offense category, even higher than auto thieves. However, escapees do not constitute a large proportion of prisoners.

Thus far, this discussion has dealt only with gross violation rates, although it has been noted that the nature of the probable parole violation may be a crucial consideration in parole decisions. The type of violation likely to be committed, if any, is a concern especially in the forefront of a parole board member's thoughts when he considers the type of offense for which a prisoner was last convicted. William L. Jacks, statistician of the Pennsylvania Board of Parole, has made one of the few studies of type of violation in relation to type of offense. This is summarized in table 5.

Table 5 indicates, first, that in Pennsylvania the offenses fell into three main clusters in terms of prospects of committing a new crime on parole, and these three clusters were much like those for overall violation rates shown in table 4. However, larceny and narcotics offenses are ranked somewhat differently in these two compilations. Burglars, forgers, and narcotic drug offenders were most likely to commit the same offenses, while larceny and robbery were an intermediate cluster, followed by felonious assault and sex offenses. Homicides were lowest, only about 1 in 250 committed a homicide on parole after being imprisoned for homicide. The gravity of this offense, of course, still makes any repetition a crucial concern.

A California tabulation of adult male parolees returned to prison for a new offense in 1959, 1960, and 1961 concluded: 26 percent are returned for a more serious offense than that on which they were paroled, 38 percent are returned for an offense of similar seriousness to that on which they were paroled, and 37 percent are returned for a less serious offense. Seriousness was measured by the length of the statutory maximum sentence for the offense in California, except

16

Table 5.—Type of Offense for Which Committed as a Factor in Type of Offense, if any, Committed on Parole (for Pennsylvania Only)

All parolees, 1946–61 [a]

Offense for which imprisoned	Percent committing new crimes on parole	Percent repeating on parole the crime for which imprisoned
Auto larceny [b]	22.5	6.4
Larceny	23.4	11.1
Burglary	22.3	10.2
Forgery	19.5	5.1
Robbery	15.9	10.1
Narcotics	8.8	2.9
Sex offenders	12.3	3.6
Assault and battery	5.7	0.4
Homicide	10.2	3.1
Other offenses		
Rates for all cases	18.4	6.8
Number of cases	29,346	29,346

[a] From Pennsylvania Board of Parole, "A Comparison of Releases and Recidivists from June 1, 1946, to May 31, 1961," Harrisburg: The Board, Dec. 20, 1961.

[b] Included in Larceny.

that narcotics offenses were classified as more serious than property offenses with higher maximum sentences.[5]

Intelligence

Intelligence tests are almost invariably administered to the inmates of correctional institutions today. They are used to determine the appropriate education, work, and treatment of each prisoner, and the test results also are reported to the parole board. Despite the convenient availability of this information, it has been found to have only a slight relationship to parole outcome. As table 6 shows, in the several jurisdictions for which we have procured statistics, there was little consistent pattern of violation rate according to intelligence. Generally, the most mentally deficient inmates did not do as well on parole as most prisoners, but usually their violation rates were not extremely different from many with above average intelligence scores.

A prisoner's intelligence test score, of course, can reflect his capacity for both legal and illegal types of behavior. It may be significant information for the parole board as an indication of whether an expected parole job is within a parolee's capacity. It may also be the basis for speculation that certain inmates would be particularly

[5] Administrative Statistics Section, Research Division, *Seriousness of New Offense with Respect to Offense Classification at Time of Parole*, Sacramento: The Department of Corrections, March 1, 1962.

17

Table 6.—Postrelease Violation Rates in Relation to Intelligence

Minnesota adult male parolees		California Youth Authority male parolees		Illinois youthful male parolees		Washington adult parolees	
Intelligence quotient	Viola-tion rate	Intelligence classification	Viola-tion rate	Intelligence classification	Viola-tion rate	Intelligence classification	Viola-tion rate
	Percent		*Percent*		*Percent*		*Percent*
145 and over__	33	Very superior_	0	Very superior_	16	----------------	---------
135 to 144_____	53	Superior_____	43	Superior_____	39	----------------	---------
125 to 134_____	42	High average__	48	High average__	33	Above average	27
115 to 124_____	49	Bright normal-	37	----------------	----------	----------------	---------
105 to 114_____	57	Normal_____	40	Average_____	41	Average_____	32
95 to 104_____	42	Dull normal___	46	Low average__	39	----------------	---------
85 to 94_____	46	Borderline____	49	Dull_____	38	Below average_	39
75 to 84_____	49	Moron_____	55	Borderline____	45	----------------	---------
65 to 74_____	51	----------------	----------	Mental deficient____	47	----------------	---------
Rates for all cases_____	44	----------------	44	----------------	39	----------------	32
Number of cases_____	525	----------------	3,046	----------------	2,689	----------------	809

dangerous if they returned to crime. However, it is surprising how often crimes reflect emotional behavior not guided by much apparent intelligent thinking, even when the offender has considerable mental capacity.

An additional consideration which parole board members should keep in mind is that intelligence tests are never perfectly accurate, and those given in a prison or other correctional institution are often exceptionally unreliable. Although the test scores theoretically reflect an inherited mental capacity, it is well known that performance on many of these tests is greatly affected by exposure to schooling, by the type of vocabulary which an individual needed in his social environment, by experience in using the type of arithmetic and mathematics included in the test, and, especially, by motivation to perform well. These tests often underrate a prison inmate's intelligence because he is indifferent or hostile to taking the test at the time it is administered, usually when he is new to the prison, and because he has not been involved in school for some time. Frequently, the scores on these tests increase if they are administered again after the inmates have attended a prison school for an extended period. It should also be noted that intelligence scores sometimes are erroneously high in some correctional institutions because of lax control in administering the tests or in recording their results.

Race and Nationality

Although Negroes in the United States have a higher rate of arrest, conviction, and imprisonment for crimes than whites, most tabulations we have encountered find little marked or consistent difference in the parole violation rates of the two groups. This is indicated in table 7. It is probable that the higher crime rates among Negroes occur largely because Negroes, more often than whites, experience conditions associated with high crime rates in all racial groups. These conditions include low income, high unemployment, low level of education, and residence in slum areas which have long had high crime rates.

These conditions conducive to high crime rates usually are also associated with high parole violation rates. The fact that Negro parole violation rates are not higher than those of whites, therefore, is somewhat puzzling. It may reflect more careful selection of Negroes for parole than of whites, or more frequent institutionalization of unadvanced offenders among Negroes than among whites. There is some evidence that the latter occurs with juvenile delinquents, but evidence as to its occurrence in prison is conflicting.[6]

Table 7.—Postrelease Violation Rates in Relation to Racial or National Descent

Ethnic classification	Wisconsin parolees			
	Juveniles		Adults	
	Males	Females	Males	Females
	Percent	Percent	Percent	Percent
White	49	37	36	21
Negro	57	49	35	23
American Indian	48	59	37	40
Mexican	71	----------	19	----------
Mongoloid	----------	----------	----------	----------
Other	----------	----------	----------	----------
Rates for all cases	50	39	36	23
Number of cases	1,037	453	2,255	206

Ethnic classification	Minnesota adult male parolees	California Youth Authority parolees	Washington adult parolees
	Percent	Percent	Percent
White	46	41	38
Negro	35	49	34
American Indian	56	----------	47
Mexican	----------	44	----------
Mongoloid	----------	----------	----------
Other	----------	43	----------
Rates for all cases	44	44	38
Number of cases	525	3,046	1,731

[6] Sydney Axelrad, "Negro and White Male Institutionalized Delinquents," *American Journal of Sociology*, Vol. 47, No. 6 (May 1952), pp. 569–574; Henry A. Bullock, "Significance of the Racial Factor in the Length of Prison Sentences," *Journal of Criminal Law, Criminology, and Police Science*, Vol. 52, No. 4 (November–December 1961), pp. 411–417.

In the southwest portion of the United States, the largest ethnic minority are persons of Mexican descent. In California, where they are most numerous, they have a parole violation rate about the same as that of whites and Negroes. American Indians generally have an average or somewhat higher than average rate of parole violation.

The differences in crime or parole violation rates for various ethnic groups could readily develop as a consequence of police or parole officers not treating every person in the same fashion for a given type of behavior, regardless of the person's ethnic descent. Statistics to assess whether or not this occurs are not available on a widespread and recent basis. A common impression is that officials tend to overlook infractions committed by minority group members in their own community, and to be unusually severe in dealing with infractions which members of minorities commit elsewhere. This, of course, could be conducive to the habituation of minority group members to criminal behavior, which they might engage in wherever they encounter an opportunity.

Japanese and Chinese are infrequent in correctional institution populations. In California, where they are most numerous, they have a lower violation rate than other parolees. This probably reflects the closeknit community and family support which they receive.

In a few portions of the country, notably New York, persons of Puerto Rican descent are a new and extensive component of the prison population. Experience with them as parolees has been too brief for confident conclusions as to how their violation rates compare with those of other ancestry.

In general, the evidence on race and nationality as a factor in the evaluation of parolees suggests that it is not of much predictive utility in itself. However, an understanding of the different social and cultural worlds from which members of some minorities come, and to which they return, may be useful in understanding their offenses and in evaluating their parole plans.

Sex

Males coming before parole boards in most States outnumber females in a ratio of about 20 to 1. This probably occurs both because females in our society commit felonies less often than males do, and because those females who are convicted of felonies are less likely to receive a sentence of imprisonment than are males. Table 8 suggests that female parolees violate less often than males, but the differences are not always marked.

Body Characteristics

In the 19th century, there was much effort to explain crime as the expression of an inherited characteristic that could be identified by a

20

Table 8.—Postrelease Violation Rates in Relation to Sex of Parolee

Sex	Wisconsin parolees		New York adult parolees	Washington adult parolees
	Juvenile	Adult		
	Percent	*Percent*	*Percent*	*Percent*
Male	50	36	37	38
Female	39	23	43	25
Rates for all cases	47	35	37	38
Number of cases	1,490	2,461	8,364	1,731

person's physical appearance. One still frequently hears people say that somebody looks like a criminal, or that someone else looks like he could not possibly be a criminal. However, parole board members often observe a fine appearance in some individuals who have shocking criminal records.

There have been popular experiments to investigate the ability to predict criminality from physical appearance. The most useless efforts involved asking people to judge character from photographs of criminals mixed with photographs of highly respected noncriminal persons, when all persons portrayed were of about the same age and wore similar apparel. These studies demonstrated almost complete failure of this approach to character judgment.

Years ago, a study found that height and weight had no relationship to parole violation.[7] Classification of people by their general physical condition has not uncovered clear and consistent findings of marked deviation from average violation rates. Some studies find those in poor health or having a handicap have slightly higher than average violation rates, while others found these individuals slightly more successful on parole than the average.

The most recent extensive research in this field has been that of the Gluecks, which compared the overall body dimensions of delinquents with those of nondelinquents from the same high delinquency neighborhoods. The delinquents were huskier (mesomorphic) in body build than the nondelinquents.[8] It has not yet been demonstrated that this is not simply the result of the huskier youth in high delinquency areas being more readily accepted in delinquent street gang activity (and perhaps, also, more readily picked up by the police), than the slender (ectomorphic) or paunchy (endomorphic) youth.

---

[7] George B. Vold, *Prediction Methods and Parole*, Hanover, N.H.: The Sociological Press, 1931.

[8] Sheldon and Eleanor Glueck, *Unraveling Juvenile Delinquency*, New York: Commonwealth Fund, 1950, chapter 15; *Ibid.*, *Physique and Delinquency*, New York: Harpers, 1956.

SUMMARY

Of the gross characteristics readily available for the classification of prisoners, those most closely related to parole outcome were found to be age and criminal record. On the whole, younger prisoners were shown to have the highest violation rates. However, the extent to which violation rate decreased with age was not uniform for all populations for which this information was available. Some sources of variation in this relationship were discussed.

The criminal record was found to have a wealth of information closely related to parole outcome, but capable of classification in many ways. Of course, an individual's prior criminality is only known from the crimes for which he was apprehended and his offenses recorded, and this record is often incomplete. Nevertheless, lower parole violation rates were consistently found for those with no prior criminal record. However, the violation rate for younger first offenders was much higher than that for older first or second felony offenders. The figures predominantly support a conclusion that the lower a prisoner's age at first arrest, the higher his parole violation rate is likely to be at any subsequent age, but some types of late-starting persistent offenders were noted.

Although persons with little or no prior contact with police, courts, or correctional institutions have a much better record on parole than those who have been in institutions before, the rate of violation does not always increase markedly with each increase in the number of convictions or commitments. This may partially reflect the crime diminution generally occurring with older age at release; the extent to which it can be credited to rehabilitative or deterrent effects of prior imprisonment cannot readily be determined.

Offenses were found to fall into three main clusters as far as parole violation rates are concerned. Those for which the prospect of violation is greatest are crimes involving the taking of someone's property by stealth or deception without the use of force. Notable here are theft, burglary, and forgery. Narcotic offenses and robbery generally were associated with violation rates near the average for all parolees, but they were inconsistent in this respect from one jurisdiction to the next. On the whole, the lowest parole violation rates were associated with crimes of violence, including rape, assault, and homicide.

23

A Pennsylvania study was cited on the extent to which persons who violate parole by committing a new offense repeat the offense for which they previously were imprisoned. Burglars, forgers, and narcotic users were found most likely to repeat their previous offenses, if they committed a new offense. Sex offenders tabulated collectively were relatively low in rate of repeating the same crime, while those convicted of homicide showed the lowest rate of repeating the same offense while on parole of any category.

Intelligence, race, nationality, sex, and body build were found not to have sufficiently marked or consistent relationships to parole outcome for large numbers of offenders to be very useful in evaluating parolees.

THE ALCOHOLIC OFFENDER

CONTENTS

		Page
Foreword		iii
Part I—Drinking and Drunken Behavior		1
Part II—Alcoholism		5
Part III—Crimes Ascribed to Drunkenness		10
Part IV—"Naive" Crimes Associated with Drinking		13
Part V—The Chronic Police Case Inebriate		15
Part VI—Parole and the Use of Alcohol		17
Part VII—Some Considerations in the Treatment of Alcoholism		21
Summary		29

THE ALCOHOLIC OFFENDER

PART I—DRINKING AND DRUNKEN BEHAVIOR

The use of alcoholic beverages is as ancient as our oldest recorded history. Foodstuffs with starch or sugar content and moisture ferment if left standing at normal temperatures. The fermentation process gives them an alcoholic content. Numerous societies have learned to prepare beverages with such natural alcohol, and even to distill the natural fermentation products to derive beverages of higher alcohol content.

We shall use the phrase "drunken behavior" to designate changes in behavior that distinctly follow consumption of alcoholic beverages. Noticeable change in behavior may not always be associated with drinking. Also, drunken behavior may vary tremendously not just with the amount of alcohol consumed, but with the person, time, and place involved in the drinking.

The usual explanation for drunken behavior is that alcohol, which is a physiological depressant, impairs operation of the higher brain centers more rapidly than it affects the lower nervous system. Consequently, it impairs reasoning and inhibition powers before it depresses the ability to act and to express emotion. However, sufficient alcohol will depress the latter functions too.

The government of Finland operates the liquor sales stores in that country and invests a portion of this income in research on alcoholism. In one interesting experiment, careful observations were made through a one-way mirror to record the behavior of four groups of four men brought into a room and provided with alcoholic beverages. Each group went through two five-hour afternoon sessions, a few weeks apart, one session with beer and one with brandy. The men were all given the same lunch before the session; they were then given blood tests at approximately 90-minute intervals. They were also given a variety of psychological tests. In portions of the sessions the men were given topics on which to reach consensus by group discussion. Similar tests and procedures also were employed with men without alcohol, who formed control groups.

As might have been expected, these Finnish experiments showed that alcohol intake was followed, for most participants, by an increase in the frequency of hostile, deflating, and otherwise negative remarks in the group efforts to reach consensus when discussing assigned topics. Such changes were greater with brandy than with beer, even when the total alcohol absorbed into the bloodstream was the same with each beverage. This finding suggests that the social expectations associated with each of these beverages, rather than just the alcohol, affected behavior. They also found that individuals differed

1

greatly in the extent of their behavior changes with each beverage, at any level of blood alcohol.

In general, the Finnish experiments showed that the most constructive participants in group discussion, and those most often preferred by members of the group as work associates, were least changed in behavior when they consumed brandy. The persons seldom chosen by the group as preferred work associates were most frequently chosen as preferred drinking companions, and they had the greatest increase in negative behavior when drinking brandy. These men also most often agreed that a person's deviant behavior should be forgiven when he is drunk. What seems to be suggested by these findings is that drunken behavior may result, in part, from the belief that deviant behavior is acceptable, and perhaps even socially expected, when a person has been drinking strong beverages. It also suggests that there is a strong contrast between persons who are popular in drinking activity and persons who are effective in getting a task done.

Certainly, a factor in the association of alcohol with crime is the social and cultural setting in which alcoholic beverages are consumed. Where intoxication connotes loud and aggressive behavior, less inhibition is expected of a person defined by others as somewhat "high." Thus, when a person thinks of himself as "drunk" he assumes—and is granted by others—some license to engage in deviant behavior without rebuke, regardless of whether or not the physiological effects of alcohol actually reduce his control over his behavior. One familiar indication of this is that many persons, when drinking in relatively formal and sedate social situations, behave with much more restraint, after the same consumption of alcohol, than at a more informal and convivial party.

No analysis of alcoholism should overlook the distinctive cultural variability in drunken behavior. On the whole, it appears that where alcoholic beverages are most widely consumed, in terms of the frequency with which they are imbibed and the proportion of the population taking them, disorderly drunken behavior as a problem seems minimal. The French, Italian, and other Mediterranean and Latin American countries characteristically use wine as a food on a daily basis and for all age groups. While alcoholism is by no means absent in these countries, problems of violent behavior associated with heavy drinking have been much more prominent in countries where alcoholic beverages are not routinely used as a food. Notable here are the Scandinavian countries and Ireland.

Within the United States, persons of certain ethnic ancestry, such as the Jews and the Chinese, have had notoriously low rates of alcoholism. Persons of Irish descent, Mexicans, and Negroes, have been disproportionately high among those arrested for alcoholism. In some parts of the country, notably the Northwest, drunkenness arrests are especially frequent among American Indians.

There is some evidence that violent drunken behavior on a repetitive basis is particularly characteristic of cultures in which there is a high level of insecurity. Two analyses of drinking among primitive peoples agreed that drunkenness was especially a problem in societies in which there was great insecurity in subsistence. The introduction of alcoholic beverages to American Indian tribes by white settlers was reported generally to have been most disturbing to tribes with a marginal existence dependent on hunting, as contrasted with tribes dependent on agricultural crops and domestic animals.

The purely physiological effects of alcohol are very much like those of fatigue. Individual personality and social and cultural influences apparently greatly determine how these effects are reflected in changed behavior as alcohol is consumed. Therefore, one can assert that alcohol alone does not "cause" drunken behavior; drunken behavior expresses personal character, cultural traditions, and social circumstances, as they influence a person's reactions to the physiological effects of alcohol on his body. For some people, and in some circumstances, these personal, cultural, and social factors may readily express themselves as criminal behavior. Before exploring further such relationships of drinking to crime, let us consider the ailment called "alcoholism."

PART II—ALCOHOLISM

"Alcoholism" has been broadly defined as any use of alcoholic beverages that causes any damage to the individual or society or both. Somewhat more specific definitions add to this personal or social damage feature the idea that the persons with alcoholism undergo loss of control when drinking has begun. Most other definitions provide little which augments these descriptions of symptoms identifying alcoholism, but add speculations as to its causes. A few definitions propose more specific criteria to distinguish varieties of alcoholism, but leave the overall concept vaguely defined. However, there is little consensus in prevailing distinctions between types of alcoholism.

It is clear from the foregoing that only a hazy borderline differentiates much heavy drinking from alcoholism. The Public Health Service describes the onset of alcoholism, as distinct from ordinary imbibing, as follows:

> One of the more obvious early signs . . . is that the individual drinks more than is customary among his associates and makes excuses to drink more often. This is an indication that he is developing an insistent need—or a psychological dependence—on alcohol to help him escape from unpleasant worries or tensions.
>
> As the condition progresses he begins to experience "blackouts." He does not "pass out" or become unconscious, but the morning after a drinking bout he cannot remember what happened after a certain point. If this happens repeatedly or after taking only a moderate amount of alcohol, it is a strong indication of developing alcoholism.
>
> As his desire for alcohol becomes stronger, the alcoholic gulps, rather than drinks, his beverage. He senses that his drinking is getting out of hand, and he starts drinking surreptitiously so that others will not know how much he is consuming.
>
> Finally he loses control of his drinking. After one drink, he feels a physical demand for the drug so strong that he cannot stop short of intoxication. Suffering from remorse, but not wanting to show it, he strikes out unreasonably at others. As he realizes that he is losing the respect of his associates and hurting his loved ones, he tries to stop or drink moderately, but he can't. He becomes filled with discouragement and self-pity and tries to "drown his troubles" in more liquor. But his drinking has passed beyond the point where he can use it as a way of coping with his problems and he is faced with the disease of alcoholism.

In several studies, alcoholics were asked to date the onset of their various types of drinking experience. Jellinek's pioneer research suggested that there is a continuous and steady progression, and a standard sequence, for different features of alcoholism, such as experiencing blackouts, drinking first thing in the morning, drinking alone, having convulsions, and having tremors. More recent studies of this sort, by Trice and others, suggest that not all alcoholics have each of these experiences, and most have several almost simultaneously. However, convulsions, tremors, and feeling that they have reached their lowest point, generally characterize the last phases in becoming clearly an alcoholic.[4]

Since alcoholism is dealt with as an individual problem, it is commonly presumed to be a defect of personality. Some have speculated that it could be a hereditary tendency, since alcoholic parents more frequently have alcoholic children than do nonalcoholic parents. However, the fact that children of alcoholics reared in foster homes do not have the high alcoholism rates of children reared with alcoholic parents suggests that social influences in the home, rather than biological inheritance, account for what tendency there is for alcoholism to run in families.[5]

Efforts to distinguish alcoholics from others by personality tests have revealed no marked and consistent distinctions in terms of standard personality categories. Rorschach, Thematic Apperception Tests, intelligence tests, personality inventories, and electroencephalograms, showed no diagnostically useful differentiation of alcoholics from nonalcoholics. Apparently alcoholics are quite diverse in terms of the personality distinctions made by such tests.[6]

In spite of these findings with traditional tests, there are several types of evidence that distinctive personality patterns characterize alcoholics. Connor gave a list of 75 adjectives to 347 alcoholics and 230 nonalcoholics, asking each to check those terms which best described them. The terms most frequent in the self-descriptions by alcoholics were "affectionate," "appreciative," "easy-going," and "soft-hearted." Non-

---

[4] E. M. Jellinek, "Phases of Alcohol Addiction," Chapter 20 in Pittman and Snyder, *op. cit.*; Harrison M. Trice and J. Richard Wahl, "A Rank Order Analysis of the Symptoms of Alcoholism," Chapter 21 in *Ibid.*; Joan K. Jackson, "H-technique Scales of Preoccupation with Alcohol and Psychological Involvement: Time Order of Symptoms, *Quarterly Journal of Studies on Alcoholism*, Vol. 18 (1957), pp. 451–467.

[5] Anne Roe and Barbara Burks, *Adult Adjustment of Foster Children of Alcoholic and Psychotic Parentage and the Influence of the Foster Home*, New Haven, Conn.: *Quarterly Journal of Studies on Alcohol*, 1945; Lee N. Robins, William M. Bates and Patricia O'Neal, "Adult Drinking Patterns of Former Problem Children," Chapter 23 in Pittman and Snyder, *op. cit.*

[6] Edwin H. Sutherland, H. G. Schroeder, and C. I. Tordella, "Personality Traits and the Alcoholic: A Critique of Existing Studies," *Quarterly Journal of Studies on Alcohol*, Vol. 11, No. 4 (December 1950), pp. 547–561; L. Syme, "Personality Characteristics and the Alcoholic, A Critique of Current Studies," *Quarterly Journal of Studies on Alcohol*, Vol 18, No. 2 (June 1957), pp. 288–302.

alcoholics differed most from the alcoholics in describing themselves by such terms as "active," "ambitious," "cautious," "curious," "loyal," "honest," "reliable," and "sincere." This suggests that the alcoholic has a conception of himself as possessing the traits necessary for success in informal social relations, but lacking the traits needed for success in most occupations, or for a responsible position in any organization.[7] Such a finding would be consistent with the cited Finnish evidence that people who change their behavior most while drinking are those most liked for drinking sociability, but least preferred as coworkers.

Peter Park analyzed responses of over a thousand college students to a long questionnaire which included inquiries on problem-drinking traits, and inquiries on the behavior they would adopt in a large variety of hypothetical situations involving action dilemmas. In general, problem drinking was associated with preferring to act in favor of a friend or relative rather than on the basis of principle, where a choice had to be made between these two types of action. Also, the problem drinkers were more likely than the nonproblem drinkers to take an action yielding immediate pleasure rather than an action yielding greater advantages in the long run, but less immediate satisfaction. These responses again seem to characterize the alcoholics as sociable and agreeable, but not oriented to the impersonal job-centered mentality demanded in most responsible work positions.[8]

It is notable that not only do alcoholics seem to be distinguished for their amiability in interpersonal relations like those of a family, but drinking characteristically occurs in a small group situation in which more familiarity between strangers is accepted than generally prevails elsewhere. One study distinguished a "social drinking," "excessive drinking," and an "alcoholic" phase in the careers of alcoholics. In comparing alcoholics in the social drinking phase with nonalcoholic tavern patrons, it concluded: "Nine out of ten alcoholics and an estimated three out of four regular patrons drink in the company of others. Some two-thirds of the alcoholics thought that the social contacts of the tavern were more important than the drinking at this stage." [9]

The role of the bartender as confidante, and as promoter of amiable conversation between patrons, is noteworthy. From this standpoint, the tavern or other drinking place can be thought of as providing a "home away from home," a home for the homeless, and a home for those who do not feel "at home" in their own residences.

This social function of drinking may be evident in the first intro-

---

[7] Ralph G. Connor, "The Self Concepts of Alcoholics," Chapter 26 in Pittman and Snyder, *op. cit.*

[8] Peter Park, "Problem and Role Differentiation: A Study in Incipient Alcoholism," Chapter 25, in Pittman and Snyder, *op. cit.*

[9] Marshall B. Clinard, "The Public Drinking House and Society," Chapter 15 in Pittman and Snyder, *op. cit.*

duction to alcoholic beverages during adolescence and may explain early steps toward alcoholism. As Maddox has observed:

> Teenage drinking . . . appears to be most adequately understood as a social act, as a mechanism of identification by which many teenagers attempt to relate themselves, however prematurely, to the adult world. Drinking is one of the available mechanisms by which the drinker may say to himself and others, "I am a man" or "I am one of the crowd." This is possible because a segment of the cultural tradition to which he is likely to be exposed has defined drinking in this way.[10]

Alcoholism in our society often seems to characterize persons insecure in making a transition from adolescent to adult roles. They alternate between adult assertion of independence and the shelter-seeking dependence of the adolescent, even decades past their adolescent years. In much usage there is a reluctance to apply the term "alcoholic" to anyone younger than about 30 years of age; before that he is a "heavy drinker" who may or may not become an alcoholic. Nevertheless, interviews with 500 successive admissions to the Massachusetts Youth Service Board Reception Center, concluded that 10 percent were "addictive drinkers" who drank whenever they could. Their modal age was 16.[11]

Two recent studies followed up as adults persons who, a few decades earlier, had been investigated by clinics and other agencies as presumed problem children. The records of these agencies permitted a comparison of the childhoods of those who became alcoholics with the childhoods of adults without alcoholism or other serious deviant behavior. Alcoholics had objectively less adequate parental care than nonalcoholics, to a significant extent; this was a difference in "the basic obligation of physical care, financial support, supervision, and provision of a socially acceptable model."[12] As children, the later alcoholics differed from the nonalcoholics in more often being described as aggressive, sadistic, and hyperactive.

From such findings, it is theorized that the future alcoholic first tries to compensate for parental neglect by asserting his independence in childhood aggressiveness. Drinking later serves as a symbol of independence. However, it is inferred that the alcoholic's basic deprivation of parental attention in childhood makes him actually have great need to be dependent, that the display of masculinity and aggressiveness in male drinking is simply a facade which hides a great need for affection. Drinking serves both to facilitate this search for affection in the sociability of the drinking activity and to express masculine inde-

---

[10] George L. Maddox, "Teenage Drinking in the United States," Chapter 12 in Pittman and Snyder, *op. cit.*

[11] James R. MacKay, "Problem Drinking Among Juvenile Delinquents," *Crime and Delinquency*, Vol. 9, No. 1 (January 1963), pp. 29–38.

[12] Robins, Bates, and O'Neal, *loc. cit.*, p. 405.

8

pendence. A vicious circle in alcoholism, therefore, may be that heavy drinking actually impairs ability to achieve masculinity and to gain affection, so that as a result of drinking, the need to seek its presumed satisfactions remains at a high level.[13]

There has been some theorizing that the chronic alcoholic is typically an individual who not only was abnormally dependent on his mother, but thereby filled the mother's need to dominate. The indulgent but rebuking mother or wife derives a sense of moral superiority over the alcoholic. The intense loyalty, often expressed in excessive indulgence, which such persons often show towards alcoholics, may be a factor in the persistence of the alcoholic's difficulty. According to this theory, these nonalcoholic persons, in a sense, aggressively keep the alcoholic dependent and morally subordinate. Many an alcoholic is in a cycle of being rebuked at home for his drinking, therefore longing for the moral equality or dominance he can enjoy with his associates in the drinking place. When the drinking spree is over, he finds solace and shelter with the indulgent family members. He then gains ascendancy over them by forcing them to care for him, and by embarrassing them, which may avenge the humiliation he receives from their rebukes.[14]

Clinical descriptions of alcoholics by psychiatrists generally employ terms like those used to describe the narcotic addict. These include such adjectives as "immature," "passive," and "dependent." (Sometimes alcoholics and narcotics addicts are grouped together as "addiction prone" personalities.) In clinical diagnoses of alcoholics, the term "dependent" is particularly prominent. The alcoholic is described as an individual who never outgrew a close dependence on mother. In this connection, the fact that alcoholic beverages are taken through the mouth leads a number of psychoanalytically oriented clinicians to suggest that the alcoholic is an individual who remains at the oral stage of development. This implies that he remains fixed at, or has regressed to, the relationship characteristic of a nursing infant.

Before exploring what may be done to treat the alcoholic, it may be appropriate to survey the relationships among alcoholism, drunken behavior, and crime.

[13] William and Joan McCord (with Jon Gudeman), *Origins of Alcoholism,* Stanford, Calif.: Stanford University Press, 1960.

[14] Cf., R. Freed Bales, "Types of Social Structure as Factors in Cures for Alcohol Addiction," *Applied Anthropology,* Vol. 1, No. 1 (April–June 1942), pp. 1–13.

PART III—CRIMES ASCRIBED TO DRUNKENNESS

A 2-year study by the Columbus, Ohio, police department involved testing for alcohol in urine samples procured as soon as possible after arrest from all persons arrested for felonies in Columbus in 1951–53. On the assumption that anyone with 1/10 of 1 percent alcohol in his urine is under the influence of alcohol to the extent that his inhibitions are reduced, they concluded that 64 percent of the persons arrested were under the influence of alcohol at the time of their arrest. These included over 80 percent of the people arrested for concealed weapons, cuttings and shootings, over 60 percent of those arrested for robbery, burglary, larceny, forgery, and auto theft, and 45 percent of those arrested for rape. About a quarter of the concealed weapons, cutting and shooting cases had more than 3/10 of 1 percent alcohol in the urine. This indicates sufficient alcohol in the blood to cause marked incoordination and confusion.[1]

The pioneer prison study of alcoholism as a factor in criminal careers was an analysis by Ralph S. Banay of over 3,000 admissions to Sing Sing Prison during a 2-year period in 1938–40. He concluded that 22 percent of these prisoners had been intemperate and 15 percent were intoxicated at the time of their crime. He found the highest rate of alcoholism for persons convicted of sex crimes, of whom 30 percent were habitually intemperate and 22 percent were intoxicated at the time of their crime. The smallest percentage of intemperate persons among the major offense groups was found in those committed for grand larceny, of whom 16 percent were classed as intemperate and 10 percent were intoxicated at the time of their crime. However, from a more intensive study of the careers of 200 intemperate criminals, he concluded that the offenses were directly related to the intemperance in 37 percent of these cases and an indirectly contributory factor in 33 percent. In the remaining 30 percent, the intemperance and crime were considered independent.[2]

Interviews with 2,325 newly committed California adult male prisoners, according to a 1960 report, revealed that 98 percent admitted using alcoholic beverages, 88 percent of these reported they had been intoxicated at some time, and 29 percent of the users said they were intoxicated at the time of the offense for which they were

---

[1] Lloyd M. Shupe, "Alcohol and Crime: A Study of the Urine Alcohol Concentration Found in 882 Persons Arrested During or Immediately After the Commission of a Felony," *Journal of Criminal Law, Criminology and Police Science,* Vol. 44, No. 5 (January–February 1954), pp. 661–664.

[2] Ralph S. Banay, "Alcoholism and Crime," *Quarterly Journal of Studies on Alcohol,* Vol. 2, No. 4 (March 1942), pp. 686–716.

then imprisoned. The latter percentage ranged from a high of 50 percent for auto theft to a low of 10 percent for narcotics offenses. The later the age of reported first drink, the lower the percentage reporting being intoxicated at some time. The percentage reporting some intoxication ranged from a high of 95 percent for those who first drank when under 15 to a low of 61 percent for those 25 years or older at their first drink.[3] This suggests that in drinking, the earlier the practice begins the more likely it is to be a problem. A more extensive study would be desirable to explore further the possible prognostic significance of drinking onset.

In conjunction with Marvin Wolfgang's study of all case files of the Philadelphia Police Department Homicide Squad for a 5-year period from 1948 through 1952, a special tabulation was made of the association of alcoholism with homicides. Alcohol was found to be present in the victim, the offender, or both, in over 60 percent of the cases. It was found somewhat more frequently in homicide cases involving Negroes than in those involving whites. As will be discussed in the next chapter, this study found over one-quarter of the homicides to be victim-precipitated, in the sense that the fatal conflict was initiated by the victim. Alcoholism was involved in 74 percent of such cases.[4]

It should be strongly emphasized that an adequate appraisal of the influence of alcohol on crime should compare the foregoing with statistics on the proportion of the general population who drink or are intoxicated, particularly in the evenings and weekends, when most crimes occur. A further analysis needs to take into account the fact that alcohol is more extensively used by the social-economic classes in which crime rates are highest. Data are not available for this. However, even with all these qualifications, it appears probable that criminal behavior is associated with drinking to a greater extent than it is with most types of nondrinking behavior.

---

[3] Austin H. MacCormick, "Correctional Views of Alcohol, Alcoholism and Crime," *Crime and Delinquency*, Vol. 9, No. 1 (January 1963), pp. 15–28.

[4] Marvin E. Wolfgang and Rolf B. Strohm, "The Relationship Between Alcohol and Criminal Homicide," *Quarterly Journal of Studies on Alcohol*, Vol. 17, No. 3 (September 1956), pp. 411–426.

PART IV—"NAIVE" CRIMES ASSOCIATED WITH DRINKING

A behavior syndrome which frequently sends men to jails and State prisons consists of crimes committed in the course of drinking to obtain small sums of money for continued drinking. These crimes are "naive" in the sense that they are almost certain to result in the offender's apprehension before long. However, they usually are successful in the short-run, and thus they permit immediate continuation of drinking.

One of the most characteristic offenses of this type is naive check forgery. In these offenses the drinker frequently has to sign a check where he is known, and he uses his own name in order to get it cashed, but it generally is drawn on a bank where he has no account or, at best, an account with insufficient funds. These are likely to be small checks, frequently cashed at the drinking place. Often such persons also write checks on the accounts of relatives or friends, whose names they sign. Generally, such forgers have committed many more of these offenses than appear on their records, for the friends and relatives repeatedly make restitution and persuade the victim of the bad check not to prosecute. Eventually, however, they lose their patience, or they are not available before the victim takes the check to the authorities. Sometimes the law enforcement officials simply become tired of allowing these offenses to be "covered up."

Forgers generally are older, more educated, and from more prosperous families, than are most other felons. In general, naive crimes associated with drinking consist of illegal acts for which the drinker does not need special criminal skills. The persons who commit naive forgeries are most often from a background where the practice of handling personal finances through a checking account is common, so they have little to learn in order to pass a bad check successfully. Alcoholic naive offenders of less education than the forgers, persons not at ease in writing and passing checks, are more likely to commit clumsy burglaries or thefts than forgeries, in order to continue drinking. Frequently they are caught when trying to sell some item which obviously does not belong to them.

Lemert has rather vividly described the "dialectical process" by which these offenders progressively work themselves into a feeling that their need for money is imperative and immediate, so that any means of procuring a few dollars quickly is grasped with little thought of future consequences:

> . . . a man . . . falls in with a small group of persons who have embarked upon a two- or three-day or even a week's period of drinking and carousing. The impetus to continue the pattern gets mutually reinforced by interaction of the participants. . . . If

13

midway through such a spree a participant runs out of money the pressures immediately become critical to take such measures as are necessary to preserve the behavior. . . . A similar behavior sequence is perceived in that of the alcoholic in a bar who reaches a "high point" in his drinking and runs out of money. He might go home and get clothes to pawn or go and borrow money from a friend . . . but these alternatives become irrelevant because of the immediacy of his need for alcohol.[1]

Often these men have great regrets after they sober up, for they are not persons who think of themselves as criminals, and they are not as stupid as their crimes might suggest. This remorse is especially evident the first few times they commit such offenses. Apparently, in the process which Lemert calls "closure," when they work themselves into the decision to commit a crime, they lose perspective on the probable later reactions of themselves and others to their offense. As he points out, evidence for this includes ". . . the tendency for naive check forgers to give themselves up to the police, in great feelings of relief on being arrested, in desires to 'pay their debts to society,' in extreme puzzlement as to how they 'ever could have done it,' and in personality dissociations attributing the behavior to 'another me,' or to a 'Dr. Jekyll-Mr. Hyde' complex."[2]

Despite these regrets, these offenses often are repeated. Lemert and others have observed that persons who commit such crimes generally have a background of conflict with family and of failure in their career aspirations; they are often the "black sheep" of their families and unsuccessful in maintaining warm acceptance elsewhere. The drinking spree seems to give them a sense of achievement and a feeling of regard and affection towards their drinking associates. They perceive these experiences as mutual, and apparently they have delusions which exaggerate in their thinking the significance of these drinking experiences for their ultimate happiness. At any rate, once they develop these delusions while drinking, they strive desperately to carry the drinking spree through to a climax of complete exhaustion, and any means of accomplishing this seems warranted to them at that time.

Sometimes the style of checkwriting or cashing seems designed to embarrass certain relatives of the offender, and psychiatrists may well speculate that this is the forger's unconscious purpose in these acts. Often subsequent apprehension and punishment seems so certain that one may readily infer that the offender has an unconscious interest in being caught. Indeed, a clearly conscious and deliberate search for some type of institutional care, especially in the winter, is readily observed in many "derelict" alcoholics on "Skid Row," who go to jail in a desperate search for shelter.

---

[1] Edwin M. Lemert, "An Isolation and Closure Theory of Naive Check Forgery," *Journal of Criminal Law, Criminology and Police Science*, Vol. 44, No. 3 (September–October 1953), pp. 296–307.

[2] *Ibid*, p. 306.

14

PART V—THE CHRONIC POLICE CASE INEBRIATE

The most frequent basis for arrest in the United States is on the charge of drunkenness, although it sometimes has a different designation, such as "public intoxication." A large proportion of other arrests, such as those for disorderly conduct and vagrancy, involve drunkenness. The individuals taken into custody on these charges are distinctly older than most felony arrestees. The median age of persons arrested for drunkenness in 1962 was 42, for disorderly conduct 30, and for vagrancy 37.[1]

An analysis of the records of 187 men committed to sentences of 30 or more days in Rochester, New York, during 1953–54 indicated that the average arrestee had a record of 16.5 prior arrests, of which 12.8 were for public intoxication and the remainder for other offenses. The most frequent other offense was larceny, which comprised about a quarter of all nondrunkenness charges. These offenders, now mostly subsisting at a marginal economic level on Skid Row, usually had committed their serious felonies at an earlier age and had a greater frequency of purely drunkenness arrests when they became older. It has been suggested by Cloward and Ohlin that such men, like many drug addicts, are "double failures"; they have resorted to a "retreatist" approach to social demands, because they failed first at legitimate and then at illegitimate (criminal) means of achieving a conventional standard of living.

Characteristically, these Skid Row alcoholics were found to be homeless men, who left the parental home at an early age following the death of one or both parents, or conflict with parents. This departure contributed to their failure to complete their studies or to progress in a vocational career. They seem to have then moved continually from one protective environment to another, between drinking sprees, being either in a correctional institution or in a shelter for homeless men.[2]

Interviews by Robert Straus with 203 men in the New Haven Salvation Army Center during 1946 concluded that they were of predominantly low education and experienced only at unskilled or casual labor. Straus inferred from his interviews that heavy drinking led to

---

[1] Federal Bureau of Investigation, *Crime in the United States: Uniform Crime Reports 1962,* Washington, D.C.: U.S. Department of Justice, 1963, Table 20, p. 94.

[2] David J. Pittman and C. Wayne Gordon, "Criminal Careers of the Chronic Police Case Inebriate," *Quarterly Journal of Studies on Alcohol,* Vol. 19, No. 2 (June 1958), pp. 255–268; David J. Pittman and C. Wayne Gordon, *Revolving Door: A Study of the Chronic Police Case Inebriate,* Glencoe, Ill.: Free Press, 1958; Richard A. Cloward and Lloyd E. Ohlin, *Delinquency and Opportunity,* Glencoe, Ill.: Free Press, 1960, pp. 179–184.

homelessness in two-thirds of the cases, and the homelessness led to heavy drinking in one-third of the cases.[3] It should be stressed, incidentally, that being on Skid Row is not synonymous with being an alcoholic; data indicate that, for many nonalcoholic homeless men, subsistence is more feasible in Skid Row than elsewhere—when they suffer extreme poverty, lack of family, or physical or mental defects.[4]

Older offenders who are homeless and chronically alcoholic have a difficult time completing a parole without committing persistent rule violations. Nevertheless, their rates of serious felony acts on parole seem to decline with age. However, their drinking makes them incapable of holding a regular job or of accumulating funds. It also is difficult to provide them with a home and employment at release from prison, except as residents in a "shelter program" such as supplied by the Salvation Army or other voluntary agencies.

[3] Robert Straus, "Alcohol and the Homeless Man," *Quarterly Journal of Studies on Alcohol,* Vol. 7, No. 3 (December 1946), pp. 360–404.

[4] Donald J. Bogue, *Skid Row in American Cities,* Chicago: University of Chicago Community and Family Studies Center, 1963.

PART VI—PAROLE AND THE USE OF ALCOHOL

The relationship between the use of alcohol and parole is one of the most recurring and perplexing problems confronting parole boards. First, they must constantly meet such issues as determining the significance of alcohol in the behavior history of many inmates being considered for parole, estimating the various kinds of risks involved in paroling inmates with drinking problems, evaluating the degree to which a given inmate may actually have overcome a drinking problem, and weighing the availability of effective treatment resources in the community. Secondly, boards establish significant public policy regarding the use of prison facilities through their decisions on the disposition of all types of offenders with drinking problems. Finally, parole boards almost universally fix as one of the conditions of parole a restriction in some manner on the use of alcohol by parolees, and constant decisions must be made regarding the practical implementation of that rule.

Many parole boards approach the problem of alcohol use by parolees through the promulgation of a rule that no parolee shall be allowed to use intoxicating liquors of any kind.[1] This action is taken on the assumption that generally the use of alcohol is involved to a significant degree with criminal behavior and its use should be strictly prohibited. One difficulty with this general rule is that, for many individual parolees, criminal behavior is not directly related to the use of alcohol, and even its moderate use is forbidden in these cases. Thus, in a number of instances, the degree of enforcement is quite variable and largely depends on the discretion of a parole officer. Complaints have been raised against this approach on the basis that it creates a general disrespect for all rules, leads to uneven enforcement, and damages the parole officer-parolee relationship.[2] A number of parole boards attempt to meet this by simply requiring that parolees not drink to excess and leave the question of excess to the parole officer. At least two parole boards make a specific decision on an individual case basis whether a parolee should be under a no-drinking rule.

Commonly, the use of alcohol by parolees involves parole boards and staffs with other troublesome issues. For example, often the parolee who has a drinking problem will also have problems with respect to failure to support his family, hold a regular job, or similar types of noncriminal but nonetheless socially disapproved behavior. As most parole systems see their function to be preventing serious

---

[1] Nat R. Arluke, "A Summary of Parole Rules," *National Probation and Parole Association Journal* (January 1956).

[2] *Ibid.*

17

crimes, rather than simply promoting generally accepted social behaviors in all areas, boards and staffs must continually decide in these types of cases whether the behavior being displayed is actually related to further criminality or is essentially socially undesirable behavior which does not seriously pose a potential criminal threat. This requires that the parole board make clear decisions relative to the relationship of drinking in individual cases and potential of further crime.

The three most common situations upon which boards are called to broadly distinguish and then to decide on an individual case and policy ground are:[3]

1. The cases of those persons who function in a relatively law-abiding manner as long as they do not drink. They may or may not be alcoholic, but in any case, when they are drinking, their self-controls are sufficiently lowered or their conduct is so irresponsible that they represent a relatively serious criminal threat. A number of assaultive individuals, chronically intoxicated drivers, and sex offenders might be placed in this general category.

2. Those persons who may use alcoholic beverages but whose criminal activity does not seem to be related in a major degree to drinking. There are a considerable number of offenders in this general category who, either because of their cultural setting or their own personal history, may drink but alcohol does not incapacitate them from pursuing what they define as their social goals.

3. Those individuals for whom alcohol poses a real problem, but their criminal threat is minimal either in terms of its likelihood or the type of crime they might commit, such as writing small insufficient fund checks.

It is clear that, in the first case, the control of alcohol is critical in terms of protection of the public, and the parolee will require a very effective plan of alcohol control and treatment. In the second case, the need to control alcohol *per se* is clearly less an issue than are other considerations.

In the third situation, alcoholic treatment is certainly indicated, but other problems are raised when persons falling into this general category show little inclination to solve their drinking problem. Some parole boards have questioned the wisdom of returning these low motivated alcoholics to a State prison for long confinement, at considerable expense, when their behavior is such that they would only be committed to an institution of misdemeanants if they were not on

---

[3] For a description of the relationship of alcoholism and crime and a much more elaborate classification system, see Selden D. Bacon, "Alcohol, Alcoholism, and Crime," *Crime and Delinquency*, Vol. 9 (January 1963).

parole. Indeed, at still less cost, this type of alcoholic might be dealt with in nonpenal treatment centers, now found in many cities.

In States where high maximum sentences are imposed for almost all felonies and a period of successful parole is required for discharge from the sentence, some men who were convicted of a felony only once in their lives are in and out of prison four or five times over a period of 15 or 20 years for the single initial offense on which their first parole occurred after only brief incarceration. Under these conditions an institution for felons is used as a rather ineffective storage place for chronic misdemeanants.

Two extreme techniques of coping with this problem have been encountered in parole board practice. One is to continue a chronic alcoholic on parole even when he is arrested for drunkenness or other misdemeanors, particularly if he is working with Alcoholics Anonymous or with some other treatment program for alcoholism. Another policy which has been employed is to offer an early discharge on re-parole to inmates who previously violated several paroles on a single sentence without committing new felonies. In Illinois during the 1950's, when some chronic alcoholics had violated three or four paroles on one year to life sentences for burglary without committing a serious new offense, the parole board exercised its option of promising discharge from the sentence in six months if they avoided drunkenness arrests during such a new parole. A number of these men earned discharges under such arrangements.

The dependent habits of these individuals make them conforming prisoners and particularly suited to an institution-like environment on parole. Placements as laborers, gardeners, caretakers, cooks or attendants in ranches, logging camps, hospitals, and other situations in which room and board are provided, often are optimum. In a few cases the usual restrictions on parolee mobility have been dropped to permit such parolees to accept employment on ships, particularly in inland waterways. In all these placements intoxication may recur periodically at scattered days of an interval of many long work days, but this is tolerated by the employer and is often traditional in such work.

The difficulties which many States encounter in recruiting employees for unskilled labor, usually at low wages, in isolated State hospitals or other institutions, suggest another promising type of placement for these institutionalized parolees. However, public employment of parolees usually is barred by State law or by parole board regulations. Since government agencies try to persuade other employers to hire parolees, perhaps the State also should adopt such an employment policy. Many States and the Federal Government have shown leadership in employing the physically handicapped. The question is

19

often raised, why should they not do the same with those who are handicapped by a criminal record, particularly those also burdened by alcoholism? Although alcoholics are liabilities in much employment, since they generally have a high rate of absenteeism due to drinking, they will be a financial burden to the State when unemployed. Public employment might augment the proportion who are rehabilitated, if the alternative is unemployment.

PART VII—SOME CONSIDERATIONS IN THE TREATMENT OF ALCOHOLISM

The most prominent methods for treating alcoholism can be divided into two broad categories: medical-psychological and social-psychological. Medical treatment often begins with hospitalization in severe cases, followed by clinical examination and counseling in the community, or it may consist only of the latter.

The purely physiological aspect of alcoholism treatment generally includes relief of the malnutrition which results from the dietary imbalance associated with heavy drinking. Sugar, insulin, and B-complex vitamins frequently are prescribed. More complex treatment may be needed for body damage distinctly ascribed to alcohol, such as cirrhosis of the liver. When the body contains a high percentage of alcohol, the expansion of capillaries near the skin (flushing) causes rapid heat loss, so winter drunkards frequently enter hospitals as pneumonia patients.

A physiological supplement to psychological counseling sometimes consists of administering drugs which promote nausea and other discomforts after one consumes alcohol. Not only is a person unable to drink without suffering extreme discomfort if he has taken these drugs, but it is presumed that he may become conditioned to experience nausea when he even contemplates drinking. This is a frequent feature of commercial cures for alcoholism.

Adequate statistics on the effectiveness of these treatments are lacking. Many conspicuous failures can be cited for these and all other approaches. Frequently what appears to be a cure turns out to be only temporary, and relapse into chronic drinking occurs at the first crisis.

A major source of difficulty in the achievement of permanent "cures" of alcoholism is that treatment of the alcoholic himself may not suffice; his social environment must also change. Particularly relevant here is the alcoholic's family, both that in which he was reared and his family by marriage, if any. With most alcoholics, close family members go through many crises before the alcoholic finally becomes a prison and parole case. The relatives suffer despair, pity, anger, disgust, guilt, hope, and disappointment with the alcoholic repeatedly, for years or even decades.

In the course of the experience of living with an alcoholic, other family members have to make some adjustments for their own welfare, and especially for the sake of any children in the family. Frequently they learn not to trust the alcoholic with money, not to give him any responsibility, in short, not to count on him. Wives of alcoholics assume the father's role in addition to the maternal role in raising their children, and they may also train the children not to place confidence in their father.[1]

These consequences of the alcoholic's prior behavior may be major impediments to changing his behavior. He cannot become a responsible person, or have a conception of himself as someone who is loved, respected, and trusted, unless he can assume responsibility and inspire respect and affection in others. When he cannot obtain these satisfactions in nonalcoholic life, drinking companionship appeals as an immediately available substitute.

For these reasons, alteration of an alcoholic's behavior usually is facilitated greatly if his decision to cease drinking is accompanied by satisfying new social relationships. These new relationships need not permanently replace family ties; they may provide a sort of framework on which the alcoholic can build a new character and reputation for himself apart from his family, which will help him to achieve a new kind of role and status in his family. Some alcoholics can find these supportive relationships with counselors or therapists, and with nonalcoholics encountered in work, church, or clubs. Some find it among relatives who have not been intimately involved with them throughout their years of evolving from an occasional heavy drinker to a chronic alcoholic. For alcoholics who have alienated all such potential sources of new relationship, however, Alcoholics Anonymous provides the most readily available and satisfying source of companionship and regard from others.

Bogue reports cases of ex-alcoholics still on Skid Row who, by seeing themselves as incapable of drinking, were able to remain in that environment without reverting to alcoholism. Frequently their change from drinking followed extreme illness, and often the change occurred in conjunction with assistance from Alcoholics Anonymous or other agencies.[2] However, prevailing impressions of those working with alcoholics seems to be that remaining in continuous contact with the setting or associates of former drinking greatly reduces the prospect of success in terminating alcoholism.

Alcoholics Anonymous is an organization started in 1935 by a physician and a stockbroker who met by chance and found they benefited from telling each other of their separate efforts to conquer their alcoholism problems. Influenced by the Oxford Group movement, an evangelical religious group emphasizing mutual aid, self-examination, and restitution for harm done, they developed the following Twelve Steps, around which the Alcoholics Anonymous program is built.

> Step One: We admitted we were powerless over alcohol . . . that our lives had become unmanageable.

[1] See Joan K. Jackson, "Alcoholism and the Family," Chapter 27, in Pittman and Snyder, *op. cit.*

[2] Donald J. Bogue, *op. cit.*, pp. 90–92, 296–297, 302–304.

Step Two: Came to believe that a Power greater than ourselves could restore us to sanity.

Step Three: Made a decision to turn our will and our lives over to the care of God as we understood Him.

Step Four: Made a searching and fearless moral inventory of ourselves.

Step Five: Admitted to God, to ourselves, and to another human being the exact nature of our wrongs.

Step Six: Were entirely ready to have God remove all these defects of character.

Step Seven: Humbly asked Him to remove our shortcomings.

Step Eight: Made a list of all persons we had harmed and became willing to make amends to them all.

Step Nine: Made direct amends to such people whenever possible, except when to do so would injure them or others.

Step Ten: Continued to take personal inventory and when we were wrong promptly admitted it.

Step Eleven: Sought through prayer and meditation to improve our conscious contact with God as we understood Him, praying only for knowledge of His will for us and the power to carry that out.

Step Twelve: Having had a spiritual awakening as the result of these Steps, we tried to carry this message to alcoholics, and to practice these principles in all our affairs.

The Alcoholics Anonymous groups meet frequently, sometimes every night, but members need not come to every gathering. They discuss each Step separately, often only one Step for many days, the members relating and interpreting their experience in that particular Step. The Alcoholics Anonymous members are always available for Step Twelve, to answer any call to help an alcoholic, at any time of the day or night. A new recruit generally has an older member as a sponsor and works through the separate Steps in succession. The Alcoholics Anonymous members believe that an alcoholic really has to "hit bottom" before he can reach out for help. This may mean different things for different people, such as loss of employment, threat of family disintegration, extreme illness from alcoholism, and so forth. Frequently there are several false starts with Alcoholics Anonymous, then reversions to drunkenness, before the member really embraces the Twelve Steps fully and consistently.

For Steps Two and Three, believing in a Power greater than themselves, and turning their lives over to His care, the organization is quite broad in interpretation; this Power may be God or it may even be Alcoholics Anonymous itself.

23

For Steps Four and Five, making a moral inventory and admitting the nature of their wrongs, members point out the rationalizations which they have employed to escape feelings of guilt and frustration. They also focus on their past selfishness and pretentiousness. Steps Six and Seven reinforce faith in the organization and in God as they see Him. Having confessed, they are now ready to take Steps Eight and Nine, of expiation to those whom they had previously wronged. Steps Ten and Eleven reiterate previous Steps and Step Twelve promotes the major source of commitment to Alcoholics Anonymous principles, that which comes from trying to convert others to them.

The Alcoholics Anonymous organization is believed by many to have brought more alcoholics to persistent sobriety than all other formal programs combined. It seems to gain its effectiveness by giving companionship to alcoholics who seek sobriety and by instilling in them a progressively more favorable self-conception as they continue participation in the organization. In addition to the Twelve Steps to guide their individual lives, the organization has the following Twelve Traditions which have been extremely effective in preventing politics and factionalism from disturbing the growth and unity of this movement.

One: Our common welfare should come first; personal recovery depends upon AA unity.

Two: For our group purpose there is but one ultimate authority . . . a loving God as He may express Himself in our group conscience. Our leaders are but trusted servants . . . they do not govern.

Three: The only requirement for AA membership is a desire to stop drinking.

Four: Each group should be autonomous except in matters affecting other groups or AA as a whole.

Five: Each group has but one primary purpose . . . to carry its message to the alcoholic who still suffers.

Six: An AA group ought never endorse, finance, or lend the AA name to any related facility or outside enterprise, lest problems of money property and prestige divert us from our primary purpose.

Seven: Every AA group ought to be fully self-supporting, declining outside contributions.

Eight: Alcoholics Anonymous should remain forever nonprofessional, but our service centers may employ special workers.

Nine: AA, as such, ought never be organized; but we may create service boards or committees directly responsible to those they serve.

Ten: Alcoholics Anonymous has no opinion on outside issues;

hence the AA name ought never be drawn into public controversy.

Eleven: Our public relations policy is based on attraction rather than promotion; we need always maintain personal anonymity at the level of press, radio and films.

Twelve: Anonymity is the spiritual foundation of all our Traditions, ever reminding us to place principles before personalities.

Persons of low economic class background and uneducated people seem more reluctant to affiliate themselves with Alcoholics Anonymous than middle class and educated persons. These nonaffiliates apparently are more readily in contact with drinking companions even after they clearly become chronic alcoholics, and are less disgraced by their alcoholism, than are middle and upper class alcoholics. Upper class and highly educated persons are most likely to use professional psychiatric assistance, and they share with the middle class more acceptance of the notion that it is not a disgrace to seek such help for behavior difficulty.

The services of hospitals, clinics, and of psychiatrists and psychologists in private practice increasingly are provided in conjunction with Alcoholics Anonymous activity. In its first few decades, Alcoholics Anonymous groups often were quite hostile to other approaches to the treatment of alcoholism, and they probably exaggerated the failure rate of all methods other than Alcoholics Anonymous. This may have reflected the selective perception of the Alcoholics Anonymous members, since each of them usually represented a failure of other methods; also, they did not see successes of other treatment methods, as these do not go to Alcoholics Anonymous. The attack on competing approaches probably also strengthened the morale of Alcoholics Anonymous groups at a time when their organization was less secure than it is at present, and this attitude has not yet disappeared from Alcoholics Anonymous members now that they are secure. Conversely, attacks on Alcoholics Anonymous still emanate from some psychiatrists and psychologists,[3] although most members of these professions seem to share the view that Alcoholics Anonymous is America's major force against alcoholism and valuable for most cases.[4]

In addition to Alcoholics Anonymous there is an Al-Anon organization for spouses and any other relatives of alcoholics who are over 21. They sometimes admit even close friends of alcoholics. Al-Anon which has grown rapidly, has also established Al-Teen organizations,

[3] For example, Arthur H. Cain, "Alcoholics Anonymous: Cult or Cure," *Harpers Magazine,* Vol. 226, No. 1353 (February 1963), pp. 48–52.

[4] For example, Chafetz and Demone, *op. cit.;* for a psychiatric interpretation of the reasons for AA's effectiveness, and observations on how it can be integrated with psychotherapy, see Harry M. Tiebout, "Alcoholics Anonymous—An Experiment of Nature," *Quarterly Journal of Studies on Alcohol,* Vol. 22, No. 1 (March 1961), pp. 52–68.

for the children of alcoholics. These groups are all modeled on Alcoholics Anonymous in many respects, but operate independently. The Al-Anon members go through Twelve Steps like Alcoholics Anonymous, but they are oriented to helping other relatives of alcoholics like themselves, as well as to helping alcoholics. Their program, like Alcoholics Anonymous, emphasizes understanding their own emotional reactions, including their self-righteousness and their retaliation against the alcoholic. As Chafetz and Demone point out:

> Gradually, because the alcoholic is unpredictable, the mate must assume more and more responsibilities. With the alcoholic's recovery, it becomes difficult for the nonalcoholic to let the reins go. Al-Anon wisely advises that life, even after sobriety, does "not stay rosy," and that AA's Twelve Steps should be practiced by both the nonalcoholic and alcoholic. . . . It also rises the possibility that the nonalcoholic partner may resent time spent at AA meetings and the fact that AA has been able to help the alcoholic where the spouse has failed.[5]

There are over 200 Alcoholics Anonymous groups in State and Federal prisons and about the same number in American jails.[6] Members of outside Alcoholics Anonymous groups visit these jail and prison groups as part of their Twelfth Step work. A major problem in the assessment of these units in prisons is that many inmates do not appear to participate with sincerity, but attend either as a diversion from prison routine or to make a favorable impression on prison and parole officials. Conversely, some participate with sincere interest, and probably benefit, who never were alcoholics, but whom Alcoholics Anonymous helps with other personal problems. It is difficult to judge the sincerity of a prisoner's Alcoholics Anonymous involvement for parole prognosis purposes.

A major positive benefit of the Alcoholics Anonymous prison chapters in many cases is that they place the prisoner in touch with an Alcoholics Anonymous group at his post-release destination. Frequently he is met at the prison gate or at his bus or train by an Alcoholics Anonymous member. Members also have rendered important assistance in procuring post-release homes and jobs for many inmates. With those alcoholics who are sincere participants, Alcoholics Anonymous seems to improve the prospects of parole success. It is difficult to assess sincerity objectively, and there has been no adequate statistical tabulation of the records of comparable parolees with and without Alcoholics Anonymous.

Most parole board members are confronted by many prisoners with a history of arrests for drunkenness or other objective evidence of alcoholism, who vehemently deny being alcoholic. It seems probable, on the whole, that they are the worst risks among men with such an alcoholic record, since they have not yet reached the condition which

---

[5] *Op. cit.*, pp. 170–171.

[6] Austin H. MacCormick, *op. cit.*

is necessary for Step One in Alcoholics Anonymous or any other treatment program, namely, recognizing that they have a problem. However, many have reached an age where their further difficulties with the law are more likely to be misdemeanors than felonies.

In Bogue's study, officials of agencies working with Skid Row alcoholics were interviewed. The points on which these expert practitioners showed consensus, according to Bogue, included:

> Little can be done to help an alcoholic control his drinking until he admits he is unable to control it, wants help, is willing to accept help, and is motivated to carry out a regimen of therapy. Some experts believe in waiting until a man has reached this point through "going down to the very bottom of the gutter," while others believe a man can be hastened to this point through counseling. . . .
>
> The men respond more quickly and more favorably to a family-like or men's-club-like situation than to a hospital or an institutional atmosphere. The feeling that he has become an adopted member, upon whom respect, affection, friendship, and genuine interest are bestowed, is an essential part of the process of helping him to realize he can "come back" and to resolve to try.
>
> The man must feel a strong belief that he will be able to stop drinking, with help. He must realize that this will require strong effort on his part and that it will not be an easy task. This belief in his own ability often is strengthened by a religious conversion. . . . This belief may also be strengthened by the testimonials of ex-alcoholics (either in a religious or nonreligious context), who are concrete and living proof that "it can be done." Counseling may also assist in establishing this attitude of hope, expectation, and determination to try. . . .
>
> Treatment for alcoholism consists of helping a man become a teetotaler. There is no such thing as assisting a heavy drinker to "cut down" on his drinking; he can be helped only to stop drinking altogether. . . .
>
> Much drinking activity is oriented toward recreational and social interests, even though it may be created by psychological tensions. Rehabilitation must also include the substitution of nonalcoholic recreation for the habits of the tavern, and the retraining to make use of such programs. . . .
>
> Some programs emphasize education and retraining. They try to teach the basic facts of alcoholism, some of the principles of elementary psychology and psychiatry, and thereby to stimulate self-analysis by the men. . . . The men undergoing treatment are made to feel like students rather than like patients.[7]

Occasional disagreement with these views is encountered among persons dealing with alcoholics under correctional supervision. For example, some contend that the authority of the parole situation can be used therapeutically, that the parole staff has an advantage in not having to wait for the alcoholic to request treatment before it can treat him effectively. A Massachusetts program for paroled juvenile delinquents with severe drinking patterns found that there was virtu-

---

[7] Bogue, op. cit., pp. 457–460.

ally no cooperation when these youth were simply asked to report to an outpatient clinic. They resisted the interviews as an invasion of privacy and failed to keep appointments. When the clinician started contact with such youth while they were still in the training school, and saw them weekly there, he established a relationship which he was able to preserve later. However, their success in maintaining contact with at least half the cases on parole is credited to the insistence of the parole officer that the parolees keep their appointments. The Massachusetts investigator asserts: ". . . it is crucial for the therapist and the parole officer to work together . . . if progress is to be made and if they are not to be caught up in the child's expert ability to play one adult against another." [8]

It should be stressed, however, that if the attendance at psychotherapy sessions were merely dependent on the coercion of the parole officer, few therapists would expect their work to be effective. From experience at a clinic for adult alcoholics on probation, Mills and Hetrick contend that the officer must not just set limits, but must augment the therapist in providing support. The alcoholic may thus see the officer "as a knowledgeable and interested authority figure whose efforts can help him avoid further legal trouble. . . . The alcoholic who is impulse-ridden, ashamed, and extremely anxious appreciates the officer's firmness and guidance in helping him secure suitable employment, keep family strife to a minimum, and check his impulses to evade responsibility by drinking." [9]

Disagreement also exists occasionally as to whether an alcoholic can be cured if he still engages in social drinking. A fundamental tenet of much Alcoholics Anonymous thinking is that the alcoholic person is biologically different from other persons; others can drink moderately, but the alcoholic is inherently incapable of drinking in any way other than to excess. This does not make biological sense in terms of the gross neurophysiological mechanisms of imbibing. However, in terms of psychological conditioning and social definition processes, it seems plausible to expect that if an alcoholic took the first steps in what previously was a strongly conditioned behavior sequence, the probability of his completing the sequence to extreme intoxication would be high. This conclusion is not contradicted by a recent study which found that 7 out of 93 long-cured alcoholics were regularly engaging in social drinking, while the others abstained completely. [10] It may be *possible* for an alcoholic to drink sociably and remain nonalcoholic, but the evidence indicates that it is *not highly probable.*

---

[8] MacKay, *op. cit.*

[9] Robert B. Mills and Emery S. Hetrick, "Treating the Unmotivated Alcoholic," *Crime and Delinquency*, Vol. 9, No. 1 (January 1963), pp. 46–59.

[10] D. L. Davies, "Normal Drinking in Recovered Alcohol Addicts," *Quarterly Journal of Studies on Alcohol,* Vol 23, No. 1 (March 1962), pp. 94–104.

SUMMARY

The changes in behavior which follow the consumption of alcoholic beverages are a function of personality, social circumstances, and cultural tradition, rather than of the physiological effects of alcohol alone.

Alcoholism generally is considered a disease. Definitions of this ailment agree in identifying the alcoholic by two features: his drinking damages himself or others, and this drinking is beyond his control. The development of alcoholism usually is a gradual process, so that just when heavy or compulsive drinking ends and alcoholism begins may be a question on which persons will have different judgments. In the advanced stages of alcoholism, however, severe physical and mental difficulties usually are experienced, such as convulsions, tremors, extreme depression and anxiety.

Standard personality tests fail to differentiate alcoholics from nonalcoholics markedly. However, several types of research evidence indicate that alcoholics are high in social skills and amiability, and low in character traits needed for success in an organization, such as responsibility, honesty, and objectivity. Indeed, the readily accessible sociability of the drinking place appears to be the major attraction of drinking in the early stages of alcoholism.

Prevailing interpretations of statistical and case data ascribe male alcoholism to an excessive dependence on the mother in early life, which is continued in adulthood. Drinking relieves such anxiety, as it expresses independence because it connotes maleness, yet at the same time, it satisfies dependency needs because of its sociable setting. Many alcoholics allegedly alternate between departing on a drinking spree to escape from the moral ascendancy of rebuking parents or spouses, then retaliating against these relatives by deliberately embarrassing and burdening them.

Tests by the police in Columbus, Ohio, indicate that a clear majority of persons arrested for felonies have been drinking appreciably when arrested, and almost a third of the armed assault and weapons possession arrestees are markedly intoxicated. Interviews with prison inmates find that fewer than this proportion admit, or are reported in prison files, to have been intoxicated at the time of the offense for which they are imprisoned. Various studies of this type report from 15 to 29 percent intoxicated at the time of their crime.

A distinctive type of crime associated with drinking consists of "naive" offenses, committed in the course of a drinking spree, in order to finance continued drinking. Prominent here are petty forgeries, often where the offender can readily be located once the invalidity of his check becomes known. These alcoholic forgers generally are

29

older and more educated than most criminals, and when sober they seem genuinely remorseful over their offenses. However, they seem to have a profound sense of failure and guilt, and once started on drinking, an exaggerated conception of the satisfaction that continued drink will give them. Therefore, prospects for repetition of their drinking and offense pattern generally seem high. Naive offenders of lesser age and status more often commit crude burglaries, thefts, or even robbery in order to continue drinking sprees. In general, not the persistence of the drinking habit so much as the character of the crime associated with an individual's drunken status, seems critical to evaluating the risks in paroling an alcoholic offender.

Chronic police case inebriates, regularly arrested for drunkeness, or for other misdemeanors stemming from drunkeness, are the largest arrest category in United States. Indeed, over a third of police arrests in 1962 were for drunkeness; if combined with disorderly conduct, drunken driving, and vagrancy offenses, they comprise a clear majority of all arrestees.[1] Persons arrested on these charges generally are older than most other arrestees, and may have a long police record, beginning with felony charges at an early age, and ending with recurrent drunkenness arrests in middle and old age. They are a burden to parole boards when a long indeterminate sentence on a youthful felony charge keeps bringing them back to prison as parole violators for years or decades after they have ceased committing crimes more serious than drunkenness. It can be contended that this procedure imposes a felony sentence for misdemeanors and burdens the prison with persons who should be dealt with in other ways. Continuing such offenders on parole despite misdemeanor arrests, particularly while they participate in anti-alcoholism programs, is a common parole board strategy.

Medical treatment of alcoholism commonly begins with relief of the vitamin and other nutritional deficiencies which accompany persistent drinking. Sometimes the attention of a physician also is required for tissue damage from alcohol, such as cirrhosis of the liver. In addition, drugs may be administered to make a person feel ill if he takes alcohol. Such medical service generally is regarded only as an adjunct to psychological and social therapy. The latter requires that one alter the immediate social environment of the alcoholic, at least temporarily, to one in which he will find social support for personal responsibility and abstinence.

Alcoholics Anonymous developed as a mutual aid fellowship in 1935. It has since grown to the point where it is believed to have been responsible for more successful cases of alcoholism treatment than all other methods combined. Its Twelve Steps emphasize confession, religious inspiration, self-criticism, restitution for wrongs done, and

[1] Federal Bureau of Investigation, *Crime in the United States: Uniform Crime Reports--1962*, Washington, D.C.: Department of Justice, 1963, Table 19, pp. 92-93.

30

service to other alcoholics. This is reinforced by the Twelve Traditions, which have kept this organization remarkably free of disruption from factional, financial, or other crises. There also is an Al-Anon organization for mutual aid by relatives of alcoholics, whose program is designed to complement Alcoholics Anonymous.

There are several hundred Alcoholics Anonymous chapters in penal institutions. These receive regular visits from members of outside Alcoholics Anonymous groups, who also meet prisoners at release and assist them in procuring homes and employment. A major problem in assessing their significance for an individual inmate's parole prospects is that many men participate in Alcoholics Anonymous in prison who do not sincerely regard themselves as alcoholics or, at any rate, would not seriously involve themselves in an Alcoholics Anonymous program if they were free. A further limitation is the relatively low rate of participation in Alcoholics Anonymous by alcoholics of lower economic class background or of very low educational attainment.

Medico-psychological agencies dealing with alcoholics increasingly coordinate their efforts with those of Alcoholics Anonymous, although there is a history of some antagonism between advocates of these different treatment approaches. It generally is agreed that an alcoholic must "reach bottom"—suffer severe emotional shock at the destruction he has wrought by his drinking—before he will be amenable to treatment. There is some contention that counseling can hasten this amenability. It generally is asserted that psychotherapy is ineffective if participation is compulsory, but several clinicians claim that effective use of parole authority to enforce attendance at treatment sessions can be supportive of anti-alcoholism therapy if the officer also achieves a supportive role in other respects.

The problems of the parole board member involve considering not just the drinking pattern of a prospective parolee, but the relationship of his drinking to his criminality. Should alcoholism seem a significant factor in a particular case, the prospect of the parolee's participation in treatment, as well as the effectiveness of the treatment in the past, are critical issues.

Evidence on these matters is never conclusive, especially not from interviews with the offenders. Reports on prior behavior should probe thoroughly into the extent and location of a parolee's prior drinking, and its relationship to his criminality. A satisfactory parole plan generally is one which minimizes the prospects of the drinking and its relationship to his criminality. A satisfactory istering parole through a prerelease guidance institution in the city of release, where prospective parolees may at least be watched on passes or furloughs from such centers before they actually begin their parole.

———

ANSWER SHEET

EST NO. _____ PART _____ TITLE OF POSITION _____

(AS GIVEN IN EXAMINATION ANNOUNCEMENT - INCLUDE OPTION, IF ANY)

LACE OF EXAMINATION _____ DATE _____

(CITY OR TOWN)　　　　　　　　　(STATE)

RATING

USE THE SPECIAL PENCIL.　MAKE GLOSSY BLACK MARKS.

	A B C D E		A B C D E		A B C D E		A B C D E		A B C D E
1	:: :: :: :: ::	26	:: :: :: :: ::	51	:: :: :: :: ::	76	:: :: :: :: ::	101	:: :: :: :: ::
2	:: :: :: :: ::	27	:: :: :: :: ::	52	:: :: :: :: ::	77	:: :: :: :: ::	102	:: :: :: :: ::
3	:: :: :: :: ::	28	:: :: :: :: ::	53	:: :: :: :: ::	78	:: :: :: :: ::	103	:: :: :: :: ::
4	:: :: :: :: ::	29	:: :: :: :: ::	54	:: :: :: :: ::	79	:: :: :: :: ::	104	:: :: :: :: ::
5	:: :: :: :: ::	30	:: :: :: :: ::	55	:: :: :: :: ::	80	:: :: :: :: ::	105	:: :: :: :: ::
6	:: :: :: :: ::	31	:: :: :: :: ::	56	:: :: :: :: ::	81	:: :: :: :: ::	106	:: :: :: :: ::
7	:: :: :: :: ::	32	:: :: :: :: ::	57	:: :: :: :: ::	82	:: :: :: :: ::	107	:: :: :: :: ::
8	:: :: :: :: ::	33	:: :: :: :: ::	58	:: :: :: :: ::	83	:: :: :: :: ::	108	:: :: :: :: ::
9	:: :: :: :: ::	34	:: :: :: :: ::	59	:: :: :: :: ::	84	:: :: :: :: ::	109	:: :: :: :: ::
10	:: :: :: :: ::	35	:: :: :: :: ::	60	:: :: :: :: ::	85	:: :: :: :: ::	110	:: :: :: :: ::

Make only ONE mark for each answer.　Additional and stray marks may be
counted as mistakes.　In making corrections, erase errors COMPLETELY.

	A B C D E		A B C D E		A B C D E		A B C D E		A B C D E
11	:: :: :: :: ::	36	:: :: :: :: ::	61	:: :: :: :: ::	86	:: :: :: :: ::	111	:: :: :: :: ::
12	:: :: :: :: ::	37	:: :: :: :: ::	62	:: :: :: :: ::	87	:: :: :: :: ::	112	:: :: :: :: ::
13	:: :: :: :: ::	38	:: :: :: :: ::	63	:: :: :: :: ::	88	:: :: :: :: ::	113	:: :: :: :: ::
14	:: :: :: :: ::	39	:: :: :: :: ::	64	:: :: :: :: ::	89	:: :: :: :: ::	114	:: :: :: :: ::
15	:: :: :: :: ::	40	:: :: :: :: ::	65	:: :: :: :: ::	90	:: :: :: :: ::	115	:: :: :: :: ::
16	:: :: :: :: ::	41	:: :: :: :: ::	66	:: :: :: :: ::	91	:: :: :: :: ::	116	:: :: :: :: ::
17	:: :: :: :: ::	42	:: :: :: :: ::	67	:: :: :: :: ::	92	:: :: :: :: ::	117	:: :: :: :: ::
18	:: :: :: :: ::	43	:: :: :: :: ::	68	:: :: :: :: ::	93	:: :: :: :: ::	118	:: :: :: :: ::
19	:: :: :: :: ::	44	:: :: :: :: ::	69	:: :: :: :: ::	94	:: :: :: :: ::	119	:: :: :: :: ::
20	:: :: :: :: ::	45	:: :: :: :: ::	70	:: :: :: :: ::	95	:: :: :: :: ::	120	:: :: :: :: ::
21	:: :: :: :: ::	46	:: :: :: :: ::	71	:: :: :: :: ::	96	:: :: :: :: ::	121	:: :: :: :: ::
22	:: :: :: :: ::	47	:: :: :: :: ::	72	:: :: :: :: ::	97	:: :: :: :: ::	122	:: :: :: :: ::
23	:: :: :: :: ::	48	:: :: :: :: ::	73	:: :: :: :: ::	98	:: :: :: :: ::	123	:: :: :: :: ::
24	:: :: :: :: ::	49	:: :: :: :: ::	74	:: :: :: :: ::	99	:: :: :: :: ::	124	:: :: :: :: ::
25	:: :: :: :: ::	50	:: :: :: :: ::	75	:: :: :: :: ::	100	:: :: :: :: ::	125	:: :: :: :: ::

ANSWER SHEET

TEST NO. ____________ PART ______ TITLE OF POSITION ____________________________
(AS GIVEN IN EXAMINATION ANNOUNCEMENT - INCLUDE OPTION, IF ANY)

PLACE OF EXAMINATION ______________________________ (CITY OR TOWN) ______________ (STATE) DATE ____________

RATING

USE THE SPECIAL PENCIL. MAKE GLOSSY BLACK MARKS.

1	A B C D E	26	A B C D E	51	A B C D E	76	A B C D E	101	A B C D
2	A B C D E	27	A B C D E	52	A B C D E	77	A B C D E	102	A B C D
3	A B C D E	28	A B C D E	53	A B C D E	78	A B C D E	103	A B C D
4	A B C D E	29	A B C D E	54	A B C D E	79	A B C D E	104	A B C D
5	A B C D E	30	A B C D E	55	A B C D E	80	A B C D E	105	A B C D
6	A B C D E	31	A B C D E	56	A B C D E	81	A B C D E	106	A B C D
7	A B C D E	32	A B C D E	57	A B C D E	82	A B C D E	107	A B C D
8	A B C D E	33	A B C D E	58	A B C D E	83	A B C D E	108	A B C D
9	A B C D E	34	A B C D E	59	A B C D E	84	A B C D E	109	A B C D
10	A B C D E	35	A B C D E	60	A B C D E	85	A B C D E	110	A B C D

Make only ONE mark for each answer. Additional and stray marks may be counted as mistakes. In making corrections, erase errors COMPLETELY.

11	A B C D E	36	A B C D E	61	A B C D E	86	A B C D E	111	A B C D
12	A B C D E	37	A B C D E	62	A B C D E	87	A B C D E	112	A B C D
13	A B C D E	38	A B C D E	63	A B C D E	88	A B C D E	113	A B C D
14	A B C D E	39	A B C D E	64	A B C D E	89	A B C D E	114	A B C D
15	A B C D E	40	A B C D E	65	A B C D E	90	A B C D E	115	A B C D
16	A B C D E	41	A B C D E	66	A B C D E	91	A B C D E	116	A B C D
17	A B C D E	42	A B C D E	67	A B C D E	92	A B C D E	117	A B C D
18	A B C D E	43	A B C D E	68	A B C D E	93	A B C D E	118	A B C D
19	A B C D E	44	A B C D E	69	A B C D E	94	A B C D E	119	A B C D
20	A B C D E	45	A B C D E	70	A B C D E	95	A B C D E	120	A B C D
21	A B C D E	46	A B C D E	71	A B C D E	96	A B C D E	121	A B C D
22	A B C D E	47	A B C D E	72	A B C D E	97	A B C D E	122	A B C D
23	A B C D E	48	A B C D E	73	A B C D E	98	A B C D E	123	A B C D
24	A B C D E	49	A B C D E	74	A B C D E	99	A B C D E	124	A B C D
25	A B C D E	50	A B C D E	75	A B C D E	100	A B C D E	125	A B C D